ERRANT PLAGIARY

The Life and Writing of Lady Sarah Cowper
1644–1720

ANNE KUGLER

Stanford University Press
Stanford, California
2002

Stanford University Press
Stanford, California

Printed in the United States of America
on acid-free, archival-quality paper

Library of Congress Cataloging-in-Publication Data

Kugler, Anne.
  Errant plagiary : the life and writing of Lady Sarah Cowper (1644–1720) /
Anne Kugler.
    p. cm.
Includes bibliographical references and index.
  ISBN 0-8047-3418-6 (acid-free paper)
1. Cowper, Sarah, 1644–1720—Diaries. 2. Legislators' spouses—Great
Britain—Diaries—History and criticism. 3. Women—Great
Britain—Diaries—History and criticism. 4. Great
Britain—History—Anne, 1702–1714—Biography. 5. Great
Britain—History—Anne, 1702–1714—Sources. 6. Legislators'
spouses—Great Britain—Biography. 7. Diaries—Authorship—History—18th century.
8. Plagiarism—England—History—18th century. 9. Women—Great
Britain—Bibliography. l. Title.
  DA497.C69 K64 2002
  941.06'9'092—dc21
                    2002006717

Original Printing 2002

Last figure below indicates year of this printing:
11 10 09 08 07 06 05 04 03 02

Typeset by Janet Gardiner in 10/13 Sabon

For Stacy

Acknowledgments

This book would not have been possible without Michael MacDonald, who first pointed me to Sarah Cowper's diary and then offered helpful advice and insightful criticism throughout the process of writing my dissertation. For his generosity and his brilliance I am forever grateful. On the financial end, thanks also go to the University of Michigan for support in the form of a Graduate Research Partnership Grant and Mellon Fellowships. The pace and fruitfulness of my research was considerably aided by the smooth professionalism of the staffs of the British Library, Cambridge University Library, London Public Record Office, and the fine archivists at the Hertfordshire Public Record Office, who were especially helpful and welcoming. During the long and difficult work of transforming the dissertation into a book, I received revitalizing jolts of enthusiasm and advice from Lynn Botelho, Dana Rabin, and the History Department of Loyola College in Maryland (particularly their Works in Progress Seminar); extremely helpful suggestions and encouragement from Anthony Fletcher and Rachel Weil; kindly patience from Norris Pope of the Stanford University Press; and all the benefits of a friendly, supportive work environment from my colleagues in the History Department at John Carroll University. In the production of this book, as in everything, my deepest thanks, admiration, and love go to my family—my husband Stacy McGaugh and children Caitlyn and Isabel, my parents Marianne and Larry Kugler, my sister Teresa Kugler, my grandparents, my parents-in-law, and my aunts, uncles, and cousins, who have all contributed to my thinking and writing in more ways than I can even begin to describe.

Contents

Contents

Errant Plagiary

CHAPTER 1

Introduction

At Saint Peter's Church, Paul's Wharf, in London, on April 11, 1664, Sarah Holled and William Cowper embarked on more than forty-two years of wedded misery. Sarah was a twenty-year-old orphan at the time, the only child of Samuel Holled, a London merchant who had died three years earlier, and his wife Anne, who died just two months before the wedding. William was twenty-four and a lawyer who at the end of that same year inherited a baronetcy and houses in London and Kent from his grandfather.[1] It seems that there had been a lengthy courtship with at least formal protestations of affection, if a valentine sonnet from William written in 1662 is any indication.[2] A stilted, formulaic piece of writing, this valentine nonetheless hints at a level of civility and mutual attraction that would never be deduced from later evidence, such as Sarah's comment in 1705: "Never met two more Averse than we in Humour, Passions, and Affections; our Reason and Sense, Religion or Morals agree not."[3] Not much else, however, survives concerning the circumstances of that ill-fated wedding.

Economic factors may have been important in the alliance, as Sarah was her parents' heir, but the marriage was not particularly successful as a financial partnership, either. It is not clear just how prosperous a merchant Samuel Holled was, but in his will, having left a third of his estate to his wife and a third to his daughter, he made bequests amounting to about £500 out of the final third. When Anne Holled died she left everything to Sarah, but in a provision that indicates she knew the marriage was impending, specified that before Sarah's "marriage to any person or persons whatsoever," £800 should be entrusted to two friends to invest for Sarah for ten years, paying her the interest.[4] Thus, while Sarah brought to the marriage whatever was left of the sum she had originally received in her father's will plus whatever she inherited from her mother without restriction, a large proportion of her dowry was out of William's reach for a decade. Moreover, with only a few remaining kin and no notably powerful friends, the relative lack of ready cash was not compensated for by a wealth of useful London connections. In retrospect, given his future career, it was not a particularly advantageous match for William. Equally, although Sarah married significantly above her social rank, she entered a gentry family whose finances were unimpressive. William's landed estate was inadequate for his high social status, and his apparent willingness to settle for the relatively small size and partial inaccessibility of Sarah's dowry are telling indications of his straitened economic circumstances. Moreover, duly producing four sons in quick succession over the years from 1665 to 1669,[5] Sarah had served her economic and biological purposes early in the marriage. Therefore, she spent the rest of her married years lacking the leverage of major and continuing contributions to the family's standing, as well as without financial security or a compatible mate.

Socially, however, Sarah was the mistress of a family that was on the rise in the legal profession and in politics.[6] She became the wife of a member of Parliament when Sir William was elected as a Whig for the borough of Hertford in 1679. He was unseated in 1681 when the Whigs fell from power but was reelected after the Glorious Revolution and served from 1689 to 1700. Following their father's career path, both of Sarah's surviving sons trained as barristers, and in 1695 the elder son, William, was elected to the other Hertford seat in Parliament. But in 1699 the family suffered a major setback when Spencer, the younger son, was tried for the murder of a Quaker woman. This event caused Sir William's defeat at the next parliamentary election in 1701, though the younger William managed to find a safe seat at Beeralston. It was consequently as a mother that Sarah saw her family rise sharply in the political world. Her son William's career took off most spectacularly; he was appointed Lord Keeper of the Great Seal in 1705, at which time Spencer took his place in the House of Commons. Then shortly after Sir William's death in 1706, William was elevated to the peerage as Baron

Cowper of Wingham in Kent. Named lord chancellor in 1707, he re-signed at the fall of the Whigs in 1710 and was reinstated soon after the accession of George I in 1714. At that point too, Spencer was appointed attorney general to the prince of Wales. The mother of the lord chancellor became the mother of the chief justice of Chester as well, when Spencer was preferred to that office in 1717. Finally, in 1718, William was created Earl Cowper. Throughout her life, then, Sarah moved up the social scale. From her origins as the daughter of a merchant, she became the wife of a lawyer, baronet, and moderately active politician, and ended her life in 1720 as the dowager of an eminent and ennobled Whig family.

The combination of a desperately unhappy marriage, insecure social standing, a lifelong habit of reading and writing, and the crisis of Spencer's trial prompted Sarah Cowper to begin a diary in July 1700. When she finally stopped writing because of ill health in September 1716, Cowper's daily entries totaled roughly 2,300 pages in seven volumes.[7] Unlike her previous writing in commonplace books, where Cowper collected selections from her reading and often attributed her extractions to their author, in her diaries, she incorporated the words of other writers seamlessly into her own personal observations. In effect, she spoke in the voice of others without signaling that fact. This habit of quoting lent literary cadences to the tone of her writing, and more important, added the weight of authoritative judgments to her own opinions. Accordingly, while the diary gives the initial impression of being an informal daily account of Cowper's thoughts, it is actually the product of not just the selection and fashioning of her own personal reflections, but of specific prescriptive texts as well. Moreover, it was a conscious process, as Cowper directly confronted the issues of attribution and originality, sometimes defensively, as when she explained, "I account Stealing to be when we altogether Transcribe out of any Author, but to borrow and alter is what most do. Since Nothing is new under the Sun." In one rare moment, when she did not feel the need to defend herself, she commented: "Like an Errant Plagiary I Cull from Books and Elsewhere what pleases my Fancy."[8]

Thus, under the stress of a particularly difficult time domestically and socially, as well as with an awareness of her advancing age, Cowper added to her usual methods of filling time and diverting energies a more personalized and introspective means of help in adversity. In beginning a journal she chose a well-known method of self-improvement but com-

bined it with her previous practice of writing out extracts from her reading into commonplace books to form an individualized, reassuring book
of self.

Because of the circumstances of her life and the way she responded to
them, Cowper's diary is an extraordinarily valuable source for addressing a number of thorny historical issues: the nature of autobiographical
writing, contemporary response to prescriptive ideology, and how women functioned in early modern England within the cultural constructs
of gender, rank, and age. Looking first at issues surrounding the production of this sort of writing, Cowper's diary elucidates the question of literary consciousness in writing about the self and cautions against the
reading of even the most "informal" self-narratives as straightforward
and unmediated. As critics have often pointed out, autobiographical
writing of any sort is never transparent. Writers select and reshape the
material of their lives, so that what they produce is necessarily partial,
constructed, informed by personal and social context.[9] But having acknowledged that it is impossible to assume an unpremeditated, uncom-
plicated expression of self, the problem is still deciding how to use these
texts, a question many scholars pose in terms of the "reliability" of the
author—that is, the extent to which the writer can be thought of as telling the 'truth,' or reporting his or her perceptions accurately, honestly,
and with a measure of objective self-awareness.[10] At the same time as the
treatment of diaries has benefited from the extensive consideration literary critics have devoted to this question,[11] their emphasis on the aesthetics of self-writing has tended to a imply a misleading level of simplicity
and accessibility in diaries in comparison to autobiographies. Even as
critics have developed the idea that autobiographical writing is interac-
tive, both with the multiple facets of one personality and with society at
large, diaries are still generally seen as at the opposite end of the spectrum from autobiography, whether the gradations are from incoherent
to coherent, formless to structured, immediate to retrospective, unpol-
ished to crafted, unconsidered to informed, realistic to imaginative, private to public.[12] Whatever the recognition of complexity in the self-
narrative does for autobiography, by making diaries the contrasting end
of the spectrum on all the scales mentioned above, it also suggests that
diaries are more artless, accessible, candid, forthcoming—in short, more
"true" and consequently presumably a better source for getting "at" the
author's outlook and historical context. Diaries, however, are also
shaped and fashioned;[13] they present multiple selves, and as Robert

Fothergill points out, they are not necessarily spontaneous, fragmentary, or even daily expressions of personality.[14]

Cowper's diary illustrates this very point: how closely personal journals can approach the complexities of formal autobiography. It is a highly self-conscious, shaped, constructed document—artful, not artless. Moreover, she herself explicitly recognized the introspective intent and quality of the journal, at one point doing so in a way that encapsulates her self-awareness, her habit of borrowing the words of other writers, and, as we shall see later, a very significant and typical trait—speaking in a voice that originally had a different context for her own purposes:

> In these writings may be Seen the Sentiments of my Mind. Sometimes I am Cheerfull, pleas'd, Sedate and quiet. Other whiles greiv'd, Complaining, Struggling with my Passions, blameing my Self, and resolving for the future . . . to Support all the Uneasiness of Life. Then by unexpected Unforseen Accidents, [I am] discomposed and Shock'd, till I have rallied . . . and by making resistance gain'd the better of my Troubles, and restored my Mind to Peace.[15]

What seems to be an observation of her own changing mental state is actually a paraphrase of the preface to Mary Chudleigh's *Poems, Upon Several Occasions* (1703). If this text was originally "dramatizing the restoration of reason as monarch of the poet's troubled mind,"[16] in Sarah's version the context is not the aesthetics of the personal drama of producing poetry, but rather her efforts to remain calm and retain the moral upper hand in her constant domestic battles with servants, her husband, and her sons. As such, her reuse of the poet's preface retained the sense of a sustained personal effort at tranquillity through subduing passion, but it is her own righteousness in struggling against anger and ultimate personal victory to which she referred. As in this instance, by reshaping culled precepts, Cowper subverted a socially approved literary format in order to furnish herself with an emotional outlet, a targeted vindication, and self-affirming portrayals of her own multiple identities.

The same tendency to think of autobiography and diary as contrasts in accessibility and complexity occurs in considerations of the audience at which self-writing is directed. The intention to publish is often taken as a defining characteristic of formal autobiography, and in assuming a contrast between this intention and the privacy of a diary, attendant assumptions can be made that diaries, because they are private, are more candid, more forthcoming, perhaps even more perceptive, having less need to be guarded in their introspection, and thus, more "authentic."[17]

This assumption of candor in private texts and of artifice and restraint in public ones has particular resonance in studies that discuss women's writing in this period, because publication had specific implications: women risked, and knew they risked, their reputations by writing for publication.[18] Modesty, women's most valuable asset, included silence in its definition, and by breaking silence, women threw their modesty into doubt, which was in turn intimately connected to their chastity. Therefore, a woman who published was morally and sexually suspect. The anticipated audience, then, clearly affected how and what they wrote.[19]

Admittedly, there are significant differences between a work written for immediate publication and one written for the author's eyes alone. But there are degrees of privacy, both in terms of the breadth of the audience and the time frame for revealing one's work. "Private" is not an absolute, in terms of meaning a total lack of audience anywhere or at any time. Between an audience of one, the writer, and an audience of the public in general are the intermediate possibilities of writing for family and writing for friends.[20] Both of these limited audiences might induce a writer to include or suppress things differently than might be the case if the work was directed at a wider public, or at no one at all. The passage of time also adds a dimension: A text might very well be constructed differently depending on whether it was to be read immediately, some time in the distant future, or posthumously.[21]

It seems that while Sarah Cowper had no thought of publication, she initially did expect members of her family to read at least some of her writings after her death, as dedications in her commonplace books indicate: "To my Daughter [in-law] Judith Cowper I leave this book desiring she would leave it to some one of the family to be kept in memory of me."[22] She was not so specific about her intended audience in the case of the diary, but it may that here too, she anticipated leaving a record for her female descendants. At any rate, she clearly assumed that she would not be the only person who read these works. In the prefatory pages of the first volume of the diary, Sarah vouched for her own reliability, directly addressing an unspecified future reader: "I will not say but there may be some things here that upon strict enquiry will perhaps appear not to be well founded, but this I will affirm that I have invented and added nothing myself." And less directly, but still suggesting she anticipated a future audience, she reflected,

> It makes me Smile when I reveiw these Notes, to See some things which at
> the time I Sett 'em down 'tis like were patt enough to present Circum-

stances; but after a while perhaps my Self can scarce tell what they mean. If hereafter then they Come to be seen of others, it must needs to them be unintelligible Stuff.[23]

She had also expected her husband would see the diary, as she commented immediately after Sir William's death in 1706:

I have Set down a great many things in my Diary's which I would never have done, but with an intention Sir W[illiam] Should See them after my Death. Not in the least imagining he would Dy before mee.[24]

In envisioning both of these future audiences, Sarah assumed that the diary would be read only posthumously. There is no indication that she let anyone see her writings during her lifetime.

Diarists' motives for writing are equally varied; they are often multiple, and can change over time. Where there are explicit statements of intent, diarists most commonly cite self-improvement, often in the context of religious duty, as their purpose. The desire to keep a record that would be reread at a later date in order to recapture information, memories, or an earlier identity was also a common explanation, and one that increased in frequency over the eighteenth century.[25] These motives, while they may be perfectly sincere, were also the conventional, laudatory reasons for journal-keeping current in this period.[26] Scholars are much more likely, however, to uncover implicit motives that suggest that autobiographers to a greater (and diarists to a lesser) extent were using their writing as a means of self-expression, self-affirmation, and self-justification.[27]

The diary clearly bears the marks of Sarah's thirty-year practice of compiling commonplace books, but it is also modeled on the genre of the spiritual journal, resulting in a highly individualized amalgam of the two forms. Its tone is generally pious, but with a strong personalized undercurrent of observation, opinion, and emotion. At the beginning of the fourth volume of her diary, Sarah acknowledged her practice of incorporating passages from her reading while quoting yet another source: "My Books are like Chrysippus'; if other Men's Sentences were left out, the pages would be Void."[28] How closely the two forms were linked is indicated by the fact that soon after Sarah began the diary, she stopped keeping commonplace books, except for very occasional addenda to a few of the volumes she had already compiled. Her habit of indexing the commonplace books accounts too for the indexing of each volume of the diaries, a practice she valorized by pointing to the eminent example of Robert Sanderson, the Bishop of Lincoln's method:

> It is Said of Bishop Sanderson His Way was to Write the Rules his Teachers Suggested, Or his Books afforded. . . . He advised to Use a Commonplace Book . . . Where What Noteable Sentence, Notion, Rule or Perticuler Soever . . . May be written and Reserv'd for Future Use, drawing Index's either in his own Paper:Book, or at the Begining and End of each Book. So have I Done for More than Thirty year.[29]

Interestingly, in her diary Sarah also apparently found it necessary to justify the act of writing itself, as opposed to pursuing the typically "feminine" activity of needlework.

> Perhaps some may think my writing so much, a very dull Drudgery. But it Sufficeth to Sattisfy me in the practice, that I find it otherwise. At worst, it may be allow'd an Employment as significant as any Sort of work I can do, and if for every stitch that others prick in a Clout, I with pen Set a letter upon paper that, as long may remain a witness to purg me from the scandal of Idleness, as the Work of a Needle.[30]

The second important influence on the form and content of the diary, the tradition of the spiritual journal, is apparent both in tone (especially early in the diary) and in selection of material. Many of her extracts were directed at improving or admonishing faults she discovered in herself through self-examination, particularly anger, with which she continually struggled and recorded her progress (or lack thereof) in mastering. She wrote out recommendations for conquering anger and achieving tranquillity in addition to recounting the "characters" of those peaceable and contented men and women she hoped to emulate. Periodically, she reviewed her progress:

> This Day 'tis four year since I began Setting down my Thoughts on those passages that Occurr in the Course of my Life. That So upon reveiw I might See what progress I make in Subduing that Vanity and Vexation of Spirit which either my own failings or the Mischeivous doings of others lays upon mee. After this Survey, I find Cause to wish the Sayings of the Apostle Concerning the Use of Speech were ever present with my Mind.[31]

In many instances Sarah offered reasons for her writing that specifically echoed the recommendations in devotional handbooks to keep a spiritual journal as an aid to leading a virtuous life. In quoting these sources she demonstrated her own commendable purposes in gathering edifying precepts and exemplary characters, enriching her devotion, and keeping a record of her progress toward salvation:

> It is advisable that thou keep a Book in which may be Register'd, for thy own private Use, whatever is worthy to be Remark'd Concerning thy Outward and Inward Life. And thou must frequently also look into this Book, and Specially at Certain Stated Seasons of Self:Examination: that so thou maist have a better and more distinct knowledg . . . of thy Advancement and Proficiency in the Spiritual Way.[32]

Furthermore, she seems to have been aware from the beginning of her diary of participating in a Protestant, elite tradition of writing, since she prefaced the first volume by saying, "Sir John Cheek praeceptor to Edward the Sixth, was the First that brought a Diary into Use; and his pupil the Next that practis'd It."[33]

With less official sanction, but potentially equal personal importance, Sarah acknowledged keeping the diary as a distraction from loneliness and boredom, as well as a safe outlet for anger. She wrote that keeping a diary "diverts me for the present, and if wee have any uneasiness that Enclines us to Sting, it is well to turn the point where it cannot wound too much."[34] and, "It Oft falls out that being Displeased at Some Actions that prudence will not permit me Openly to Reprove, I discharge my Self upon paper, Such Lashes imprint themselves best there."[35]

The expectation Sarah had of an eventual audience is also a crucial motivating factor in her writing and helps to explain her self-justification and concern to present herself in the best possible light. For Sarah's descendants, the diary, like the commonplace books, was to serve as a source of advice and edification. As such, it was testimony to Sarah's own virtue, to her benevolent desire to assist her family, and to the value of such a record for the self-improvement of future generations of Cowpers. More important, with regard to her husband, the diary was to function as a weapon in her marital battles. It would vindicate her life and actions after her death, an unanswerable reproach that gave her the last word in a long-running argument.

Because Sarah's reworking of ideology took place within the much broader context of her considerations of and assumptions about the family, society, politics, and religion, her diary resonates aspects of the culture of which she was a part. This diary, then, not only serves to further the interpretation of early modern journal writing as a consciously constructed effort that both conformed to and contested literary forms, but addresses a fundamental problem of historical methodology as well: Whenever historians attempt to explore the mental worlds of people living in previous centuries they run into the issue of disparity between social theory and individual reality—a gap that is mirrored in the sources. While plenty of material survives that attempts to inculcate ideals of human attitude and behavior, and while personal documents still exist that indicate the perspective of the writer, making the connection between prescription and practice remains an elusive goal. Uniquely, Sarah explicitly made that connection as she reflected upon various aspects of her life. Her diary offers a specific link between the ideologies that institutions and authorities were concerned to promulgate and the outlook of the individual.

This linkage is most valuable in two related areas of historical debate: the extent of women's internalization of early modern ideologies of femininity, and the nature of family relations. In their efforts to spell out the hierarchical structure of early modern English society and the obligations it entailed for each of its members, prescriptive writers devoted a great deal of attention to the question of women's place in the social order.[36] Drawing upon scriptural authority especially, writers argued that women were inferior and thus subject to men on the basis of natural and divine law, and consequently owed obedience to their superiors—their husbands, since it was assumed women would marry. It was essential to convince wives of the validity and necessity of their submission not just for the smooth functioning of the family, but because the relationship of governor and governed within the family was considered the foundation of the political order as well.[37] But if these conduct books, printed sermons, tracts and treatises are abundant evidence of the ideology those in authority hoped to impart, they are not necessarily descriptive of social reality, nor do they indicate what their audience thought of their arguments.[38]

When trying to discover how women themselves understood and responded to these prevailing ideologies about their gender, historians are confronted with several difficulties. The first and most obvious is that while directions for living could be disseminated to the illiterate through catechisms, prayers, and sermons heard in church, evidence for reaction is mostly limited to the literate[39]—and consequently to the upper social orders—and furthermore, to those who were inclined to write and wrote in ways that at least indirectly shed light on their attitudes toward what was being propounded.[40] Within this small subset of the female population are further disparities in the type of evidence, which ranges from published literary contributions to the formal debate on the "woman question" in which women (and men) argued for a higher valuation of the female sex, to passing comments or indirect indications of opinion in diaries or correspondence.[41]

Given these problems with the sources, it is not surprising that when historians have attempted to develop a general picture of female mentalities in this period, their interpretations have differed significantly. Although scholars have generally moved away from identifying the beginnings of modern feminism in these challenges, historians and literary critics alike have generally reaffirmed the idea that early modern women contested the notion of female inferiority, although there are still differences of emphasis as to the degree and manner of this resistance.[42]

At the most cautious, most conservative end of the range of interpretations, Harriet Blodgett considers the act of diary-keeping itself to be the response, the opposition, that "counters the patriarchal attack on female identity and self-worth. A diary is an act of language that, by speaking of one's self, sustains one's sense of being a self. . . . " But in her interpretation, this is by and large the limit of women's dissension: "remarkably few Englishwomen of the past used their diaries for active self-creation . . . " and although they "reserved certain rights to themselves, most of them adjust to what their contemporary life allows them and observe the codes. The subtexts they encode are not subversive."[43] For Patricia Spacks, however, the picture includes much more anger and resistance, much less satisfied acceptance. She contends that "letters, diaries, memoirs sketch a drama of self-defense. Women writing about themselves defend integrity both by the declaration of the self implicit in the writing process and by the retelling of what they have endured, individually and generically." Nussbaum accords women more active involvement in a struggle, arguing that even diaries, though not public records of resistance, "bear witness to the plurality of the gendered positions" and "register opposition to circulating notions of 'self.'"[44]

Although acknowledging the small section of the population to which these surveys can claim to apply, these studies often treat their collections of literate, elite women as representative of the whole,[45] a tendency that is also associated with a one-dimensional examination of women's experience on the basis of a single hierarchy, that of gender, when in reality, women in England were positioned on multiple, sometimes conflicting, interwoven scales,[46] including rank most importantly, and to a significant degree age and attendant life stage. Contemporaries were perfectly aware of the operation of multiple hierarchies. In 1694, Mary Astell summarized the consequences at the logical extreme of this positioning in her argument against men who asserted total feminine inferiority:

> For if by the Natural Superiority of their Sex, they mean that every Man is by Nature superior to every Woman . . . it wou'd be a Sin in *any* Woman to have Dominion over *any* Man, and the greatest Queen ought not to command but to obey her Footman.[47]

Members of the elite were not only predominantly the ones writing, they were also experiencing the hierarchy of gender differently from women further down the social scale. And because of the privilege of rank, it is this very same group of women whose experience of the gender hierarchy was most likely to be mitigated so that they might accept or even further the doctrine of female submission.[48] The picture is therefore already skewed by the potential for adherence to the social order by conservative women for whom it was the least onerous. Even those women who addressed themselves to the problems of women's place might be limited in their analysis by the perspective of their privileged position.[49]

Alongside the problems of limited and unevenly weighted evidence in attempting to examine the influence of prescription on women's attitudes is the question of how we regard the production and dissemination of ideology itself. While sermons, devotional manuals, and conduct books were copiously produced and distributed in large numbers, their arguments and authority were not monolithic.[50] Loopholes, undefined boundaries, and contradictions might be exploited; meanings might be contested. Prescriptive literature, and the mainly religious foundation on which it was built, were not immune to individual interpretation.[51] Despite being imbued with a patriarchal and paternalistic view of society, Christianity offered affirming, equalizing ideas as well. The assertion of the equality of souls and the need in cases of conflict to obey God rather than human authority might be made into liberating, empowering concepts.[52] If women internalized a negative biblical view of their sex, they could still attain the highest states of humanity, "salvation and sainthood," in contrast to their exclusion from the achievement of civic virtue in humanistic ideals.[53] And at the same time as the church purveyed a very restrictive ideal of marriage for women, it might provide them with compensation, meaning, and an outlet of escape from the rigors of the married state.[54] Moreover, the cultivation of virtue could offer for women the chance of righteousness and the potential for authority stemming from confidence in their unassailable piety.[55]

Although Lady Sarah Cowper quite clearly inscribed the codes of her time, it is in the active, transforming, subversive purpose of women's writing that Sarah's diary is to be found. Her diary records the reworking of ideology and the construction of self-validating female identities in response to and by means of addressing prescriptive texts, within a written format that subverts conventional literary forms and models. The conditions of her family life were the basis for some of her most striking responses to prevailing ideologies of womanhood. Prescriptive literature set forth a vision of the ideal woman that assumed her most fundamental relationships and occupations were to be found within the home. Correspondingly, it is in this arena, in her interactions with the authoritative texts that she collected to direct and justify her outlook and behavior, that Sarah most drastically reshaped and appropriated prescription. Her life is an instructive example of the ways women, especially as wives, could react to and reshape a repressive system of principles while still accepting the existence and validity of that system.

Two interrelated elements of her response to domestic ideology stand out especially. First, her contentious relationship with her husband revealed contradictions between the prescriptive vision of women within the family and her own experience of married life. Sarah considered this gap between the ideal of household relations and the reality to be not just unfortunate but personally injurious, both as a deprivation of the authority and respect owed to her in her domestic capacities, and as an impediment to her religious development. This impediment is the second important element of her response: Sarah's investigation and creation of the identities of wife, mother, and mistress of servants were based in large part on an overarching need to discover how to live well and to demonstrate that she was in fact performing as she should in the domestic arena in order to be deserving of salvation. It was in attempting to demonstrate the injustice of these contradictions and redress them that Sarah managed to derive a conception of herself that reaffirmed both her sense of worthiness as a Christian and her sense of moral ascendancy over her husband.

With regard to the second historical issue, the nature of English family relations in this period, Sarah's response to her marital situation again bridges a problematic gap in the material. Responding to Lawrence Stone's seminal book, *The Family, Sex and Marriage in England 1500–1800*, historians have argued over questions ranging from the reasons for making a marriage, through power relations in the family, to the influence of religion, society, and politics on conceptions of family and its operations, to the timing and character of any changes in family structure or interactions. Stone portrayed the English family before about 1680 as a harshly authoritarian entity where parental control extended to arranging marriages for their children mainly for reasons of economics rather than affection.[56] He argued that because of the influence of "affective individualism," family relationships warmed and became more free and equal as more people were able to choose their own partners for reasons of love more than money, without interference from kin and friends, and that wives in particular experienced improvement in their positions, as marriage more nearly approached an egalitarian emotional partnership.[57]

Historians initially responded to Stone's sweeping scenario by arguing that a wider selection of evidence from personal sources demonstrated that the picture of stern authoritarian domesticity in the seventeenth century was neither so uniform nor so extreme as he had asserted. Diaries and correspondence indicated a variety of experiences of family life, including situations in which patriarchal authority and companionability could and did coexist. For Stone's critics, the family did not change appreciably over time from coldly authoritarian to lovingly egalitarian, but rather remained by and large both hierarchical and affectionate.[58] More recently, Margaret Hunt and Amanda Vickery have shown the persistence in the eighteenth century of the participation of family and friends in matchmaking as well as the continuation of the value placed on economic considerations in marriage. Moreover, both Hunt and Vickery have very effectively criticized the presumption that love and equality are necessarily connected, pointing out that even if marital relationships could be proven to have grown more affectionate in the eighteenth century, tighter emotional bonds hardly precluded continuing inequality in a relationship: Love does not mean liberation.[59]

Historians have also turned to conduct books for evidence of continuity or change in early modern family life, focusing in particular on the implications of the redefinition during the Reformation of the best human state on earth as marriage, rather than celibacy. It has been suggested that Protestant writers correspondingly reshaped the purpose of matrimony beyond procreation, emphasizing companionship and deepening the emotional significance of marriage, and that such an emphasis might create the potential for increased power and equality for women in marriage.[60] This idea has been criticized in a number of ways. Kathleen Davies has doubted that mutuality in marriage was a new or especially prominent concept among Protestant writers and theologians.[61] But further, and perhaps more significantly, Susan Amussen and Patrick Collinson have detected an uncomfortable inconsistency in these conduct books, seeing on the one hand increased value on affection in marriage, yet on the other continued insistence on the primacy of husbandly authority, so that wives' first duty throughout the early modern period was still to obey, husbands' still to rule, though preferably benevolently.[62]

In these discussions of the family, there is a noticeable division between theoretical and actual conditions in descriptions of patriarchy itself, and in the sources used to back the arguments. On the one hand, theological, advisory, didactic, or literary texts are used to explain the theory of patriarchal marriage, while on the other, diaries and letters are most frequently used to investigate the actual experience of marriage. Both sides to the question do not normally appear in the same study. The division is understandable, given the available evidence, but it does frustrate attempts to understand the interaction between the literary texts and "real life" as seen in fragments in a diary, and to arrive at a picture that is more than idealized and abstract (in handbooks and theological treatises) or anecdotal (in diaries). Here the evidence for Sarah's life and outlook is especially useful. In her case, the rigors of patriarchy are clear in her frustration in marriage, her continual, frequently futile power struggle with her husband, and the consequent motivations to describe and justify herself as a wife. It is therefore salutary to keep Stone in mind and remember that mutuality may have been an attractive aspect of matrimony, but marriage was still based on, and people still acted on, a conception that included inferiority and submission for one member of the partnership. On the other hand, if we look at the influence and application of theoretical writings to actual attitude, Sarah's case shows the extent to which patriarchal conceptions could be malleable, or at least understood in a way that allows for an expectation of power and respect as a wife.

Unlike descriptions of the ideal man, where his life and duties as a public citizen of the state and as a professional were discussed as part of his identity, conduct books organized their directions to women according to the domestic roles of wife, mother, and mistress of servants.[63]

By marrying, women entered into a relationship where they were to adopt the needs and interests of their husbands as their own. In their role as loyal subjects, they were above all to be obedient and sexually faithful to their husbands.[64] Once they had children, wives were responsible for the upbringing and education of sons until the age of about seven, and for daughters throughout childhood. In general, mothers were to be a living example of virtue for children to emulate.[65] As mistresses of the household—the domestic delegate of the supreme head of the family—women were to oversee the servants and instruct them in religion.[66] For Sarah this organizing principle had a resonance in reality. In the course of constructing her wifely persona she explicitly examined herself according to those capacities and advanced claims that were derived from her reading of prescriptive explications of the duties and rights of those roles. Building a case for her proper role as a wife was of particular concern to Sarah because her marriage was such a disaster. Throughout the diary, she indicated the level of marital friction and her opinion of her husband with comments such as, "I do from my Soul beleive him to be the most difficult humour to live at Ease with this world ever afforded."[67] Correspondingly, her construction of domestic identities not only validated Sarah's conception of her self-worth, they justified her criticisms of her spouse and formed part of her indictment of Sir William's performance of his duties as a husband.

This citation and appropriation of texts makes Lady Sarah Cowper a uniquely informative source for discovering how people in early modern England understood social doctrine; however, it is also remarkable that in her family life, the ideal as laid out in texts and then reshaped by Sarah was thwarted by those with whom she interacted. Whether from a position of inferiority or as the superior member of the relationship, Sarah's difficulty in getting others to acquiesce to a vision that was in many ways very conventional warns that not only is it necessary to be cautious in evaluating the extent to which women might internalize the depiction of their sex as inferior and submissive, but it is important to remember that husbands, sons, and servants too might not see their roles precisely as they were formulated either in prescriptive texts or in the interpretations of their wives, mothers, or mistresses. Sarah managed to value herself and demand power and respect based on the ideology of family relations. She challenged yet worked within patriarchy, a cultural system that defined her and simultaneously offered strategies of resistance. But her success in exercising the authority she claimed was decidedly mixed. Becoming a widow was more important to her control of household management than proving her case for wifely jurisdiction, and moreover, even after the death of Sir William, those in theoretically inferior positions could prevent Sarah from realizing her own ideal domestic roles. Historians have already noted that the variety of personal circumstances and the elasticity of interpretation made ideal family relationships much easier to envision than to enforce. Sarah's example illustrates both aspects of this process: the success of her formulation of self-validating domestic roles, and the mixed results of her attempts to enact them.

In her approach to dealing with the world outside her immediate family, where rank was especially significant in governing her relationships, Sarah used prescriptive material to buttress her insecure social position and assuage her anxieties about her standing. In constructing an image of herself as a pious gentlewoman she could both assert her own honor and deflect criticism of her family. In addition to visiting and patronage, Lady Sarah Cowper made churchgoing and charitable giving into means of social empowerment, vindicating her choices and strategies through prescriptive texts. Here too her life stage was important in enabling her to see herself as a matron defending the interests of the family, and as a pious widow devoted to good works.

In all forms of public participation—visiting, churchgoing, charitable giving, and involving herself in patronage—Sarah took advantage of ideas of piety, gentility, and motherhood that allowed her to claim a place of personal authority and to bolster the tenuous prestige of her family in the social world. As a historical document, this monument to self-justification illuminates not only one English gentlewoman's reaction to her family and her society, but her implementation of a number of strategies for claiming domestic, public, and intellectual authority. In her complaints about her family, her comments on visiting, and her ruminations on politics and church doctrine, Sarah both reflects the controversies and ideals of late Stuart society and demonstrates some of the ways in which the disenfranchised could assert their membership in the intellectual realm and the political nation. The ideology of rank was at once empowering in that it gave her an alternate means to think of herself than as female, but it was also destabilizing: As a recent arrival to her level of social eminence Sarah constantly had to reinforce her honor—an effort hindered by male relatives who based their prestige more on the risky supports of political activity and government service than on birth or (especially landed) wealth.

Moreover, in her associations with the church establishment, played out in every sphere of her public activity, Sarah chose a means of reinforcement in opposition to the strategies employed by her husband and sons. It was a practice that caused friction in the family, especially in conjunction with her attempts to appropriate her son's material and symbolic capital for enhancing her personal prestige, but on the other hand, as a strategy, it enjoyed some notable successes. As a visitor and churchgoer Sarah declared her public image as a pious gentlewoman, and apparently reaped the benefit of good reputation and a number of obliging, respectful acquaintances, though she only infrequently managed to move to the level of real friendship. In these public activities she also built up a network of connections that served her well in her more direct efforts at exercising power through the ties of reciprocity and gratitude created by charity and through the ties of friendship and motherhood in terms of her one notable patronage success. Sarah managed a remarkably affirming and empowering implementation of the ideology of rank to enhance both her own and her family's standing in the political and social world, despite the impediments afforded by opposing visions of the ideology of family, the Cowpers' shaky social status and consequent dangers of misplaced political involvement, and the Tory ascendancy during much of the period of her diary.

In the intellectual arena, where gender relegated her to the sidelines, rank enabled her to think that she was entitled to consider and make judgments about current theological and political debates, and it gave her access to privileged information. Moreover, the social ideal of dignity and wisdom in old age encouraged Sarah to envision an attractive, admirable retirement into a contemplative life where her preparations for death would benefit from her long experience of and consequent distaste for worldly affairs. Alongside the redefinition of feminine domestic roles and the assertion of social selves in her diary, Sarah devoted a good deal of thought to theology and politics. Her selection from and comments upon her reading in these areas allow insight into Sarah's formation of a personalized theology and political stance and chart her increasing cynicism toward the worldly aspects of politics and religion. Both her extensive reading and her personal contact with the shapers of political and social discourse are important factors in the fashioning of her outlook. She observed the affairs of church and state from the privileged position of someone who had kin and friends in the highest echelons of church and state. Although as a woman she was denied political participation in any formal sense, she had the advantage of being able to base her opinions on "inside" knowledge as well as on more generally accessible texts.

Sarah claimed she was entitled to make those judgments because of a combination of social position and, most important, her image of herself as a contemplative sage—a mature woman who with the benefit of age and the experience it brought, and the knowledge she had gained over the years from the study of "men and books," could legitimately claim an elevated perspective, one that realized the essential vanity of this world and so had its priorities in order. Thus, while working out her own salvation, an imminent concern, she could claim to evaluate religious and political doctrine and events objectively. As Sarah herself commented, in the words of *The Spectator*,

> As to all the Rational and worthy pleasures of our Being, the Conscience of a Good Fame, The Contemplation of another Life, Our Capacities for Such Enjoyments are Enlarged by Years while Health endures; the latter part of Life in the Eye of Reason is Certainly the more Eligible. Age in a Vertuous Person of either Sex carry's in it an Authority which makes it preferable to all the pleasures of youth.[68]

By virtue of her rank, age, knowledge, and piety Sarah was secure in her authority to consider and judge matters of religion and current affairs. Theologically, Sarah sided with moderate Anglicanism, a set of tenets that provided her with moral criteria by which to evaluate ideas and people, and by which to measure her progress toward salvation (in comparison, no doubt, to her husband's lack of progress). She focused on many of the same themes in and same threats to religion as did the eminent Latitudinarian divines, though with certain reservations and omissions in the applications of these themes to her own devotional life. Politically, she was understandably most interested in the many issues in which church and state were intertwined. Despite the clear Whig allegiance of her male kin, Sarah asserted a nonpartisan identity that both reflected her distrust of the ethics and purposes of both Whig and Tory politicians and combined a general principle of moderation with the attributes she preferred from each party: the Tory message of conservatism, order, and deference, and the Whig commitment to the preservation of the rights of Parliament and the Protestant succession.

In the political as well as domestic realm, then, Sarah's diary stands as an exceptional record of intellectual activity and interaction with contemporary ideology in which one woman reacted to her position—initially middle-aged and unhappily married, then elderly and widowed—and to events in her world. It served as a space in which to work out a redefinition of feminine domestic roles in order to assert her own righteousness versus her husband, to construct social selves that contributed to family status, and to formulate conceptions of the religious and political world both for spiritual reassurance and as an assertion of intellectual authority. As such, Sarah's diary provides lengthy and fascinating insight into the mind of an extraordinarily articulate and self-conscious Englishwoman, while at the same time vividly illuminating the early eighteenth-century gentry society that she inhabited.

Sadly enough, while of exceptional value to historians, this remarkable document owes its production to the profound discontent and leisured social position of its creator. A happily married or otherwise occupied woman would not have had the need, time, or resources to produce such a testament. As the next chapter of this study explains, Sarah's family life appears to have been full of conflict throughout the thirty-six years of marriage that preceded her commencement of the diary in 1700. Money and the lack of it, the risky political choices of her husband, and the upbringing, marriages, and living arrangements of her sons produced nearly constant tension, to which Sarah initially responded in writing by compiling commonplace books. What may have prompted her to develop this activity into diary form was the crisis of her youngest son Spencer's trial in 1699 and the resulting intensification of both family and social pressures, as well as her own consciousness of her advancing age and need to prepare for death. The rest of this study traces the conditions of Sarah's life and her responses to them in the period of the diary—from 1700 when she first appeared as an angry, fifty-six-year-old wife, disapproving mother, frustrated mistress of servants, defensive gentlewoman, and pious Anglican, through her gratifications and mortifications at the spectacular rise of her son William to the lord chancellorship, and her years of freedom and benevolence in widowhood—to 1716, when after her alienation from the political and social world during the Sacheverell trial and Tory ascendancy, she stopped writing because of her increasing physical infirmity in late old age.

CHAPTER 2

"The Unhappy Accidents of My Life"

I have lived with Sir W[illiam] (upon Computation) almost 14000 daies, and from the bottom of my Soul do believe I never past one without Something to be forgiven him. . . . [1]

As this retrospective comment from 1702 demonstrates, Sarah perceived her marriage to have been unhappy from its beginning. And it does appear from the fragmentary evidence for Sarah's married life in the years before she began the diary that family relations in the Cowper household were fraught with hostility, conflict, and tension, most visibly over tight finances, political choices, the children and their marriages, and just basic temperamental disparity. While Sarah managed on one occasion at least to effectually further one son's career, demonstrating some of the rewards and powers of motherhood, the general picture of her married life is one of frustration and resentment. Sarah seems to have responded to this marital situation by reading extensively and writing profusely, a practice that served as an emotional outlet, productive project, source of comfort and guidance, and testament to her personal virtue in difficult circumstances. For the first thirty years this activity was in the form of collecting and extracting the writings of others, but in 1700, under the added strain of the fallout of her youngest son Spencer's trial for murder, this habit of responding to family tension moved into a new arena—personal expression in the form of a biblical commentary and, most important, the diary.

Sarah Holled married into a family where the men had followed a typical economic trajectory, using banking, government office, professional training, and mercantile marriages to amass capital with which to buy land, thus qualifying themselves for moving up the social scale and into the gentry through wealth, real estate, and political service. The earliest Cowper of whom much at all is known, John (d. 1609), was at least a second-generation Londoner, and seems to have been a prosperous notary public and moneylender.[2] His son William became a customs farmer whose lucrative perquisites included the right to collect a new (1622) tax on French and Spanish wines. William invested in London houses and then began buying land, mostly in Kent, but also in Surrey, Essex, Lincoln, and Wiltshire. In 1631 he acquired a county seat, Ratling Court, in Kent. A royalist, he was created a baronet in 1642 and suffered heavy financial and personal losses for his support of the king.[3] In fact, his eldest son, John, who had been educated at Lincoln's Inn, married a merchant's daughter, and was a customs farmer alongside his father, died imprisoned in Ely House for fighting in the royalist cause.[4] At least one other son was trained in the law; Sir James Cowper was a barrister and became the first member of Parliament in the family.[5] At William's death in 1664, his grandson, Sarah's Sir William, inherited through his father, John, the title, the Kent and Surrey lands and leases, and the houses in Cornhill in London.[6]

In marrying Sarah Holled that same year, Sir William was continuing the family tradition of contact with London and mercantile marriages, but as mentioned in the Introduction, he did not achieve a particularly impressive infusion of mercantile wealth into the Cowper family. From the size of this inheritance, Sarah's father, Samuel, appears to have been moderately prosperous—perhaps what Gregory King would consider a "lesser merchant"—with an average annual income of about £200. Though Geoffrey Holmes warns that King is at his most unrealistically conservative in his conception of the numbers and income of that part of the population involved in commerce,[7] the general scale of his estimate indicates that Samuel Holled's daughter was not a particularly profitable catch. Presumably, the attractive aspect of her inheritance was that part of it would have been available as ready cash. Otherwise, in order to provide a more permanent endowment, Sir William ought to have been seeking a bride who would bring land into the family.

C. G. A. Clay says that with the succession of William Cowper, second baronet to the title, "the transformation of the Cowpers from London financiers and property speculators to rentier gentry was complete. There is no suggestion that he had any business interests or any sources of income other than the rents of his various estates, and he appears to have lived as a politically minded county gentleman."[8] This description is primarily on the basis of the absence of evidence; Sir William was educated at Grey's Inn and may have occasionally practiced law, especially before the death of his grandfather or before his first election to Parliament in 1679.[9] But in the main, it is quite true that he lived as a gentleman. The problem for him and his new wife Sarah, though, was that he was not notably successful as a rentier. Not having large amounts of capital to invest from his part of the inheritance from his grandfather, he bought fifteen houses in Blackfriars, but seems to have sold his Surrey and some of his Kent holdings. Rents on his remaining Kent properties did not rise much, and worse yet, the Cornhill houses in London were destroyed in the Great Fire of 1666 and then rebuilt on terms favorable to the tenants.[10] Clay calculates that Sir William's income was about £1,200 per annum in 1675. This is an unimpressive showing for a baronet—the top of the gentry socially—given Clay's estimate of £1,400 as the average annual income of baronets in Kent thirty-five years earlier, and especially keeping in mind Wrightson's suggestion that the top end of the range of gentry income in 1640 was about £10,000.[11]

The financial and social status of each party to the marriage, then, was not particularly conducive to marital harmony. Sarah married out of her social rank shortly after being orphaned by the death of her mother, and she brought a dowry suspiciously restricted from her husband's use by the terms of her mother's will. Economic difficulties may strain a marriage but are hardly guarantors of marital misery. But there are indications that differences in temperament were a serious and public source of tension by 1678, when Anthony Ashley Cooper, first earl of Shaftesbury wrote to Sir William, his friend, political ally and kinsman soon after the Cowpers' departure from a visit to the Shaftesbury country estate in Dorset:

> Since I profess I have that opinion of my Lady Coopers excellent good quallityes, and that upon great tryall that if there be a fault you must leave it; and I lay no worse imposition on you than I am ready to take on myselfe; for it is not possible that men of our Hethrodox opinions (having Ladyes so Othrodox that they tyre the very Country Parsons, with Common Prayer and [illegible word]) should not bear the whole burthen of faults; and we need not much grumble to doe it; since the accomodation we have from their vertue, discretion, and good humour, doth more than doubly repay us.[12]

This passage indicates that Sir William had complained about his wife to Shaftesbury and that both men had wives who were much more devout and wedded to the Church of England than they were. Unlike the Cowpers, however, the earl of Shaftesbury and his wife, Margaret, appear to have had a happy marriage despite their religious differences.[13]

This letter from Shaftesbury also hints at another potential bone of contention between Sarah and William related to their general outlooks on life. Lord Shaftesbury is famous as a contentious "forefather" of the nascent Whig party, notable for his resolute anti-absolutist, pro-religious toleration stance, and Sir William appears to have been equally staunch in his adherence to the Whig agenda and in his support of Shaftesbury's activities in government. When William became a member of Parliament for Hertford in 1679, he strongly supported Shaftesbury's efforts at exclusion of James, duke of York, from the succession to the throne of England.[14] In the Oxford Parliament of 1681, during the anti-Catholic hysteria of the Popish Plot, Sir William seconded two incendiary resolutions—Sir John Hotham's motion to publish the House Resolution that "the weight of England is the people and the world will find that they will sink popery at last," and the resolution to have votes printed—clear attempts to appeal to the people, and alarming republican and disorderly acts associated with Shaftesbury's beliefs and reputation.[15] Furthermore, in the Oxford Parliament William served on the committee to draw up the Third Exclusion Bill. This political stance may well have been a source of discord in Sir William's marriage. In a later comment indicating both her conflicting loyalties and her political divergence from her husband, Sarah expressed her fundamental opposition to her husband's political and intellectual leanings, even as she acknowledged her obligation to support the political choice of her husband:

> It greives me I no offner Can Comply with his [Sir William's] Sentiments about Government, being enclin'd to Love Order and Obedience, I think him too much a favorer of licentious Liberty, so that these debates make me somewhat uneasie, since the interest of my family bends me to wish well to the party he is engag'd with, and my opinion leads me to think the Contrary best for the good of the Community.[16]

While Shaftesbury was a powerful ally when political times were favorable, Sir William paid for his friendship by undertaking serious political, financial, professional, and even personal risk in the frequent periods when Shaftesbury's opposition to Charles II and the duke of York proved costly. During the later years of Lord Shaftesbury's contentious political career, Sir William repeatedly supported him in concrete, visible ways that were potentially dangerous to Sir William himself and to his family. In 1677, when Lord Shaftesbury was sent to the Tower of London by the House of Lords on the basis of the dubious accusation that he had asserted Parliament was dissolved (raising the uncomfortable question of whether a member could rightfully be prosecuted for voicing his opinion in the course of a debate in the House of Lords), Sir William acted as his trustee and was on the list of people given regular access to him in the Tower until being struck off by the king in early 1678. In 1681 Sir William served on grand juries with patently political inceptions as a Whig manager: once on the Middlesex grand jury indicting Tory Lord Treasurer Danby for the murder of Godfrey in the Popish Plot, and once trying to delay the indictment of Edward Fitzharris for a treasonous libel against the queen associating her with the Popish Plot, an indictment and trial that was a power contest between Shaftesbury and King Charles II.[17] Unfortunately for Shaftesbury and for Sir William, the king was eventually victorious, and upon Fitzharris's execution in July 1681 Charles had Shaftesbury arrested on charges of high treason for purportedly having said that he would compel the king to accept exclusion, that he had armed men prepared, and that the king deserved deposition.[18] Sir William did not escape the fallout. Though the case was not carried further, he was indicted that same year "for reflecting on some of the Hertford magistrates and was alleged to have said that if Parliament voted a supply the King would bring in arbitrary government and popery."[19] Nonetheless, upon the grand jury bringing in a verdict of Ignoramus against the Crown's evidence regarding Shaftesbury, Sir William helped stand surety for Shaftesbury's bail at the end of 1681.[20] In the violent political atmosphere that followed, Shaftesbury went into hiding in October of 1682 and in late November left London in secret for Holland. Perhaps a week before his departure, Shaftesbury put into execution a deed he had drawn up in May 1680 devising to Sir William and three other friends as trustees his whole personal estate and his property in Carolina and the Bahamas in trust to pay debts and provide cash and investment income for his wife.[21]

Even after Shaftesbury's death in January 1683, William was still perilously closely associated with malcontent Whigs, especially Shaftesbury's ally William Lord Russell. In that same year, the Rye House Plot was uncovered, an alleged plan to assassinate both Charles and his brother James on their way back from Newmarket in March 1683. In hopes of clemency, Lord Howard confessed to involvement, and extended the scale and history of conspiracies against the king in ways that implicated not only Lord Russell, but also the recently deceased Lord Shaftesbury. Lord Howard asserted that not only had there been an assassination plan set for March, but that there had been a previous plan for insurrection to take place in November 1682 led by Shaftesbury, who undertook to raise London, Lords Howard and Grey to raise Essex, and the duke of Monmouth and Lord Russell to raise the West. Lord Howard's incriminating testimony was the basis for the executions of Lord Russell and Algernon Sidney for treason in July 1683.[22] Sir William himself did not escape unscathed; he was required to find bail of £3,000.[23] Moreover, there was a political cost to be paid for his support of these Whig leaders; after the Oxford Parliament was dissolved in 1681 he did not regain a seat in the House of Commons until the Glorious Revolution, at which point Sir William reaped further dividends in being named as a justice of the peace for both Hertfordshire and Middlesex, and deputy lieutenant for Hertfordshire from 1689 until his death.[24]

That Sir William made his most risky political choices in a period when his three surviving sons were still children with futures to provide for and school fees to pay may well have been alarming to his wife Sarah. Moreover, given the couple's contrasting opinions on religion and politics, the husband's choices may have been difficult for the wife to support on an intellectual as well as familial level. The education of the children was already apparently an issue in and of itself. The eldest, William, was sent to boarding school in Saint Albans from the age of seven, and the other two presumably followed at similar ages.[25] From there, they went to Westminster School. William entered Middle Temple in 1682; Spencer entered in 1687.[26] From Sarah's comments years later it is apparent that Sir William took sole charge of the children's formal education and that she was not entirely pleased with the course he chose. In general, she seems to have thought Sir William had denied them advantages they ought to have had, and she believed that both sons considered themselves deprived as well:

> The Circumstances of our Sons is greatly Advanc'd . . . Sir W. imputing it to be the Effect of his own good Managment in the Disposal of their Education, Magnifys Himself Exceedingly. I can perceive they rather Ascribe it to the Excess of good Fortune that has Help'd them to Surmount

the prejudice and Disadvantage some parts therof gave them; and so ffar I must needs think 'em in the Right.[27]

What precisely it was in their education that Sarah found so prejudicial is not clear, but there may be some relevance in her simultaneous disapproval and satisfaction over a much later event, when Spencer removed his own son William from school early:

> At this time W[illiam] C[owper] not Sixteen till November, yet his Father hath taken him from Westminster School without, nay against the Consent of his Grandfather. May not I observe the Retaliation is just?[28]

The early and problematic marriages of all three sons, within roughly two years of each other, also caused family discord. John was first to marry in 1686, having barely turned eighteen. Presumably he met his wife, Ann Roberts, while at school, since her mother kept a boarding-house for Westminster Scholars. Certainly the marriage was not approved by the Cowper side: Sarah commented much later "none of our family ever owned her," and after John's death only four months later, the Cowpers did not maintain contact with his widow.[29] In that same year, while he was still a law student, the eldest son William married Judith Booth, with whom he had been carrying on a partly clandestine courtship.[30] In this case, however, the match was to the Cowper family's advantage, as Judith brought with her £5,000 pounds down and £4,500 in trust for any children on the death of her father.[31] In fact, Robert Booth expressed strong reservations about the match before it occurred, warning his daughter that William was too young and too poor, and that she would be forced to live with his parents.[32] He was quite right about this; William and Judith lived with Sir William and Sarah in Hertford and in London for the next twelve years,[33] an arrangement indicative of the financial straits of the Cowpers, since normally a newly married couple set up an independent household.[34]

From their letters to each other during this period, a picture emerges of frequent friction between all four members of this household, exacerbated by living together for so many years, with so many consequent opportunities for disagreement brought on by close proximity and issues of authority. Judith and Sarah argued over housekeeping jurisdiction and kept tabs on observation of the proprieties of correspondence and asking after each other when they were apart.[35] Judith and her husband William were at odds over the need for William to account for his movements (and possibly implicitly over his adultery). Tensions existed between William and Sarah over the degree of respect he owed to each parent and over his infidelity, and between the two Williams over money, down to the amount spent on letters.[36] Even Sir William and Judith were not always on good terms, as in one letter Judith told her husband, "Pray give my Duty to my Lady and Sir William if he be in humour to except of it."[37] Between Sarah and Sir William in particular, there are hints of the themes of marital conflict that surfaced more explicitly in the diary, for instance Sir William's refusal to supply her with money when she felt she needed it. There is only one occasion where the evidence points to concord between Sir William and Sarah, and unsurprisingly, it is agreement directed against Judith, whose complaints about Sarah were discounted by Sir William.[38]

Housekeeping jurisdiction was an especially difficult matter to resolve, since nowhere in prescriptive texts or general notions of hierarchy was there a specific recipe for how to deal with two women in the house, both with claims to authority. Judith was at a disadvantage on two counts: First, while the appropriate relationship between mother-in-law and daughter-in-law was ambiguous, especially in the case of co-residence, the general notions of seniority by age and deference to parental figures gave Sarah a theoretical upper hand. Second, William the younger was frequently absent on the legal circuit, and later had political duties too, once he joined his father in representing Hertford for the Whigs,[39] so Judith was on her own with her in-laws a good deal of the time, without the moral support that she might expect from her husband's presence. On the other hand, in the later years of this arrangement, Sarah might have felt pressure from the idea that the elders should retire to make way for the new generation. It is also unlikely that Sir William backed up her claims to precedence, as his attempt in 1690 to ease both financial and jurisdictional problems shows. He drew up an itemized plan to split costs and authority in the Hertford and London houses, proposing that Judith keep house in London, and that "I will keep house (or my wife) at Hertford."[40] It is notable that the counterpart to assigning Judith preeminence at one house is his awarding himself control at the other, while Sarah is mentioned only secondarily. At any rate, this plan seems not to have taken effect, for in 1692 William commented that Judith "had often threatened that if you [Sarah] kept not house at Hertford she would not meddle in Town."[41] Perhaps both sides preferred to be in control at the Hertford residence, since it was the official family seat. It may also be that without the entertainments and society of London, they had more time on their hands and thus more temptation to "meddle" in Hertford; apparently, Judith disliked summers there as much as Sarah did. In any case, they both seem to have been willing to give up London jurisdiction.

The suspicions, shifting alliances, and clashes on all sides of this family arrangement are particularly well illustrated in a vituperative letter Sarah wrote to her son William, answering complaints Judith had about her mother-in-law:

> To Mrs C[owper's] charge in general that I have endeavor'd to make difference between you, your self knows that I never went about it with you, and that ever I did endeavor it with her I give it under my hand 'tis altogather false. . . . But granting that if formerly her complaint and bitter resentments have extorted from me a compliance with her passion that I might asswage it by not seeming partial to my Son, it must needs be thought disingenious and ungratefull in her to make use of what I might then say to my prejudice. What I am to blame you for is that you should lay your ear so open to such suggestions against your Mother. . . . These practices begat in you a Cold and Neglectfull behavior toward me . . . which stirr'd up disdain and indignation in me, and thus the winter past while the agitator of these mischeifs laugh'd in her Sleeve and by throwing her Crackers among us has Blown us about Briskly.[42]

Further on in the letter, Sarah touched more directly on the reason for Judith's resentments against William, saying,

> Nor need you fear to meet any rubbs about former matters while I think of 'em not as I once did injurious to a good Woman. I confess it abates much of the offence with me for your fault is but fleshly, hers is —— .

The correspondence between Judith and her husband also hints at this problem. Judith demanded frequent letters and accounting of William's activities[43] and though his replies were affectionate, they also show annoyance at her expectations. Very frequently he commented that he would not have written with so little news if she were not so "importunate," or that she would see him so soon it was only to satisfy her that he wrote at all. In one case he was more direct:

> I was sorry to let you part without a satisfaction I could so easily have given you, but am as jealous of having my reasonable liberty suppresst, as you can be of any other matter. . . . It is a little hard, you should give way to discontent, unless I will become accountable at my age for my time. Which the more you exact, I must be the tenderer of doing. Pray entertain

no more such thoughts, as your letter hints at, and give me Cause to continue pleased with no circumstance of my life so much, as in that I am
your affectionate husband.[44]

Judith, however, had every reason to be suspicious: It is unclear when
the affair started, but Elizabeth Culling, member of a prosperous family
in a neighboring village, had a son and a daughter by William in 1697
and 1700 respectively.[45] The existence (and nearby presence) of these
children must have been particularly difficult for Judith, since some time
between 1691 and 1700 her only child died.[46]

The pressures of continual cohabitation and contention and the prospect of the summer move to Hertford apparently became intolerable to
Sarah in 1692. It is not clear what precisely prompted her drastic action,
but when Sir William and his son came home on the day of the departure to Hertford, expecting to find Sarah ready to go with them, they
found instead that she had left for an extended visit to the by-then
dowager Lady Shaftesbury. William acted as go-between for Sarah and
her husband, expressing the shock of father and son at her abrupt disap-
pearance (while assuring Sarah that Sir William was not furious, as she
had expected), and deploring the inconvenience to Lady Shaftesbury.
William also mentioned an arrangement for supplying Sarah with money
during her stay, implying a bemusement and reproach but also immediate acceptance of her action.[47] Near the end of her three-month stay,[48]
however, there are indications that the financial arrangements were not
carried out, or at least not to her satisfaction. Having first specified
where money should be sent, Sarah complained in a second letter to her
son of Sir William's refusal to comply, and demanded he at least send
what was due as her quarterly allowance.[49] In this marital conflict, and
probably in others, Sarah and William put their eldest son squarely in
the middle. In fact, he seems to have been caught in the middle of an argument between his parents early in that very summer, possibly about
his career, which may have been a precipitating factor in Sarah's flight
from London. At any rate he felt he had to reassure her of his respect
while maintaining his father's authority, saying,

> Let me beg you not to think that I can not preserve my Love and Duty to
> you, at the same time, that I unfeignedly behave my self so to my Father,
> as I should and must expect of my self.[50]

But it was a hopeless attempt at conciliation, to which Sarah indignantly
replied,

I cou'd not have imagin'd that when I said it was farr from me to insti-
gate or approve the least undutyful behavior to your father you could
wrest my meaning [so] . . . that I should seem to expect it from you.[51]

An even deeper level of discord is evident in the relationship between
Spencer and his parents. In the tradition of his brothers, Spencer married
young, to Pennington Goodere, a relative and close friend of Judith.[52]
While Sir William had consented to the marriage, it does not seem that
Sarah was consulted, as Pennington wrote to Judith, "I acknowledge my
Lady had cause to be displeased with me for presuming to marry without her consent (a fault for which I heartily ask her pardon)." Judith
seems to have been displeased as well, since in this letter Pennington was
writing to ask why Judith was shunning her.[53] Apparently this marriage
caused a major family estrangement, at least among the women, since it
is not until 1696 that Pennington and Judith began a rapprochement,
Pennington hoping "that all those unkind suspicions which have been
for several years so industriously suggested to us both by those who to
be sure had no good will to either, shall be laid aside." Even then, however, Sarah does not seem to have been on good terms with Pennington,
as the letter goes on to ask to visit Judith "at such times as it will be no
offence to my Lady."[54]

Lady Sarah Cowper responded to her domestic situation in these difficult years by compiling and indexing eleven commonplace books of
collected verses, precepts, extracts from sermons, scripture, biblical commentaries, and essays.[55] Comprising over 3,500 pages of notes and
comments, these books record Sarah's continual intellectual development and efforts to divert herself during the long three decades 1670 to
1700, and reflect her interests in politics, history, philosophy, poetry,
and religion. Moreover, her commonplace books suggest that in the
1670s, at least, she did not pursue her interests in isolation, but ex-
changed ideas and material with her friend and neighbor Martin Clifford, who was a writer, secretary to the duke of Buckingham, master of
the Charterhouse, and friend of Abraham Cowley.[56] It was probably
through him that she obtained material, including the longest extant version of Cowley's epic poem *The Civil War*, and verses by Buckingham
that were only finally been published in the twentieth century from the
copies in his commonplace books.[57]

This vast collection of extracts from her reading is testimony to
Sarah's intellectual energy, endurance, and interaction with important
literary figures. Even more notably, however, it displays her self-

conscious awareness of the reasons for, and the changing focus of, her endeavor. In the first two books she compiled, Sarah collected topical political and historical material, satirical and panegyric verses, short sayings on a variety of subjects, and accounts of foreign countries.[58] The second of these indicates in a retrospective preface that through the activity of noting what she read, Sarah was making a conscious effort to find an emotional and intellectual outlet in those years. She wrote, "If in the Dayes of my Youth, I had not Diverted my Thoughts with such Stuff as this Book Contains; the unhappy Accidents of my Life, had been more than Enough to ha' made Me Madd."[59] In 1675, Sarah started work on her first collection that concentrated exclusively on scripture and moralists.[60] This shift in her search for sources of mental stimulation signaled the subjects that were to be most prominent in the rest of her commonplace books. Aside from one volume consisting of a 600-page extract from a history of the world and a life of Mohammed, and a scrapbook of engravings, lampoons, and eulogies,[61] the remaining books were concerned with religious and moral topics.[62]

The prefaces and dedications to several of these volumes reaffirm the notion that Sarah undertook this work to channel her intellectual energies away from the unhappiness of her life, but in these later efforts, she specifically focused on improving her mind by selecting edifying material, and encouraging a regular habit of industriousness, as she explained in the preface to her "Thoughts and Meditations":

> In the year 1690 I began to make these Collections being then in Affliction and under great disturbance of mind . . . I task'd my self to write one page every day, and were it possible (as I hope it is not) that I should never reap other Benefitt from the perusing of the best thoughts and meditations of learned and good men, yet the present diversion from my own troubled thoughts may render it sufficiently worth my time and labour.

In the preface she also cited the examples of Queen Elizabeth, who to "allay her greif" read scripture, theology, and philosophy, and of Caesar Augustus who transcribed out of his reading "such wholesome precepts, or examples, as might serve him either for publick or private use which upon occasion he produced for instruction or admonition as he thought himself or any other had need."

Even as the Cowpers were sniping away at each other at home, and as Sarah was creating a productive outlet for her frustrations, Sarah's two sons made notable headway in their careers, capitalizing on both their own talents and on the political rewards to be reaped from early support of William of Orange (who would become King William III). The elder son, William, was called to the bar in early 1688 and had begun practicing on the home circuit (apparently made somewhat nervous by his mother and wife's attendance at court in Hertford and sitting near the judge to hear him plead).[63] Hearing of William of Orange's landing at Torbay, William and Spencer raised a party of twenty-six or so volunteers to ride to support him. They met the prince at Wallingford, outside Oxford and accompanied him in his progress from there to London.[64] Just as their father had acted in potentially risky ways to support the Whig cause, so too did the sons, but with considerably better results.

It is in the context of claiming reward for this political bravery that Sarah made at least one significant contribution to the family standing by her involvement in patronage for the benefit of her son William's career. She successfully used the symbolic capital she had personally amassed by her friendships and moreover offered the rationale of the compelling impulse of motherhood as a legitimating image for her participation in the patron-client system that staffed all the major institutions of early modern England.[65] Because it was a system that relied on personal relationships to fill offices and bestow favors, despite their official exclusion from the professional and political world, women could exercise significant influence.[66]

In 1689, Sarah's son William sought to gain the place of king's counsel on the basis of his Whig credentials and his prompt declaration for William of Orange when the prince landed in England in 1688.[67] But the commissioners of the great seal opposed his appointment, and King William himself objected to William's youthfulness. Rather than placing her faith in the just rewards of political service, Sarah acted to tip the scales in William's favor by enlisting the help of the connections she had cultivated with Margaret, the dowager Lady Shaftesbury, and Lady Rachel Russell especially, who was a formidable ally in her reserves of power, prestige, money, and influence. Both of these ranked significantly higher on the social scale than Sarah in all possible ways: they were of impeccable lineage, wealthy, and profusely well-connected—in fact, they were cousins themselves.[68] They were also both the widows of important Whig politicians with whom Sir William had had links. Lord Shaftesbury, as mentioned earlier, was Sir William's patron, and Lord Russell had been a friend and ally of Shaftesbury's. But both Shaftesbury and Russell had paid very high prices for their Whig principles; in 1683

Shaftesbury had died in exile and Lord Russell had been executed for treason, so Rachel Russell had the important additional symbolic clout of her status as the widow of a Whig martyr. Their wives in some respects had made similar choices to Sarah in being associated not with the strident Whiggery of their husbands but with a more cautious approach and, moreover, with the established church.[69]

Sarah did not take the lead in the effort to secure her son's place, but nonetheless wrote twice to the lord privy seal, the marquess of Halifax, to state her case.[70] Her letters show her reliance on the model of the devoted mother to justify her involvement, initially excusing her "presumption" by saying "my near concern for my son will not let me rest," and in the second letter, "Your Lordship has done me too much honour to pardon and take so favorable notice of a mother's impertinence. Nothing but the ease and content of my dear son . . . cou'd move me to be I fear so undecently importunate in this business." She might well excuse her presumption by alluding to her motherly concern, since in these letters she argued against Halifax's tactics in favor of her own:

> My son tells me your Lordship desires to have my Lord Bedford join with you in further pursuit of this favour. But (with due submission) it seems most proper to obtain some great Lawyers Opinion that may Convince the King's judgment. . . . In order to this I apply'd my self to Sir Robert Attkins who . . . has promised me to assist in what manner your Lordship shall direct.

She also directed him to a section in Montaigne's *Essays*, to represent her arguments (and implicitly his) that William was not too young for the position. In postscripts to both letters, she warned him that no one was aware of her actions for her son, perhaps implicitly insisting on her modesty, and asking that he not reveal her machinations to her husband.

In contrast to Sarah's stealth and ostensibly deferential style, Lady Rachel Russell's letters to Lord Halifax and to the attorney general, Sir Henry Pollexfen, on behalf of William Cowper demonstrate the confidence of a woman very high up the social chain addressing her equals or inferiors. Moreover, Lady Russell was in a position to recompense the favor from Halifax, since at that time he needed her public approval to sustain his own career in the face of attacks from vengeful Whigs who associated him with the execution of Lord Russell.[71] In her letter to Halifax, Lady Russell politely dismissed the condescending gallantry of the king's eventual agreement:

> If his Majesty, when he was pleased . . . to express his sense of that favour as a thing extraordinary, and to make the irregularity of it as an instance of his grace to Lady Shaftesbury and myself, we are ready to embrace His Majesty's concession in the largest sense . . . and therefore would not controvert that point, tho' very understanding men and several eminent and disinterested persons of the profession of the law, are of a contrary opinion; and the frequent instances that are given of its having been done before, seem rather to prove it has been used as an encouragement for young gentlemen to serve the King in that difficult profession.

She then smoothly cast aspersions on the motives of the commissioners of the great seal who were blocking the appointment: "Sure this is a matter below the envy of the Lord Commissioners; and what other reasons they can have in suppressing him, we think it not proper to enquire into." Her closing lines are equally graceful from a position of strength: "The readiness your lordship has expressed to undertake this matter, first in compliment to Lady Shaftesbury and myself, and since to the family, makes it unnecessary to urge zeal."[72]

Lady Russell was far more severe with the attorney general, once she had discovered that he was the main obstruction. Essentially, she demanded that he implement the appointment, but rather than argue for its legitimacy, or the worth of William Cowper, she intimated his obligation to obey the wishes of his superiors, whom he was inconveniencing. She began by reminding him of the artificiality of his high station:

> What I offer in this paper to Mr. Attorney General, I should with a better will do personally, if I were not very sure it would be very much more a trouble to you to tell you in your chamber my true joy for the eminent station you are in.

She then recounted the course of the appointment and cast his reluctance to agree to it as defiance:

> And now it stops at the Commissioners of the Great Seal, and, as they tell me, because Mr. Attorney General is not contented at it. I am sorry if it is so; and if the business had not proceeded so very far, I would not urge it. But the reflection will be very heavy upon Mr. Cowper, and not easy to my Lady Shaftesbury and myself; as for a favour to us, the King expressed he did it, and after some difficulty at the irregularity of it. . . . I undertake very few things . . . but I do not love to be baulked, when I thought my end compassed.

Finally, she threatened to bring Sarah to plead the cause in person:

> Let me know, if you please, how it stands, and if you can be inexorable
> to the earnest solicitudes of a mother, who I must bring to you, I know
> not what to say more, but that I am sorry they were ever made to hope
> for it.

This was solicitation on behalf of a client by a woman who was of such lofty status that regardless of her gender, she expected acquiescence to her requests. Lady Rachel Russell's involvement in patronage indicates the level of political power that women of the highest rank might hope to wield, if circumstances were favorable. Sarah, on the other hand, felt it necessary to deplore and conceal her actions, despite their justification on the grounds of concerned motherhood, since she was reaching beyond her remit in approaching the cabinet minister, especially without the sanction of her male relatives. Nonetheless, she knew how to make the most of her friendships with more powerful women, and in this endeavor for her son was notably successful in using the patronage system to the family's advantage.[73]

From this promising start, Sarah's son William spent the next decade building up his legal business on the home circuit and the court of chancery in London, where he attracted the positive notice of the lord chancellor, Lord Somers, while serving in his government position, and starting in 1695 sitting with his father (who had regained his seat in Parliament in the first election after the Glorious Revolution) as the two members for Hertford in the House of Commons. In the House, he established a reputation as a firm Whig and eloquent speaker in favor of electoral reform (he was on committees on bills to prevent election expenses and regulate elections in 1695 and 1698) and sympathetic to the trading interest, against standing armies and Jacobitism, chairing the committee on the bill to prevent correspondence with the deposed King James II.[74]

Spencer too did well professionally in these years; immediately after being called to the bar in 1690 he was appointed by the corporation of London as comptroller of the Bridge House estates in Southwark, which brought him residence rights at Bridge House as well as a respectable income and civic responsibilities. He became a justice of the peace for his district and traveled the home circuit as well.[75] The crisis that developed in 1699 then, was entirely unexpected, terrifying to Spencer and the entire Cowper family, and briefly catastrophic for their political fortunes.

It was also a major catalyst for Sarah's beginning not just yet another commonplace book, but a diary.

On March 13, 1699, in the course of his travels on the home circuit, Spencer stopped in Hertford and had supper at the home of Sarah Stout, the daughter of a recently deceased Quaker brewer. The Stouts had been an important part of the Dissenting alliance that supported the Cowpers, father and son, in elections, and the two families were friendly socially. Spencer then spent the night at his lodgings, a Mr. Barefoot's house, and left the next morning for Chelmsford, the next stop on the circuit. That morning after his departure, Sarah Stout's body was found in the river that ran through town. Even as Sarah Stout's body was being pulled from the river by local parish officers, a rumor apparently started that she was pregnant. Accordingly, in the course of preparing the body for burial, Sarah Stout's mother, the widow Mary Stout, called in a midwife to establish that Sarah was not pregnant. At the coroner's inquest, Spencer testified to having been the last person to see Sarah Stout alive and said he knew of no reason why she should kill herself. The inquest resulted in a verdict of suicide while not of sound mind.[76]

To the Cowpers that must have seemed to be the end of the matter, but six weeks later widow Stout, without a warrant, had her daughter's body exhumed and examined by six physicians, all of whom signed a certificate that they found "the uterus perfectly free and empty, and of the natural figure and magnitude, as usually in virgins. We found no water in the stomach, intestines, abdomen, lungs, or cavity of the thorax."[77] The first the Cowpers heard of this development was when in early May widow Stout and her stepson John Stout brought charges against not only Spencer, but two attorneys and a law clerk as accomplices, for the murder by strangulation of Sarah Stout and subsequent disposal of her body in the river. On the basis of the physicians' certificate, and the further testimony of five of the six doctors signing it that the lack of water found in the body meant that Sarah Stout did not die of drowning, and that there were discolorations of her skin near her ear and collarbone, as well as testimony that the three alleged accomplices had talked of Sarah Stout in a suspicious manner on the night of March 13, Lord Chief Justice Holt committed the four for trial. The other three men were then freed on bail, but on May 19 Spencer was remanded to King's Bench prison, where he remained until the trial in Hertford that July. In slightly over two months, then, Spencer had gone from being a successful and busy lawyer, perhaps regretful but otherwise unaffected by the suicide of a young woman in his hometown, to imprisonment, facing trial for a capital crime, in the spotlight of scandal and contemplating the possibility of death by hanging.

The trial that commenced July 16, 1699, was a travesty of judicial process. The prosecution was clearly perpetrating a malicious attack on Spencer Cowper. It totally lacked in concrete positive evidence and was aided by the presiding judge, Baron Hatsell, whose direction of the proceedings hardly qualified as impartial. The prosecutor, Mr. Jones, began by trying to give the impression that Spencer's behavior at supper at the Stout's had been suspicious, and his manner of leaving downright sinister. His questioning of Sarah Stout's servant, Sarah Walker, emphasized that Sarah Stout had been under the impression that Spencer was going to spend the night at her house and that in the maid's hearing at least, Spencer had not contradicted that impression. Furthermore, the prosecutor established that the maid left Spencer and Sarah together alone at ten-thirty that night, that at roughly ten forty-five she heard the door slam shut, and when she returned to the room a quarter of an hour later, both were gone and neither returned that night. Then, using "expert witnesses" (the physicians who had signed the certificate at the exhumation) plus witnesses who had been nearby when the body was pulled from the water, Mr. Jones claimed that Sarah could not have drowned because her body had been found floating and she had neither been seen to discharge much water, nor found to have any in her body cavities upon exhumation—these signs being, supposedly, the classic marks of death by drowning.[78] The final element of the prosecution's case was the lengthy testimony of the Gurrey family, with whom the other three defendants (Mr. Stephens, Mr. Rogers, and Mr. Marson) had lodged. The Gurreys testified that the three had arrived at eleven or a bit later that evening and while drinking together and gossiping, they had said "Mrs Sarah Stout's courting days were over" and that her "business was done." Mrs. Gurrey also testified that the next morning after the three had left, she discovered a cord in the room where they slept. From this testimony, which at least in the transcript was never summed up and explained by the prosecutor, the jurors were apparently supposed to make the truly huge leap that somehow all four men desired to kill Sarah Stout, conspired to do so, and that between ten forty-five and eleven, one or all of the men had actually accompanied or met Sarah Stout at the river, strangled her, and thrown her in.

Spencer was not allowed counsel at the trial and so defended himself. He argued that he was not guilty of murder because no murder had occurred, but rather the suicide by drowning of a depressed and lovesick woman, and that in any case, he had no motive for murder and no opportunity. Spencer suggested instead that the whole prosecution was motivated by party politics and sectarian pride. He began testimony for the defense by calling the parish officers who actually pulled out the body to establish that Stout was in fact found under four or five inches of water in the four-foot deep river, driven up off the riverbed proper by running into the stakes that lay across the river at one-foot intervals at a slant upward in the direction of the current. Those parish officers also testified to a significant amount of water being discharged from Stout's nose. Moreover, testimony made clear that while there were two skin discolorations, one on Sarah Stout's collarbone, the other near her ear, no witness saw any marks at all on Sarah Stout's neck.[79] Then, Spencer offered the testimony of his own battery of expert witnesses, seven respected London physicians including Dr. Garth and Dr. Sloane.[80] They argued that there is much variability in how much water is found inside a drowned body and that a little water in the lungs is certainly sufficient to suffocate, and that at any rate, one would not be able to establish water content or drowning in a body after six weeks' decay. Spencer thus cast serious doubt on the supposedly scientific prognostications of the prosecution about the nature of the physical indications of drowning, having already suggested that Sarah's body manifested those indications anyway.

Following up with a plausible explanation for Sarah Stout drowning herself, Spencer brought in eight witnesses to Sarah's persistent depression, to her statements that it stemmed from her hopeless love of an unavailable man, and to her hints of an early death. In a blockbuster of a revelation, Spencer then presented the court with two letters he had received, in Mistress Stout's handwriting, in which she asked Spencer to come visit her in Hertford in terms that intimated her love for this married man, and that suggested that thus far, Spencer had resisted her overtures.[81] Witnesses attested that Spencer had shown these letters to friends and to his brother William when he received them, the week before Sarah Stout died.

Concluding his case, Spencer demonstrated that the timing meant that it was impossible for him to have carried out the alleged murder, even if it had taken place. Witnesses placed him going into the Glove Inn at eleven, visible there for at least a quarter hour, and by half past eleven at his lodgings and in bed. Eminent London financier Sir William Ashurst then testified that he had timed the walks from the Stout house, Glove Inn, and Spencer's lodgings to the riverside site. Each of these walks had taken half an hour or more—far too much time for Spencer to have squeezed a murder into the maximum fifteen minutes unaccounted for in traveling between the Stouts' house and Glove Inn, or between Glove Inn and Mr. Barefoot's.[82]

In a very brief footnote to the main defense (remarkable for a trial in which four men could be hung if found guilty) the three other men (who had not been connected by evidence with the death in any way) simply testified as to how they happened to be in Hertford that day and about their movements. Witnesses placed them at a coffeehouse, a tavern, and their lodgings for the entire evening from their arrival in town until going to bed. As to the suspicious comments the Gurreys claimed they made, the men admitted to inquiring about Sarah Stout's character because they knew her suitor, a Mr. Marshall in London; but they categorically denied any further or more ominous conversation about her.[83]

After some pointed questions from the prosecutor as to why Spencer had not mentioned Sarah's unrequited love at the coroner's inquest as an explanation for the suicide (to preserve her modesty, was the answer), the trial concluded with an egregiously biased summing-up. Throughout the trial, Baron Hatsell had allowed the prosecution pretty much free rein. In contrast, he had consistently restricted Spencer's defense, even on points not pertaining to law. For instance, when in his opening statement Spencer noted that one ought to prove a murder occurred before trying a man for it, Hatsell warned, "do not flourish too much, Mr. Cowper."[84] Likewise, Baron Hatsell's account of the evidence was a ridiculously brief, stunningly irresponsible depiction of the significance of the testimony, which judging from the transcript probably took under five minutes to speak in its entirety. Beginning by dwelling on the testimony of Sarah Stout's maid about Spencer's intentions as to where to spend the night, he cast it as sinister that Spencer did not deny he would stay at the house and that "Mr. Cowper was the last person seen in her [Sarah Stout's] company." Hatsell totally ignored the issue of the whereabouts of Spencer and the three men at the presumed time of the presumed murder, and the fact that witnesses accounted for all four men's movements in a way that made it logistically impossible for them to have murdered Stout. In similar fashion, in his brief summary of the problem of how reliable water in the body was as evidence for drowning, he accepted, despite witnesses to the contrary, that no water emerged from Sarah Stout's nose, and that one could actually determine how much water was in a body that had decayed for six weeks. Furthermore, when in a mere two sentences he considered the question of motive, Hatsell declared he saw no motive for either murder or suicide, discounting the evidence of Sarah's melancholy state except as evidence of distemper of the brain that would excuse Sarah from what would otherwise be an immodest crush on a married man. Lastly, Hatsell gave total credence to the reports of the Gurreys and none at all to the denials of the three accused men as to how they had spoken of Sarah Stout. He concluded by reflecting on their alleged conversation, and on the case in general:

> What you can make of it, that I must leave to you; but they were very strange expressions; and you are to judge whether they were spoken in jest, as they pretend, or in earnest. . . . Truly, gentlemen, these three men, by their talking, have given great cause of suspicion; but whether they, or Mr. Cowper, are guilty or no, that you are to determine. I am sensible I have omitted many things; but I am a little faint, and cannot repeat any more of the evidence.[85]

After about half an hour, the jury returned a verdict of not guilty. As Edward Foss in his *Biographia Juridica* said of Hatsell, "by his querulousness at the trial, and the stupidity of his summing up, the prisoners certainly had no cause to thank him for their acquittal."[86]

It seems that many people were perfectly convinced of Spencer's innocence,[87] but unfortunately for the Cowpers, the matter did not end there. There was still on the books a law that "allowed an appeal for murder to be instituted within a year and a day after the death by the next heir of the deceased."[88] Widow Stout, with the assistance of her stepson John Stout, sought out the heir, Henry Stout, who turned out to be a boy of ten. Then, in March 1700, just three days before the term set for such appeals would expire, widow Stout pretended to be the heir's guardian and obtained a writ from the sheriff without the knowledge or consent of Henry or his mother, the rightful legal guardian. A month later, in order to get the child to make an appearance before the lord keeper for the appeal to proceed, the widow Stout and some of her kin fraudulently intimated to the mother that the legal proceeding was to help settle Sarah Stout's estate on the boy Henry. When the mother discovered what was actually going on, she and her son obtained the writ from the sheriff and burned it.[89]

Undaunted, widow Stout petitioned the lord keeper for a new writ of appeal. The heir and his mother counterpetitioned, disowning the former writ and requesting that no new writ be issued. At a hearing in May 1700 before the lord keeper, widow Stout and her stepson John, the heir Henry Stout and his mother, and Spencer and his brother William all appeared to argue over the possibility of a second writ of appeal. During the hearing, another issue arose that briefly derailed the proceedings and illustrated the remarkably dire convergence of circumstances in law, politics, and personal emotions under which Spencer labored. The "appeal of murder" was a very infrequently used process, allowed only as a limited preventive to "faint prosecution."[90] In this case the prosecution was manifestly not faint, and generally, the judiciary disapproved of the use of this device. But there was some dissent, and Spencer was nearly caught in the middle. In the course of the arguments, some of the judges present asserted that the notion of an appeal for murder cases "was a revengeful, odious prosecution, and therefore deserved no encouragement."[91] To which Chief Justice Holt (the magistrate who had denied Spencer bail at the outset of the case) "with great vehemence and zeal said that he wondered that any Englishman should brand an appeal with the name of odious prosecution; that for his part he looked upon it to be a noble prosecution, and a true badge of English liberties."[92] While Holt was outnumbered, the risk was that judges arguing over a legal principle might allow widow Stout's efforts to succeed. Despite this distraction into questions of legal principle, with the advice of four other judges, Lord Keeper Wright refused another writ because the first one had been fraudulently obtained, without the knowledge or approval of the supposed plaintiff, and after such delay as indicated that it was meant to spin out scandal "maliciously and vexatiously" and not to obtain justice.[93]

After the lord keeper refused the writ, the indefatigable widow Stout brought a petition to Parliament for a new trial. But her petition was never heard there, and it seems she finally gave up, as there is no record of further action after June 1701.[94] But meanwhile, the trial proceedings had been published, and the case and its further developments were the subject of numerous pamphlets on both sides from July 1699 through 1700, keeping the Cowper family in the spotlight of public scandal. Moreover, for those nearly two years the Cowper family was never sure that Spencer might not have to stand trial yet again.

Those pamphlets bring up another notable issue: If Spencer had no motive to kill Sarah Stout, what motive could widow Stout have had to be so energetic in her prosecutions? Spencer himself in his defense pointed to political and sectarian motives, intimating that no prosecution would have occurred had it not been for the machinations of a political enemy, the Quaker Mr. Mead, and local Tories hoping to make gains at the next election against the two Cowper men holding the Hertford seats in Parliament.[95] In the pamphlet he wrote shortly after the trial, Spencer again pointed to political motives and suggested that matters of religious honor operated as well: "Nothing but the zeal of some Quakers for the reputation of their sect, to clear it from being liable to the same infirmities the rest of the world are, assisted by the heat of faction, which is in most boroughs, could ever have stirred up a prosecution."[96] The "infirmities" he mentions have usually been taken by commentators as the shame of suicide, both in and of itself, and also as Spencer further elaborated, as it would reflect on people who believed themselves possessed of an "inner light" of revelation from God. And while issues of politics and corporate religious honor may well have been operating, and apparently were widely considered to have a major bearing, they do not explain why or how party politics or Quaker pride could necessarily have been effectually forwarded without the agreement of the main agent in carrying the prosecution forward, namely, the widow Stout. She may well have been an avid partisan (though one would have presumed for the Whigs, who were associated with Dissenting creeds, not the Tories) or a staunch defender of her sect, but the pamphlet entitled "The Case of Mrs. Mary [Widow] Stout" also points to what may have been for her the definitive motivation: "they would do well to consider, if it were their own case, to have an only child murdered and her reputation rendered infamous to posterity, whether nature and duty would not oblige them to use all means to make a discovery of the cause thereof?" From the moment of discovery of the body, widow Stout's daughter's name had been dragged through the mud—not, to begin with, by the sin of suicide and its imputation on the Quaker's spiritual pretensions, but by casting aspersions on Sarah Stout's sexual virtue. It is worth noting that her mother's initial attentions were to establishing that Sarah had not been pregnant, in response to rumors to the contrary. Of course, in bringing a prosecution, even if she intended to defend her daughter's reputation, widow Stout ended up causing it to be besmirched further. In the trial itself, extending this destruction of her honor as a woman, Sarah Stout's own letters depicted her as immodestly throwing herself at a married man. Those letters were then published with the trial transcript, in one more violation of the code of modesty surrounding women's bodies and expression.

In the pamphlet war that followed the trial, both sides attacked each other's credit and reputation in the arenas where it would hurt most— for Sarah as a woman, her sexual virtue; for Spencer as a man, his professional honesty with clients in money matters. In a pamphlet arguing Spencer's side, in a departure that had nothing to do with impartial evidence and everything to do with smear tactics, the concluding paragraph pointed out that certifying that Sarah's uterus was free from conception did not also certify virginity: "She might not be a virgin, though charity should oblige us to hope at least that she was."[97] On widow Stout's side, a pamphlet claimed Spencer had taken £1,000 in cash from Sarah and promised to invest it but had subsequently embezzled the money. This charge could be seriously damaging to a young lawyer like Spencer, who was building up a practice on the basis of his reputation for creditable dealings with his clients. The publicity of the trial and subsequent developments rendered both parties notorious and brought their families into the censorious public eye as well. Spencer's brother and father were anticipating an election soon, and all the Cowper kin faced social ostracism and very uncomfortable moments in company.[98]

In this period of grave personal and political threat to the family, the Cowpers drew together to present a united front to the public. They supported Spencer through the ordeal in a number of ways, most important of which was probably William's help with the management of his defense. William and Judith also testified on his behalf regarding Sarah Stout's character and state of mind. Sarah visited her son in prison, attended the trial (along with the rest of the family),[99] and retired from the round of social visiting as much as possible, both to avoid stirring anything up and to keep her own character above reproach.[100] Moreover, it may be that the pressure of the Sarah Stout case was a factor in the amelioration of Sarah's relationship with her daughters-in-law. In November 1700, Sarah mentioned spending an evening with them, "perfectly easy and unconcern'd at all that's past." The next year she went so far as to tell Pennington that she had forgiven her.[101]

Perhaps also in response to the pressure of this trial and its aftermath and to the publicity and family solidarity, in May 1700 Sarah resorted to her standard escape valve and began another commonplace book.

This was her most ambitious project to date: her own commentary on scripture. In the preface, Sarah simultaneously insisted on her originality and disclaimed any pretense to scholarship:

> I began to read two chapters a day in the Holy Bible, one out of the Old, and one out of the New Testament, taking notes and observances entirely from my own memory and meditation, without looking into the interpretation of others, or any commentator whatsoever. This I say because the mistakes or errors there found, may be imputed to my own weakness and ignorance, to which indeed they will wholly belong. As the flat and low conception, with the unskillful style might abundantly testify, without this confession.

In this move from transcribing to recording her own observations, Sarah was trespassing on clerical territory, though not without some uneasiness at her presumption. Furthermore, she was aware of a future audience to whom she ought to justify her excursion into the province of male authors.

But it was two months later in July of 1700, when Sarah was fifty-six years old, that she started to write her most important work. When William and Sarah returned to their Hertford house to spend the summer, the scandal was still simmering, the Cowpers were still ostracized, and living as they did in the center of town, every time they ventured outdoors they were in the public eye. At the best of times, Sarah disliked summers in the country, finding Hertford provincial and boring. At the same time, Sarah felt her two sons were neglecting her, and that her domestic arrangements were in total disarray, so even more than usual, she was bored, lonely, and under siege. It is apparent that she initially turned to the idea of the spiritual diary as a strategy to occupy her hours, to provide solace and support, and to work on dealing more effectively with her situation, as can be seen in the very first entry and on succeeding days:

> July 25. My Custom hath been of late, to be in Bed from Nine to Six, the other 15 Hours I am 12 at least, alone. When I arose this Morn: I mett with a snare laid for me by an Instrument of the Enemy of Souls. . . . Since it is not possible for me to redress these Domestick greivances, I wou'd notice them to no other purpose, but to find by what means to sustain and bear them well. What if I try this expedient? Never to speak any thing but what is necessary to be said for some Use or End. that so my Mind may be kept more Close to the One thing Needfull, from which these vexations too much Distract it. Oh my God do Thou assist me, I

can find no sattisfaction from my own Conduct, nor Hope from any
thing but thy Mercy.

July 26. I Escap'd till Noon, but then was hugely provok'd; however with
some performance of my resolution I made shift to gett over it pretty
well. Oh that I cou'd live one Day so as to be pleas'd with my own doings, tho' I had no reason to be so with others.

August 11. I mett with an Extream provocation from servants . . . to divert the Thoughts of it I went to walk, taking a Manuscript wherein long
since I had writ precepts, etc., opening the Book where I did not intend,
lit upon this. Shou'd a Wise man reason with unprofittable talk, or with
Speeches wherewith he Can do no good? Methought this was a Divine
admonition which put me in Mind I had Fallen from the Resolution made
July 25th. See—I must reinforce it or I am lost to all peace.[102]

As with the biblical commentary, this diary was another sort of work
she could accomplish that became in the process an important vent for
her own feelings and frustrations as well as serving as a spiritual journal
in the more formal devotional sense. Four months after beginning the
diary, Sarah herself articulated both the causes of her profound personal
dissatisfaction at this point in her life, and her identification of a way to
occupy her days that would afford her comfort and authority:

Most things of this world are to me as tho' I had them not. A hus[band] I
have without mutual complaissance or right correspondence. Children
without society or kind conversation, a house and servants without
authority or command. . . . My sattisfaction must arise from the contentment of my own mind, or I shall be totally disconsolate and void of
all comfort. A pious life gives power, liberty, ease and peace.[103]

CHAPTER 3

The Angry Years: Married Life, 1700–1704

When I hear the Bills read at Church for any disease or distress whatever, it Shocks me less than the Banes of Matrimony. Cou'd I fourty years ago ha' foreseen what hath Since happen'd, I shou'd sooner ha' Choke (were it no Sin), to leap into a Whirl:pool than suffer as I have done in that State.[1]

While there are strong indications from the Cowper correspondence and the prefaces to Sarah's commonplace books that her family life was not happy, it is only once the diary starts in 1700 that it is possible to assess the level of friction and explore its causes. As her dire assertion above indicates, it is clear that Sarah often regretted marrying Sir William. Moreover, this intense regret and resentment is a key factor in not only her impulse to write in the first place, but in her practice of borrowing from and subverting prescriptive texts as a strategy for coping with her marital struggle and justifying her actions in her relations with her husband and children.

What was it about her relationship that made Sarah so vehemently negative about marriage in general and about Sir William specifically? From her perspective, William was a disorderly, irreligious, avaricious, tyrannical fool. In his turn, Sir William probably regarded Sarah as insufferably proud and smugly pious. In addition to the constant sniping at each other because of differences in character and opinion, the main bone of contention in their married life was power in the household, especially, though not exclusively, authority over the servants. From numerous incidents related in the diary, it appears he refused to let her hire, fire, or discipline the servants at her discretion; exercised very tight control over money, household supplies, and furnishings; and criticized her in front of servants, relations, and guests. Since her language regarding the "wicked" servants is vitriolic, and since she did not often mention what, exactly, their perfidiousness entailed, one might suspect this conflict had more to do with her dislike of Sir William than with the bad behavior of servants. Equally, given her constant vehement diatribe against her husband's character, one might think she was overstating the case for his tyranny over even trivial aspects of housekeeping. But there are enough specifics to indicate that as well as the run-of-the-mill insolence and disobedience that might well have seemed to deserve discipline or dismissal, Sarah was fearful and furious over actual episodes of embezzlement, violence, drunkenness, and situations where her mobility and safety depended on servants. In the space of three years, two coachmen kept part of the money Sir William gave them to use for feeding the horses (either billing him more than the feed cost and then not paying the final bill, or not feeding the horses); one cheated her grandson, twelve-year-old Spencer Cowper, out of money given him by his uncle; two menservants beat two women servants and one of the men beat up the gardener too; and one coachman came in at noon, so drunk he could hardly stand, much less drive.[2] In no case did William immediately dismiss them or even, according to Sarah, punish them; and he overruled or undermined her attempts to do so. In the case of the coachman who cheated his grandson, Sir William admitted to Sarah that the man was a rogue, intimated she could fire him, and then invited him to remain. When a cook complained to William about being beaten, he told her to get a warrant and did nothing further; when the gardener's mother came to express her worries for her son's safety, Sir William told Sarah to close the door to gossips. To make matters worse, outsiders could see what was going on, which infuriated and embarrassed Sarah. She was particularly chagrined when one visitor told her someone had called her a bad mistress to her servants.[3] As Sarah saw it, Sir William both deprived her of her management rights and did a terrible job of governing the servants himself. As she put it, "Sure to live with S^r W and his Tools must be the Emblem of Hell where is Confusion and every Evil work."[4] By implying that husband and servants were actually in alliance against her, in drawing the parallel between infernal chaos and her own household, Sarah was expressing her disturbance at what she felt was a fundamentally out-of-order family hierarchy.

There are enough specific examples, even though taken from a biased source, to suggest that Sir William was extraordinarily controlling of even the smallest of household matters. Sarah wanted sheets for an ar-

riving visitor's bed, but Sir William would not give her the key to the
linen cupboard. Sarah wanted to have dinner served an hour later but
could not enforce her command, and Sir William complained about how
much it cost for her to have breakfast and a midmorning snack.[5] The
pettiness of some of the bickering, the intensity and fury of Sarah's response, and the underlying point of their disagreement are illustrated in
the following entry:

> With taking out a Table that Cumber'd up a Room, Sir W[illiam] saith I
> have spoil'd the Uniformity of it. 'Tis mervellous to hear him talk how
> much he is for Liberty . . . when at the same time there is not a more ab-
> solute Tyrant, where he hath power (which indeed he has not over any
> one but me) than himself. He restrains me in all my due priviledges, so far
> is he from giving me Ease or Liberty. . . . I just now mett with a Note that
> tells the difference between a wife and a Concubine. The wives adminis-
> ter'd the affairs of the Family, but the Concubines were not to meddle
> with them. Sure I have been kept as a Concubine not a Wife.[6]

What was at issue in this and many of their arguments was the correct
conception of marital roles. Based on her own observation,[7] experience,
and her reading of conduct books and other prescriptive literature, Sarah
held firm ideas about the authority due to her as a wife. While her expectations of the wifely role were conventional in the sense that she accepted the general assumption of women's lesser capabilities and their
consequent necessity for subordination to their husbands when married,
she was also acutely aware of the "due privileges" allotted to wives in
the patriarchal ideal of the family. There was the discussion in *Domesticall Duties*, for instance, where William Gouge was very specific in his
division of responsibilities in the home into male and female domains.
Husbands were in charge of the "great and weighty affairs" of directing
the religious life of the family, supplying a house, income, and other
major necessities, keeping older or stubborn children under control, and
"ruling men-servants." Wives were to deal with "some less, but very
needful matters as nourishing and instructing children when they are
young, adorning the house, ordering the provision brought into the
house, ruling maid-servants, with the like."[8] It was therefore not only a
sign of ill temper, but unjust and wrong in the natural and divine scheme
of things for a husband to withhold from his wife the powers of her jurisdiction. This deprivation was additionally troubling to Sarah because
it lessened her ability to perform the duties associated with women's domestic roles—duties that were part of her Christian obligations. Sarah,

then, did not so much feel repressed by patriarchy as she was outraged that its prescriptions, as she understood them, were not being fulfilled.

If Sarah was to follow patriarchal ideology to the letter, applying it equally to her own obligations and to her husband's, her behavior toward Sir William ought to have been quiet, cheerful, and submissive, despite his failure to live up to his duty as a patriarch. Rather than gracefully bowing to Sir William's style of governance, however, Sarah aired her grievances and claimed her rights both in her writing and in actual arguments. A vivid example of the hostile depths these skirmishes could reach, and of Sarah's paradoxical portrayal of herself as long-suffering martyr at the same time as she clearly answered back in anything but the prescribed deferential manner of a wife, is in this very nasty encounter:

> Woe is mee, how Short and uncertain are my Sattisfactions? After passing two Hours this Morn: with more Content than Usual; Came Sir W in a rage for my Ringing a Bel at 5 a Clock, which he Said disturbed his Rest; and would not have Patience to hear me give the Reason which was this. The Whole family goes to Bed before Ten if they Will. So I desire to rise at 7 but Cannot, unless my Maid gett up at 6 to make my Fire. If I Call not till then, they Come not till 7, making divers pretences, as they Cannot Strike Light etc. So I meant till that habit was broke to awake 'em as aforesaid. but in much wrath he Swears I Shall not; if I make a noise to disturb him he'le throw me and my Bell to the Devil. I cou'd not forbear to Say Sure 'twas not to be forgott how many 100 Nights Rest his Base Usage had lost me; and I did also remember how oft he had bragg'd that all the Disasters of his Family never Robb'd him of Sleep for an Hour; then Sure 'tis hard to imagine a litle Bell at that distance it is, wou'd do it. He Swore—Damn mee for a Bitch did I Hector him, he wou'd fell me to the ground. This I must own was more than I Cou'd decently bear, so I set up to out dare, it being the only way to deal with it. Now the lasting Sting of this is, that it Comes from one who insults only poor me like a Slave; wheras any Rascal or Drab he has kept, may with all imaginable Insolence Pluck him by the Nose and he tamely takes it to a Wonder—[9]

If the idea of wifely obedience and meekness should have proved in theory a major obstacle to such behavior, in reality, Sarah found herself in circumstances that seemed to demand that she ignore, rationalize, or circumvent this part of the prevailing social code. Sarah considered her husband morally and intellectually inferior to herself. While acknowledging her duty to obey cheerfully, even in such a situation, she evaluated her performance of that duty more self-righteously than accurately. Sarah's treatment of prescriptive texts that deal with marriage, therefore, needs to be understood in the context of her experience of life with Sir William. Sarah selected and interpreted Scripture, history, poetry, devotional works, sermons, and conduct books to formulate and buttress her claims to domestic authority. Many of these works were written in order to legitimate and reinforce the existing social order by demonstrating its natural and divine origins and explaining the appropriate relationships of superiors and inferiors in families and the respective duties they entailed. But when Richard Allestree or William Gouge detailed mutual rather than one-way systems of obligation, and assigned spheres of influence to husbands and wives, they provided a small but significant opportunity for someone like Sarah to use them for purposes of self-justification by focusing not just on their own performance of duties, but on their rightful share of power and on how well or badly other members of the household fulfilled their obligations. Thus, when writers addressed the problem of allegiance to bad husbands, yet insisted on the necessity of submission to them, Sarah generally focused on the unfavorable descriptions of such husbands rather than on the continued requirement of obedience. While ostensibly relying on such books to shape her conduct, she managed to understand these writers in a way that vindicated more than directed her expectations and behavior. In reading and selecting these sources, she did not choose socially radical works, or criticize the prescriptions she found in the standard sermons and manuals. Rather, she looked to the socially sanctioned authority of the Bible, the Church, and eminent men to support her conception of what marriage should be like and for practical tactics to alleviate her situation. But in both searches her intrinsic sense of self-righteousness reshaped the theories and directions she found.

Occasionally, Sarah's appropriation technique can be seen just by looking at her comments about what she was reading. Now and again, she directly referred to tracts that outlined wives' duties and rights in order to describe and justify her position and behavior as a wife and to point out the injustices that prevented her from fulfilling her duties completely. In January 1701, she wrote:

> A Book Coming in my way, wherin was Contain'd the Duty of Wives, I read that particuler, and find I have discharg'd the Negative part punctually well not being guilty of any thing forbiden. As to some positives such as Education of Children, governing the house and Servants, I have not been in Capacity to perform that well, the power being taken from me by him who shou'd have invested me with it.[10]

In conduct books, the primary emphasis is on the wife's duty to obey the husband. The husband's responsibilities to the wife are much more briefly described (he must love and govern her), and the duties of governing children and servants are put more in terms of parental authority and the authority of masters than specifically what a wife ought to do. In entries like this one, however, books that were supposed to direct the readers' thoughts and actions (in this case, toward submission) became sources that supported her critique of her husband, making manifest his tyranny and wrongful deprivation of her rights. On numerous occasions, rather than examine herself as a wife and conclude that she had misbehaved in not fulfilling her obligations, Sarah redirected the onus of performance onto her husband. From practical, patriarchal guides to her behavior as a wife, Sarah managed to extract meanings that affirmed her own conception of herself while condemning her husband's performance of his role.

There are many instances where Sarah repeated this condemnation of her husband's poor performance of his role as husband and master of the family and absolved herself of responsibility for miscarriages of duty. In some passages, Sarah also indicated that not only did she accept the convention of wifely obedience, but she considered herself to have fulfilled that duty and was comforted by the thought of a reward in the next life for having done so. Clearly, she thought of herself as being properly submissive, and therefore deserving of the prize held out by handbook writers to sweeten the prospect of subordination in this life. Quoting one of Richard Allestree's works, she reminded herself that, "How uneasie soever the perversness of the husband may be, he Cannot make the Duty less but more rewardable by God. This is thank worthy if for Conscience toward God ye endure greif suffering wrongfully."[11] Allestree is not unusual in his emphasis on the rewards of the afterlife, and Sarah frequently echoes the distinction between the attractions and desirability of heaven and the contemptible, changeable nature of this world. In this aspect of her attitude, again, she accepted the conventional depiction of the way the social order was supposed to work and the need for piety, patience, and resignation in her place in it. She often repeated the dictum that devout meditation would, through communion with God and the promise of a better life in the next world, provide consolation here on earth. Accordingly, abridging a passage in *Reflections Upon Marriage*, she spoke with Mary Astell's voice, passionately denouncing Sir William's chief failings and describing what her response ought to be:

> To be yoak'd for Life to a disagreeable Temper; to be Contradicted in every thing, and bore down not by Reason but Authority of a Master whose Will and Commands a Woman Cannot but despise at the Same time She Obeys them, is a Misery none Can have a just Idea of but those who have felt it. If this be a Womans hard Fate She is as Unhappy as any thing in this World Can make her. A Man in the like Case has a hundred ways to releive himself, but neither Prudence nor Duty will allow a Wife to ffly out: her Business and Entertainment are all at home and though he make it never So uneasie to her, She must be Content and make her best on't. Indeed the provocation is great, yet nothing Can justify the revenging the Injurys Wee receive from others upon our Selves: If you wou'd be Reveng'd of your Enemies, Live Well.[12]

Here too, Sarah ultimately pointed to a refuge in piety at the same time as she implied her own satisfactory behavior. The intensity and reiteration of this theme in her diary shows again the importance of religious belief to Sarah's life and outlook, and the fact that religion could offer a powerful level of comfort to women dissatisfied with their circumstances.

Emphasizing the fruits of piety in the next life is part of a characteristic pattern of writing about her marriage: Sarah complained about her husband, often in the words of people she had read; consoled herself with the thought of a heavenly reward for her blamelessness; and frequently neglected to acknowledge the actual advice authors gave for wives in situations such as she perceived her own to be (that is, that her husband was inferior to her in nearly every way possible). A remarkable example of this strategy of appropriation is visible in Sarah's treatment of George Savile, the marquess of Halifax's *The Lady's New Year's Gift*. In order to criticize one of Sir William's specific faults (avarice) and to deplore the laws of matrimony, Sarah detached passages from what is normally seen as the epitome of the oppressive prescriptive text and recast them in a very different context. In the process, she dramatically subverted Halifax's text.

Halifax wrote this book as advice to his daughter on married life and on how to deal with various flaws in husbands. Sarah, however, did not quote his advice about all of the character defects she thought her husband had. Halifax advised his daughter to smile at and yield to a bad-tempered husband; or to run things tactfully, giving the impression the husband was giving the orders, even if he happened to be a fool.[13] Halifax also commented unfavorably on avaricious husbands, but then went on to detail the appropriate response to that flaw. First, a wife must make sure she was not mistaken in her judgment of her husband; then she was to go along with his behavior, seizing opportunities when he was in a good mood to persuade him to generosity.[14]

This same passage, quoted in part in Sarah's diary, has a very different sense. In her entry, she shortened Halifax's ideas on avarice and combined them with his views on the impossibility of divorce. Starting with his comments on the undesirability of such a husband, she repeated Halifax's remark that

> If in the Lottery of the World you Draw a Covetous Husband it will not make you Proud of your good Luck; yet Such a One must be endured tho' there are few passions more Untractable than that of Avarice.[15]

But then she went straight on, without mentioning his advice about how to act with such a husband, to quote him on divorce:

> The Causes of Separation are now so very Coarse that few are Confident enough to Buy their Liberty at the Price of having their Modesty so Expos'd. And for Disparity of Minds which above all other Things requireth a Remedy, the Laws hath made no Provision; so litle refined are Numbers of Men by whom they are Compiled.[16]

Here, too she left out Halifax's answer to the problem. He went on to warn his daughter that while the laws of divorce might seem to be cause for complaint, in reality, "the institution of marriage is too sacred to admit a liberty of objecting to it"; and even though the laws were made by unrefined men, women, "being the weaker sex . . . maketh it reasonable to subject it [lawmaking] to the Masculine dominion." Furthermore, Halifax added, no law is perfect, and the very few cases of injustice were far outweighed by the necessity of keeping such a fundamental social institution intact.[17] As well as leaving this second half out, Sarah reversed the order of the passages: In the original, Halifax's observations about divorce come from an earlier section of the tract, before the discussion of husbandly flaws. Her method of reordering and combining emphasized, therefore, not what she should do to accommodate or circumvent Sir William's shortcomings, but just how unpleasant his faults were, and that she had no legal recourse, should they become intolerable.

There were practical strategies related to these intellectual exercises. Sarah's understanding of her identity as a wife, and her characterization of her husband as a tyrant, enabled her to arrive at a temporary but remarkable experiment to try to solve one of the problems of her marriage. Since she could not bring Sir William to allow her to manage the household, Sarah went on strike. In December 1701 she declared:

> One Experiment more, and if that fails mee I Shall despair of having peace from this world. Since the priviledg of a Wife, and a Mistress is deny'd mee, nay the Common power of all housekeepers it is; to dispose of the women Servants; methinks it resembles the tyrrany of pharoah to demand Brick without Straw . . . I will resign the whole to the Managment of Sir W and resolve to live quiet in my Chamber.[18]

This is an impressive leap from sources that advocated obedience, and from sources that merely established certain household rights, to refusing to fulfill expectations because of obstacles, even if the obstacles seemed insurmountable. Sarah took action in a passive sense—refusal to act—but it was nonetheless radical action, and required a certain amount of ignoring, or reinterpreting, or taking advantage of loopholes, within standard texts on the role and duty of wives. So in addition to using handbooks to define and defend herself as a wife, Sarah (and, presumably, other women) could employ a strategy of withdrawal or retirement to resist what she considered unreasonable demands or situations. Thus, at the same time as the larger ideological framework of the patriarchal vision of wives generated grievances for women whose husbands insisted on and misused their prerogatives, it offered a means of resistance, albeit one based in passivity. Nonetheless, while the results of Sarah's strategy were mixed, her husband was the one to capitulate. Several months later Sir William asked her to return as housekeeper and promised he would behave better.[19]

The exercise of this strategy in the battle over servants was at least partially responsible for further defiance. The following June, she refused to accompany Sir William to Hertford. The combination of motives and justifications surrounding this event is interesting: First, her aversion to Hertford was long-standing, well known, and as described earlier, had resulted in her fleeing at least once before. Second, one factor in her husband's acquiescence to her refusal may have been that in early spring of that year, Sarah had been seriously ill and lost all sight in one eye. Naturally, she was extremely depressed by this loss and worried that she would eventually go completely blind.[20] And, in an indirect acknowledgment that her abdication of domestic responsibility was not socially sanctioned, Sarah did not want it to be known that Sir William had formally taken over her duties. She cited all of these reasons and also managed to include a claim to having been a diligent wife in the family political interest in telling Sir William that she would not accompany him:

> Sir W began to talk of going to Hartford, which I can by no means think to do; Considering all circumstances. It is a great folly to go there, to Expose our Selves, be letting the Town know, he is turned House:keeper and Misrules the Maids; . . . Besides; the loss of my Eie, will make the deserted life we lead, intollerable, since I cannot divert the dismal hours by reading, and Scribble as I was wont. These three last Summers lay heavy on mee, but I forc'd my Self to endure, while I thought it might serve his interest to be a Member of parliment. but now that is at an End, I took the courage to tell him (for the reasons aforesaid) I did not mean to go there this year.[21]

The very next entry reinforces the idea that she considered herself a dutiful, obedient wife, as (remarkably enough) she declared, "This is the first time (I may truly Say) that ever I design'd to Contradict his Will."[22] It appears that Sir William accepted her reasons for not going, since while they were apart, he voiced concern for her health and fear of "Spleen and Melancholy" had she been in enforced idleness at Hertford, unable to read and write much during her recovery. Two letters that Sir William wrote during his absence still exist,[23] and Sarah recorded her reaction to them in her diary—the only instance where it is possible to see interaction between them that is not reported by Sarah alone. In the first letter, Sir William wrote pleasantly of missing her and solicitously of her health. In her diary she described the letter as "fraught with kind expressions," and although her answer is not preserved, she must have been quoting her reply when she commented, "'twas great pity so good meaning should be spoiled in the management"[24] because Sir William referred testily to this phrase in his next letter, where he promised to send her fruit as soon as it was ripe, and protested,

> you shall be sure to partake of it, as you shall of every thing that I enjoy in this world, which I must needs say is somewhat more than good meaning spoiled by ill management; I am very sensible my faults are great, and many, and that I have failed very much in my good Intentions

toward you, but I can truly say; that I never Did or Spoke any thing Designedly to Disturb your peace or quiet.

Sarah happily quoted his acknowledgement of faults in her diary, and wrote back:

> I have more hopes of you now than ever, ffor Confession of faults imply's Repentance and that leads to amendment which be Sure Shall produce its due Effects with all grateful returns from mee.[25]

In justifying her actions in withdrawing from housekeeping duties, Sarah alluded to the Jews in Egypt to point out both the unreasonableness of her husband and the possibility of, if not armed rebellion, escape. This reference to the Bible is typical; Scripture and scriptural commentary are among the main sources Sarah used to conceive of herself as a wife. The process took place mostly in her commonplace books, where she collected interpretations of specific scriptural passages as she was reading the Bible. In these collections and in diary entries that refer to these collections, Sarah went further than setting out the specifics of proper duty and behavior for herself as a wife as the conduct books detailed; she extended her examination to the philosophical and theological underpinnings of marriage and wifehood, of women's nature and lot in life as a Christian. In the course of her collecting and commenting, Sarah not only claimed a sphere of power, but went on to contend, on the basis of scriptural examples of marriage and of illustrious women, that as a wife, she deserved respect as well as accordance of certain rights. Here too, she was a long way from the original context by the time she had finished; and here too, there are some interesting cases where she both constructed an intellectual justification of herself and actually took what could be called radical action. This is not, however, to say that there was a cause-and-effect relationship between her intellectual justifications and her actions. The episode discovered from the family correspondence, in which Sarah fled to Lady Shaftesbury's in 1692, shows that Sarah employed tactics of flight and refusal regardless of whether she provided herself with a written justification. It may be that once she began writing about her daily life in a journal ostensibly devoted to self-examination, she felt it necessary to represent herself as righteous after the fact, in order to make her argument for deserving salvation in the face of behavior that plainly contradicted religious and social prescription. Whether she felt she had reasons on her side before her actions or legitimated them afterward, her reading of Scripture shows an independence of mind and willingness to overlook what were theoretically compelling demands on her as a wife.

On some important theological points regarding women's condition in the world, Sarah noted down her own observations and not just what Anglican divines had said on the matter. The tenor of her comments on passages related to women in marriage suggests that she was going to the original, authoritative source because she believed in spite of her disclaimers that she was perfectly capable of interpreting for herself what the Bible said, and that in a number of cases having to do with gender relations, especially, she had valid contributions to make to scriptural commentary. Sometimes she thought the commentator's gist was correct but derived different implications from the passage. Starting at the beginning, over the question of Eve's part in original sin and its practical implications, Sarah cited Genesis 3:16, where God said to Eve that for her sin, "thy desire shall be to thy husband, and he shall rule over thee." Sarah commented on this verse: "Had Eve obey'd God, her daughters had not fallen under the curse of being subject to, and ruled over by unreasonable men."[26] Sarah was not doubting the standard interpretation of the Bible nor the reasons given there for female subjection. Nonetheless, her own attention to and characterization of the practical consequences of Eve's disobedience focused on the misery of the punishment and the unfitness of men (probably the unfitness of her husband in particular) rather than on Eve's guilt.

She continued this redistribution of guilt and worth in her notes on Genesis 26:10, where Isaac admitted he had lied in saying Rebecca was his sister, not his wife. The king replied, "What is this thou hast done unto us? One of the people might lightly have lien with thy wife, and thou shouldst have brought guiltiness upon us," about which Sarah commented, "See the guilt of adultery. This may silence such as account it no great fault in men, laying the guilt only on the woman."[27] She went further in her observations on Judges 13:22, where after having seen an angel, Manoah said "we shall surely die, because we have seen God," but his wife responded that if God had intended to kill them, he would not have accepted their offerings nor shown them the angel. And to this Sarah said, "Here the man's fear was greatest and the woman's reason clearest, which may serve to shew that men have no such advantage as to the faculties of the soul, which they so imperiously pretend to."[28] Hers is not a radical theological position; writers knew and cited Paul's letter to the Galatians (3:28), that in Christ there is neither male nor female. But Sarah's position emphasized aspects of scripture that affirmed either the equal value of women in relation to men, or at least the equivalent sinfulness of men as compared to women.

In other cases Sarah both copied down selections from churchmen writing on the Bible and interpreted the same scriptural passage herself. She extracted a great deal from the commentary and paraphrase of Simon Patrick, the bishop of Ely, not just adding to his thought but construing certain parts differently, as in Genesis 16:5–6. In this chapter, Sarah, Abraham's wife, gave her maid Hagar to Abraham to conceive a child. But then Sarah said to Abraham, "My wrong be upon thee: I have given my maid into thy bosom and when she saw that she had conceived, I was despised in her eyes: the Lord judge between me and thee." Abraham responded, "Behold thy maid is in thy hand; do to her as it pleaseth thee." The narrative continues, "And when Sarah dealt hardly with her, she fled from her face." In Bishop Patrick's interpretation of this passage,

> tho' Sarah showed too much wroth to her maid and too little reverence to her husband (for some take her words . . . as a threatening to recompense his wrong with some ill requital) yet he gives her the respect of a wife, and the authority of a mistress with out any return of intemperance or contumely towards her.[29]

In her own commentary, however, Sarah ignored what Patrick had to say about Sarah's faults of wrath and irreverence. Though she acknowledged the possibility of a threat, she cited Abraham's acquiescence as an indication that Sarah did not intend her words to be understood as such. She went on to quote Patrick on Abraham's respect for his wife. Then, in contrast to Patrick's view of the phrase "dealt hardly with her" about Hagar's treatment, Sarah translated "'Dealt hardly'—that is corrected her no doubt," and said of Hagar "how apt are servants to presume upon their power with their master."[30]

In another case, she took a different tack from Bishop Patrick entirely. In 1 Samuel 1:22, Hannah said she would not go up to sacrifice to God until her son was weaned; her husband agreed. Bishop Patrick clarified this passage by saying this was a reasonable action, "Because women are not bound by the law to go up, but the men only, tho they often accompanied them."[31] Sarah, on the other hand, took this as an example of a good marital relationship and proper behavior of a husband, noting, "She gives her reason, and he without contradiction gives his assent. So is amity and unity reserved among good people who are lovers of peace."[32]

But it is in the sexual arena of her marriage that the most drastic of Sarah's reinterpretations of standard doctrine took place. Sarah vested the word "chastity" with a double meaning in order to contrast her performance of the marital duty of fidelity with that of Sir William, and, more radically, to cast sexual abstinence within marriage as a virtue. In the face of conduct books' specific admonitions not to do so, she equated chastity with celibacy and on the basis of this redefinition claimed to be deserving of praise for her behavior as a wife:

> [I] reckon my Self a Mirrour of Chastity, Even beyond the most intact virgin, ffor to Conceive four Children without knowing what it is to have an unchast thought or Sensual pleasure and being but 26 when the last was born have Ever since then remain'd pure—is a thing Scarce to be match'd by a married woman, and a Reflection that without Vanity may justly delight me.[33]

Sarah may have found an opening for this redefinition in a commentary she had read on the New Testament, regarding the end of Paul's first letter to Timothy, 2:11 . . . 15. The biblical text itself reads:

> Let the woman learn in silence with all subjection. . . . For Adam was first formed, then Eve. And Adam was not deceived, but the woman being deceived was in the transgression. Notwithstanding, she shall be saved in childbearing, if they continue in faith and charity and holiness with sobriety.

In his paraphrase, Henry Hammond added "purity" as another reading for "holiness" in this verse, and explained,

> but by means of the seed of woman, the messiah which should be born from her posterity, she had a promise of redemption, and so all others of her sex, upon condition of their perseverance in faith, love and obedience to Christ, and performance of those great Christian duties of Chastity and modest behavior.[34]

Hammond himself was not advocating abstinence, but his explanation of the text may have suggested to Sarah the possibility of a conflation of the words "pure" and "chaste" to mean "celibate." In her collection of scriptural commentaries, she copied Hammond's annotation to these verses and drew a pointing hand in the margin beside it.[35]

Here again, as in her retreat from attempting to manage the household, she withdrew from her duties as a wife. But in this case, having essentially failed to fulfill her sexual obligation, she went on to dramatically misconstrue, or at least willfully ignore, two basic Protestant doctrinal points regarding marriage: first, that chastity should not be equated with celibacy; and second, that celibacy is not a virtue.[36] Being chaste meant being a modest, sexually faithful wife, while celibacy was associated with superstitious, papist doctrine. It is all the more remarkable then, that in another entry where she praised herself for abstinence, Sarah did so in the context of ridiculing an excessive trial of celibacy in an anti-Catholic account of monastic orders that she was reading:

> The Order of the Countess Guastalla instituted 1537 was made up of Monks and Nuns who to overcome fleshly lusts did lay together a Monk with a Nun in one and the Same Bed putting a big Wooden Cross between both which (as they gave out) had the Vertue to quench Rebellious Concupiscence. But this cross being but a very low wall of partition and Several Scandalous disorders and works of Darkness arising from this foolish institution this infamous Order Came to an End being destroy'd all over Italy. I know a Man who at 30, and a Woman but 26 lay 16 year in a Bed yet entirely Chast (they were husband and Wife indeed which might help somewhat) without any partition, vow, or other Reason than to avoid having many Children. Had the La: been of the Romish Church perhaps she might have been Canonized, no doubt but Some have for less Matters.[37]

In this remarkable discussion, Sarah mocked the idea of monks and nuns attempting to affirm their renunciation of "fleshly lusts" through the superstitious use of a cross. At the very same time, she completely ignored the implied attack on the idea of celibacy as a valid religious goal and instead actually drew an analogy that valorized sexual restraint in her own marriage. Moreover, she explained that this practice had been to limit reproduction, a reason that was specifically rejected in conduct books.[38]

It is worth remembering, however, that at the time when Sarah and Sir William ceased to have sexual relations, their fourth son Spencer had just been born. Therefore, despite the death of the second son in infancy, a male heir was very likely.[39] Furthermore, between the births of these children there was an average interval of roughly a year and three months. This testimony to Sarah's fertility might well have been worrisome on both health and economic grounds, since she would have had many childbearing years ahead of her. It is not clear what weight was given to either of these factors in the couple's choice to "avoid having many children," nor indeed the extent to which either partner was responsible for the decision.[40] And it is important to note that Sarah first offered her rationalization of wifely celibacy more than forty years after the birth of her last child, so that our source for reconstructing the situation is already far distant from the actual event. Certainly, Sarah took all the credit (due or not, prescriptively speaking) for their celibate marital life, but given Sir William's worries about their finances,[41] it is possible he agreed to or even initiated their practice of abstinence. After all, society's sexual double standard meant that for Sir William as a man, ending conjugal relations did not necessarily mean ending sexual activity.

If so, Sarah's insistence on her own continence, which implicitly isolated and elevated her behavior over her husband's, might be understandable as a reference to Gouge's discussion of conjugal duties, in which he declares (having previously denied the equation of chastity with celibacy) that in marriage, the opposite of chastity is not abstinence, but adultery. It may be that Sarah was both distorting the word "chaste" to mean "celibate" and also using it in Gouge's terms as meaning "sexually faithful to a spouse" in order to contrast her "chastity" inside and outside the marital bed to Sir William's infidelity outdoors. That their sexual life (or lack thereof) was a continuing point of contention is evident in Sarah's reports of two arguments that are ostensibly framed as religious debates but clearly have a personal subtext. In the first, Sir William spoke in Sarah's language to deny the validity of her measure of her own virtue, comparing it unfavorably to the very thing from which Sarah distanced herself—sexual license. "Chaste" here could mean either celibate or faithful, or both; what Sir William was objecting to most was her self-righteousness. In response, Sarah insisted in biblical terms (perhaps asserting her superior command of the language of piety) that not only was she righteous, but she deserved admiration, not criticism for it:

> In the Evening Sir W fell into a wrangling discourse wherein he Compared, or rather wou'd level me with a Liar and a Whore, saying, pride was a worse Sin than either, and a Chast Woman that overvalued herself was in greater fault. However I shall not be perswaded, but the Vertuous have some Reason to Value themselves, and to Expect Esteem from Others, and I spared not to tell him, that my manner of living with him did deserve all the praise, Love and Respect, that he cou'd give me. But my

Comfort was if I miss'd of that I had a sure promise. Do that which is good and thou shall have praise.[42]

A second quarrel, which started out as a dispute about the servants, quickly escalated to a battle over religion and sex. Arguing against frequent church attendance (Sarah's practice) Sir William said that

he found nobody the better that went so much there, nor for making such a stir against whoring which he thought the least of Sins. I could not forbear to say that he ought not to Reproach Religion, but Love the Effects, which was 'twas like had prevented him knowing to his Cost, the difference between a Chast wife and a Whore as he very well deserv'd to have done.[43]

Sir William's rejection of the gravity of "whoring," and Sarah's implication that her piety saved him from what would have been his just deserts (that is, the dishonor of an unfaithful wife and perhaps her illegitimate children) indicate that in this case, chastity was understood to refer primarily to sexual fidelity.

In these arguments, as in all of her writing, it is as if Sarah were building a case to prove to God that she deserved to be saved on Judgment Day. Assuring herself of her own eligibility for salvation may have helped her to stand her ground against her husband and to preserve a strong sense of self, but at the same time, her assertions of righteousness and authority exacerbated her marital situation. Although patriarchal ideologies were a source of strength and self-respect for Sarah, patriarchal reality as expressed in her family was, ironically, the source of much of her conflict and unhappiness in the first place.

As a mother, Sarah also had to confront the difference between ideal and real in her relationship with her children. Although as a parent Sarah could claim much more authority than as a wife and could find direct backing for her position in conduct books and sermons, she still was faced with the intervening authority of her husband and with the resistance of her adult sons to her demands for deference and support, since fathers, not mothers, were the final word in command.

In criticizing the treatment she received from her sons, Sarah generally kept to a few main themes. First, they did not visit her or invite her to visit them frequently enough; second, during visits they were not sufficiently attentive or polite; third, they did not include her in their good fortune; and finally, they persisted in bad moral habits, particularly adultery. In Sarah's complaints, it is possible to see both the quality of her relationship with her children and the expectations she had as a mother from that relationship. These expectations seem to have mirrored the prescriptions of conduct books concerning the respective duties of parents and children as well as the assumptions of her acquaintances about the way children and parents ought to behave to each other. Because in this interaction Sarah was theoretically in the position of authority and superiority, she had less need to subvert and reinterpret her sources in order to buttress her claims to respect than she did when justifying her performance as a marital partner. So in this case, she was more straightforward in her use of literary prescription to reinforce her condemnation of her sons' performance of their duties.

As is her conception of wifeliness, her conception of motherhood is fundamentally conservative, echoing the description set out in Scripture and elaborated by numerous divines in sermons and conduct books. In these works, mothers were depicted as naturally tenderhearted and selfless and likely therefore to be indulgent.[44] As a parent, they were second in authority to fathers, but children were still to obey them in all things, unless contrary to the command of either God or the father.[45] There were slight variations in writers' descriptions of the extent to which adults still owed their parents obedience, but it was consistently reiterated that the children continued to be obligated to show reverence for their parents, since they could "never recompense the pains and cost" of their mothers and fathers.[46] For that same reason, adult children ought, in gratitude, to assist parents financially should they need it and care for them in their old age.[47] Parents, on the other hand, were bound to care for and educate their children, mothers being most concerned with the early years of education and fathers with the later years, especially in setting their sons up to earn a living.[48] Once children were grown, parents' remaining obligations were to set a good example for their children, pray for them, and watch over their souls—to "exhort, encourage, or reprove, as they find occasion."[49] Sarah subscribed to these precepts both by portraying herself as the tender, suffering mother who continued to fulfill what remained of her duty to her children and by citing sources to show that children ought to try to please their parents and show them all possible respect and honor.[50] In her reporting of family interactions and in her correspondence, however, Sarah undermined her representation of herself as patiently silent, but provided illuminating indications of her conception of the nature and correct operation of the relationship between grown children and their parents. In this role, there were even rare occasions where Sarah actually sided with Sir William, when she felt that the prerogative of parents had been abrogated by her sons, for instance, when William refused to accompany Sir William to the election at Hertford in 1701, which Sir William lost.[51]

Unsurprisingly, given her marriage, Sarah was interested in the question of the relative loyalties to each parent. In the back of Volume 2 of the diary, she copied out a long extract from an "eminent divine" that insisted on the equal duty owed to each parent and cited multiple scriptural passages to back up this assertion. This section may very well be a paraphrase of Gouge, who cited Scripture and particularly Proverbs to establish the equal respect due to mother and father. Nonetheless, Gouge clarified his position by unequivocally coming down on the side of the father in cases where parents were in opposition, though while preserving "reverence and humility" toward the mother.[52] If this was in fact the source to which she was referring, Sarah did not acknowledge this final clarification.

As she did in her behavior as a wife, Sarah as a mother employed a strategy of withdrawal—of refusal to accept responsibility for the behavior of others—while representing herself as having perfectly fulfilled her own duty:

> I find this Comfort, that my Conscience doth not accuse me of having begun the Offence with any relation whatever, and do render Thanks to the Divine Goodness, for that I am so well Come off and have so gracefully bore with those of Others.[53]

It was important to be able to fend off the burden of sin with a conviction of her own blamelessness, since Sarah knew she should first assume she was at fault. In her collection of "Thoughts and Meditations," Sarah copied out Allestree's warning that if children misbehaved, their mother should examine herself to see if (as was most likely) the fault lay with her for setting a bad example. If so, she should consider it a just punishment and amend her ways.[54]

Occasionally an implication surfaced that there might be a connection between her demeanor and her sons' treatment of her, but she attributed such a connection to her moral superiority and their discomfort in having to confront their sins by her allegedly silent reproach:

> I cannot imagine why they so studiously Shun me, unless being Conscious they have lived in a way I do not like, they are Shy and fear to give me oppertunity to reprove them, though I have Carefully avoided all occa-

sions to rubb upon their Sore . . . however distrust has no bounds, and
they Cannot think themselves secure from blame, therefore avoid me.[55]

Interestingly, while there are frequent instances where Sarah pointed out
her restraint in not reproving her sons[56] (presumably reinforcing her image as a tender, forgiving, peacekeeping mother, as well as acknowledging her impotence), there are also passages where she described her own
silence as retaliation for the negligent conversation of her sons.[57] Here
too, her silence was that of an ill-used, discreet mother, but also carried
an aura of coldness and disapproval: As in many of her other actions to
deal with her married life, withdrawal and refusal to interact provided a
strategy with which Sarah could express her discontent, while still
claiming the moral high ground, albeit having to overlook prescriptive
sources in many cases.

This refusal even held when she was directly pressured by a member
of the church establishment to accept responsibility, at least indirectly,
for the behavior of her sons. She denied culpability regardless, not only
claiming impotence, but throwing back a counterargument furnished by
another favorite authority, Bishop Patrick:

> In Discourse a Severe Divine [Dr. Manningham, her parish priest?] did
> insinuate as if I did not Sufficiently lament the faults of Some persons nor
> did it trouble me enough. But at that rate we Shou'd lose the Enjoyment
> of our own innocence. If my Relations do not as I wou'd have 'em, it is
> none of my fault, and therfore there is no Reason it Shou'd be my Misery,
> or that I Shou'd depend on the Will of another for my peace and not
> upon my own. I can advise 'em but not make 'em good and so the matter
> must rest.[58]

In Patrick's *The Heart's Ease*, there is slightly more emphasis on the responsibility of parents; Sarah skipped the second half of the sentence,
which in the original ran: "If our children be not as we would have
them, *if we endeavor they should be so* [my italics], we may comfort
ourselves. . . . "[59] More important, however, is the whole tone of this
work, which advocated complete knowledge of one's duty and its limits
as a means of comfort in times of trouble. Patrick advised, "Let us consider what is in our power and what is not."[60] Sarah seems to have relied
extensively on this book as support and ammunition, since it encouraged
and validated her strategy of self-examination as vindication or absolu-
tion from bearing any responsibility for those faults she condemned in
her husband, sons, and servants.

It may be that the "faults" hinted at by the "severe divine" had to do with sexual licentiousness on the part of her son William—blame for which she may well have been particularly unwilling to share, given her marital history. Her encounter with the cleric and subsequent distancing occurred later in the month (March, 1703), when she noted the mortifying publication of what she accepted as accurate gossip about her son:

> There is now Come out a Satyr to expose the personal Vices of ye Whigg party. It bestows two lines on the Fault of my Son. In Secret I lament that he gives 'em any handle but to such as tell me of it, my Answer is, It is a Manifest Sign he has Some Considerable Vertues, ffor no body minds what they do who have None; and it must needs be apparent Envy that picks out him from among So Chast and pious a generation as this.[61]

Her caustic defense of her son to outsiders demonstrates her strategy of closing ranks at the same time as it hints at the sexual nature of his transgression. It is probably no coincidence that in February 1703 William Nicolson, bishop of Carlisle, had recorded in his diary, "Mr Cowper's perswadeing his Mrs to think her self his other wife."[62] This reference also reiterates the theme of bigamy and the idea that this scandal was known to the clergy. Sarah herself already knew of William's affair with Elizabeth Culling;[63] on this new occasion of bringing it up she lamented:

> I know a Female that lives in Open Adultery, if to have Children by another Womans husband be So. Yet She wipes her Mouth and with an impudent Face of Brass saith She is his Wife and doth the other no wrong. . . . St Paul Shews the reciprocal tie that is between the Man and the Wife, by w^c it appears that a Man Can no more have two wives, than a wife have two Husbands—I truely am Sett in the plague, and my heaviness is ever in my Sight. Yet am I become as one that heareth not, and in whose mouth are no Reproofs.[64]

Here too, she depicted herself as an uncomfortable but long-suffering, silent parent, a position she acerbically denied to her husband when their son William's relationship to Elizabeth apparently foundered:

> I won't say who; has been arguing about a Wench y^t hath had two Children and now her pretended Spouse is run from her. 'tis maintain'd to be better for her if She is not married to him than if She really be, which I Cannot admit of, but think of two Evils the last to be much the least. There Can be no Excuse for any one to justify and approve what he knows to be Evil; here is no room for passion or Surprize. It must be the

Evidence of a Soul harden'd in Wickedness, not only to do what is Evill but to take pleasure in it, and to applaud and encourage the practise of it. Be not pertaker of other Mens Sins.—[65]

Just as when Sarah and Sir William argued in the hypothetical about whether pride or promiscuity were a worse sin, here, in a more concrete case having to do with sexual virtue, there is the strong subtext of a long-running marital argument over chastity and righteousness as well. Moreover, Sarah's comment after Elizabeth Culling died in November of the same year suggests that Sarah was privy to more than just the vague outlines of her son's affair:

A Decent or as Some Say Stately Monument is Rais'd att Harting-ford:Berry to preserve y᷄ Memory of E.C.—I desire to be laid in the Same Church:yard more East:ward, and expect the Example Shou'd be taken to do the like for mee. They who have Seen her last Will, tell me it was her Express Order to be Bury'd Close by the Ew:Tree ffor Which Fancy I can imagine no other Reason; unless it be to Suggest this Motto.
     Where I lost my Virginity, I lay my Body.[66]

When she was faced with conflicting demands, on the one hand to lament the sins of her family yet on the other to hide those sins from the world through her discretion and to loyally defend their perpetrators, she chose the position that allowed her to represent herself as a good, protective mother, yet still distance herself from culpability for her children's faults. This idea of keeping silent as a long-suffering mother, both to decrease contention within the family and to defend it from contempt from outsiders, resurfaced more than once. Sarah observed that examples of other publicly quarreling families:

Teach me to conceal so much as possible the Dissentions of our ffamily, ffor to expose them by Appeals or Complaints doth but multiply discourse, and serves no purpose but to aggravate the misfortune. If wee can Support the Reputation of those who have used us ungratefully after wee have loved and serv'd them, then indeed the Spirit of peace abides in us.[67]

A case in point, perhaps because of the gravity of the threat but also because the danger came from outside the family circle, is Sarah's surprisingly muted criticism of Spencer shortly after his trial.[68] Instead, her anger was almost wholly directed toward the "malicious Quakers," Chief Justice Holt (who had refused to grant bail to Spencer), and Mrs. Stout, Sarah's mother.[69] After the attempts at appeals had failed, however,

Sarah's comments on the negligence and bad behavior of her younger son are by far the most frequent terms in which she refers to Spencer.[70]

Sarah's third domestic role was as mistress of the servants in an irritatingly subordinate role as lieutenant governor of her "family" of five domestics.[71] As with her other household selves, Sarah expected a particular framework and set of rights and responsibilities to hold true. Here again, she drew on prescriptive sources to determine and describe the correct workings of servant/master relations and the way each party should behave. Because this relationship was based on a hierarchy of rank rather than gender, and because Sarah's position in it was as ruler rather than ruled, her consideration of the theory of master-servant interaction was not only conservative socially (as it was for her roles as mother and wife), but it also involved still less reinterpretation of sources and less justification of her own actions. The conflict in this relationship was first between her husband and herself over the power accorded to mistresses while there was a master; and then between her servants and herself as she tried to impose a conservative, paternal order on a group of people who resisted her control. Since Sarah did not have radical ideas about the social place of her own gender, it is not surprising that she did not question the deferential, hierarchical ideology of social rank in general, and master and servant in particular. But it is interesting that when she applied prescriptive literature to her own case as a wronged wife, she appropriated it to a much more empowering vision of her own place in the family, whereas when she cited prescription in the case of servants, it was either to insist on the rightness of the relationship as it was described by clergy and others or to point out the failure of methods suggested for managing servants. Characteristically, these failures were, in her view, not because she was in some way at fault nor because the writers of handbooks were necessarily wrong, but because servants were essentially incorrigible—a lost cause. Their refusal to act as it was set out in the literature does not seem to have crossed Sarah's mind as in any way parallel to her own refusal to think or behave as a private woman in exactly the way it was prescribed, perhaps because she did not think of herself as having refused.

That there was a conflict between Sarah and the servants over her attempt to impose a deferential, pious family order is not surprising, especially if, as historians see it, the eighteenth century was a time of particularly heightened tension between masters and servants, as a paternal, originally medieval concept of the relationship contested with a more recent, individualistic, contractual notion.[72] While servants were in reality employed on a contractual basis, usually in yearly units, the paternal ideal survived in the theory of the duties of each party. Servants were obliged to put their time entirely at the disposal of their masters, and further, they owed their masters obedience, deference, and fidelity. Masters were to provide for their servants materially (pensioning them in old age) and to guide them morally. The imbalance in duties respectively owed was explained (and supposedly mitigated) by the idea that the master-servant bond was in essence familial, so that the master was not just employer, but father, and the servant was child, implying a higher level of affection and mutual help than in other business relationships.[73]

If the evidence for public and private complaints by those who employed servants is any indication, Sarah was not alone in her unsuccessful struggle to impose control. Masters frequently complained about (and sometimes tried to reform legally) insubordination, disloyalty, theft, embezzlement, and frequent job-leaving.[74] Overall, Sarah seems to have been one of many employers who "sought to impose the extensive control and exact the perfect allegiance to which in theory [they were] entitled; the servant, on the other hand, sought to limit his obligations and preserve . . . independence."[75] Certainly, she thought of herself as a generous, reasonable mistress, as complaints of her servants' ingratitude indicate. She never mentioned the amount paid in actual wages, but clearly felt that the provision of food and clothing for the servants was more than adequate.[76] Beyond performing her duty to provide for servants' material needs, Sarah reported on one occasion her generosity with actual money when she gave her coachman fifteen shillings with a promise of another fifteen for good behavior to help him pay for a "coach glass" he had broken.[77] This reimbursement probably says more about what expenses servants were expected to bear than it does about Sarah's largesse, but it does suggest some of the ways, other than wages, in which Sarah could, and felt she did, treat her servants well.

In accordance with the conduct books, Sarah expected in return obedience, deference, and loyalty. These duties, laid out time and again in prescriptive literature, were far from the reality of her household, however.[78] As mentioned earlier, she records specific instances of theft, embezzlement, violence, disobedience, and insubordination. Another recurring problem seems to have been that the menservants, especially the coachman, stayed out all night or all day drinking, or stranded Sarah when she was out visiting.[79] In the first year of the diary, one additional sin that "disorderly servants" committed provoked one of her most extreme reactions of fright and anger: Her maid got pregnant. Sarah recounted the episode in terms that indicate the maid's previous sexual history and suspected abortion. She also hints at forms of intimidation a servant might exercise over her nominal employer in situations where the mistress of the household was known by servants not to actually exercise discretion in matters of hiring and firing: "My Old greivance holds me in Continual terrour, I sometimes fear she may give me at least the dregs of the phisick she kept in her Trunk wherwith last Winter (as I have Reason to believe) she destroy'd her Conception." And the next day, "At night S^r W and I fell into Sharp Contention about this wicked serv^t, who I fear bears me Malice because she Suspects I discover her Crimes."[80] Finally, the servant left of her own accord, but in circumstances that rekindled Sarah's fury and intense alarm (justified or not) at the maid's transgressions and the likely publicizing of the event through the gossip of other servants:

> The Female Servt so oft mention'd had a Month before given warning to Sr W. (having pressing occasion to be gone) without taking any notice to me. the day of her own setting being now Come, himself told me he had paid her wages but withall bid her take her own time to begone. O prodigious! After I had acquainted him the irresistable fears I had, least she and her very lewd fellow shou'd Robb and fire the House to run away by the light. That I cou'd take no food peculier to my Self, without the fancy she might mix some of the vomits she kept in her Trunk w^c she used to Clear her Self with, but at this time had fail'd her, that I had not slept quiet in my Bed from the Apprehension she wou'd be deliver'd in ye House . . . however I persisted to be rid of her that night and was so, upon w^c S^r W was so reserv'd that we supp'd together without Speaking one Word, a pretty sight to ye fellow that waited, who no doubt will make a good use on't.[81]

Sir William's lenient treatment of these offenses infuriated Sarah, both because he often undermined her authority as a mistress when she attempted to punish or direct servants, and because he completely failed to fulfill the intangible duties of the master to her satisfaction. He neither governed well (that is, strictly, or at least in a manner that resulted in an orderly household), nor did he guide the family morally and spiritually. Masters were supposed to set a good example, and furthermore, actively to instill piety in the whole family by enforcing church attendance, catechizing, and reading prayers aloud daily.[82] As in other facets of her domestic life, Sarah summoned scriptural authority to justify her position. In her own commentary on 1 Samuel 2:29, pointing to the destruction of Eli's family because of his failure to reprove his impious sons, she warned, "This sin of Eli in being so remiss . . . is a severe admonition to such as use not their utmost authority to restrain the vices of such children or servants as are under their government."[83]

But despite the ideological backing Sarah could marshal for her vision of orderly governance of the household, except when a servant's behavior was so bad it seemed worth the fight to prevail in getting Sir William to dismiss him or her,[84] Sarah could only propose to herself strategies of avoidance and withdrawal. Resolved to interact as infrequently as possible with the household staff, she had to live as well as she could manage in a family where, as she saw it, the hierarchical order had been inverted.

CHAPTER 4

The Angry Years: Social Life, 1700–1704

Domestically, Lady Sarah Cowper was challenged to construct identities as a wife, mother, and mistress of servants by which she could hope to fulfill or at least justify her quest for authority within the family. In the social world she was equally motivated to explore and manipulate ideas of social standing to create public identities for herself by which she could garner personal status as a woman, and by that same means acquire honor for the family and help to buttress their precariously elevated position. On the one hand, Sarah's position as a jumped-up member of the gentry offered her opportunities as a woman for participation in the world outside her home. But on the other, because of the circumstances of Sarah's membership in the elite, her participation was precarious. In this context Sarah spent less time subverting prescription than referring to it for support in negotiating the pitfalls and dangers of social interaction. While Sarah's high status offered opportunities for participation in the wider world, the discrepancy between the Cowpers' high rank and their landed estate rendered problematic the concurrent requirement that she participate in society in order to maintain that status. Notwithstanding this difficulty, given a broad definition of "public" that includes all the spaces where social interaction and demonstrations of status take place, Sarah created a personally powerful and family-affirming "public" self that relied especially on religious notions of the pious gentlewoman to exploit the avenues for public action that were open to her through visiting, churchgoing, and charity. Visiting and churchgoing were visible means of accruing status, expressing political affiliation, and maintaining family and personal reputation through acting out claims to eminence in front of an audience. Equally, the social links forged by these activities opened other, less visible channels for accumulating power and prestige within and outside the construct of female piety. If the social round and public worship were theaters for self-presentation intended to uphold family or personal honor, the exercise of benevolent giving and patronage were behind-the-scenes counterparts in which the strings of influence, interest, and obligation that were in part manufactured on the public stage could be pulled to achieve the same end.

As Keith Wrightson puts it, "The most fundamental structural characteristic of English society was its high degree of stratification, its distinctive and all pervasive system of social inequality."[1] The population of England is often described as forming a pyramid of rank divided into three layers of increasing size: the landed elite at the top (uppermost politically, socially, and economically); the middling sorts, including merchants and yeomen farmers; and the lower orders, that is, small farmers, artificers, and the laboring and unemployed poor. Unlike continental aristocracies, the top layer was divided into a hereditary peerage and a lesser nobility—the gentry. This group comprised four ranks: baronets, knights, esquires, and gentlemen. In theory, membership of these ranks was determined by lineage, officially recognized through the grants of titles and coats of arms by the College of Heralds. But practically, the essential qualifications for belonging to the gentry were landed wealth and appropriate comportment.[2]

As for the second attribute—comportment—it was education, manners, and conspicuous consumption that marked out the upper ranks of society. To live and behave as a gentleman was both a requirement for admission to the elite and a badge of membership. Physical display of wealth in housing, number of servants, clothing, and hospitality asserted claims to social status, reaching extraordinary levels of expenditure in the upper levels of the peerage, where wealthy landowning nobles demonstrated their place in society with elaborate country houses, lavish entertainments, and armies of servants.[3] It was equally important for members of the gentry to maintain the appearance of living according to their status through the graciousness of their surroundings and of their demeanor. In addition to social display, since the landed nobility was the ruling class in England, being a member of the gentry also meant participating in both local and national government.[4] Moreover, the relative prestige of each office was simultaneously an indicator and a bestower of social status. Since the most substantial of the gentlemen were in offices such as members of Parliament, justices of the peace, and Crown commissioners, while the lesser gentlemen held the less important, more local positions such as high constable,[5] obtaining government office both reinforced and advertised claims to specific levels of gentry eminence.

That comportment, not merely birth and wealth, was an ingredient in the requirements for admission to the gentry meant that the English aristocracy had a relatively high level of social mobility in comparison to its counterparts on the continent. While hierarchical, no rank was a completely "closed caste."[6] There was, however, a sharp difference in ease of access between initial admission to the gentry and consequent attempts to obtain higher ranks within the upper echelons. At the bottom, because of the fluidity of the idea of manners as a membership criterion, a prosperous merchant, yeoman, or professional could gain entrance to the gentry as a gentleman or esquire simply by living as one. If he bought land, built an appropriate house, and dressed and acted in a manner befitting the station he claimed for himself, the assertion of that status was often enough to gain it, especially if there were family connections to the gentry already. But while one generation was usually sufficient for entry into the gentry, further movement up the social scale was far more restricted. Beckett emphasizes that possessing the attributes of landed wealth and suitable behavior was no guarantee of progress up the hierarchy. Although appropriate education, intermarriage with the elite, and service to state or party in local or national office were all useful in furthering a family's social ambitions, it was normally a long-term, multigenerational process of advancement, even for those who did actually achieve a title.[7] In fact, the greatest degree of social mobility was actually downward, since primogeniture, reinforced by the strict settlement after 1660, meant that younger sons of the nobility did not inherit titles or estates, and so generally sank into the lower orders of the gentry or even out of it altogether, turning to the professions to support themselves.[8] Overall, Stone concludes from his study of movement into the peerage that "the actual volume of social mobility has turned out to be far less than might have been expected. Moreover, those who did move up were rarely successful men of business. Most of the newcomers were rising parish gentry or office holders or lawyers, men from backgrounds not too dissimilar to those of the existing county elite."[9]

As Stone pointed out, while moving up the hierarchy was generally a lengthy, difficult, and uncertain prospect, there were avenues to follow that did offer some hope of advancement. The legal profession was especially conducive to social mobility, as those practicing the law were often already from gentlemen's families. Barristers, in particular, could translate their sometimes very considerable earnings into landed wealth. They were also well-positioned to acquire power and status through becoming judges or holding other state offices.[10] Indeed, Prest asserts that during this period, the law was the profession "which offered the greatest opportunities of acquiring wealth and exercising power."[11] A prosperous London barrister might earn over £1,000 a year,[12] and as the gulf grew between barristers and solicitors, and the upper ranks of the legal profession became more removed from routine legal dealings with clients, those at the top could present themselves as "honorable counselors" rather than men of business, an image of an "elevated, intellectual, and even non-mercenary" calling that enhanced prestige.[13]

The opportunities for advancement provided by the legal profession were crucial to the social rise of the Cowper family over the course of the seventeenth century. But having followed the path of upward mobility provided by the law, office-holding, and political service, at the end of the 1600s William and Sarah found themselves in a position where their social rank exceeded the landed income they required to maintain that status. By choosing the road of political allegiance and preferment, Sir William was following a risky, but perfectly acceptable means of furthering social status. In terms of material display of wealth, however, Sir William did not cut nearly the figure that was expected of someone holding the highest rank in the gentry. His housing arrangements were very modest; the original family seat at Ratling Court does not seem to have been a residence even for the first baronet and is described in the next century as a "very mean farmhouse."[14] Rather than residing in a suitably elegant country seat, the Cowpers lived in Hertford Castle, leased for a peppercorn rent from the Earl of Salisbury.[15] The castle had originally been a Norman building and was used by royalty until James I, but by the time the Cowpers occupied it, the gatehouse was the only habitable part.[16] Nor were Sir William's London residences large or fashionable. He consistently rented houses in the Holborn area, ending up in Bedford Row, next to Gray's Inn.[17] While the general direction of his moves was to the west, as was the trend for the upper classes in this period, he stopped short of the new property developments in Covent Garden, Bloomsbury, St. James, and eventually Mayfair.[18] It is likely that Sir William's last house was also his most expensive; Sarah was worried that should he die, she would not be able to manage to pay from her annuity the £80 yearly rent.[19] According to Peter Earle, prosperous members of the middle class typically paid £50 to £60 per year for a house in a good city center neighborhood, occasionally rising as high as £80.[20] So on this measure, the Cowper standard of housing in London, while comfortable, was completely inadequate to their social rank, an insufficiency of which Sarah was acutely aware, as her disparagements of the small size of the Bedford Street house and her embarrassment at the concurring opinion of an acquaintance indicate.[21]

In Sir William's case, this fiscal conservatism seems to have been dictated by a real lack of resources with which keep up the proper appearances. He often worried about the expense of even basic amenities, and even if his complaints about Sarah's spending on her meals and his refusals to heat rooms were as much provoked by general marital tension as real economic worry, Sir William's targets of attack show a concern about spending money out of proportion to what a gentleman should be able to afford.[22] And actually, despite complaining about Sir William's parsimony, Sarah was equally frugal. Making a virtue of necessity, she was particularly restrained in her expenditure on clothing, while uncomfortably aware that she was transgressing the rules of dressing according to her station:

> On my Self I lay out as litle as may be, and am no way enclin'd to Costly Apparel, least of all in this place where I cannot stir out but must meet with many Naked backs which I had much rather Cloth were I able then lay too much on my own as is the fashion of some who I perceive blame me for visiting them in a Garment Cost but 24[sh:] and perhaps they are not quite in the wrong.[23]

It also appears from contemporary comment that outsiders assumed Sir William was worth significantly more than actually was the case. Narcissus Luttrell reported that Sir William left an estate worth £2,500 per annum to his eldest son, but in his account of his father's estate, Spencer calculated a disposable income of only £694 for the first three quarters of 1707, which did not even cover the expense of the £1,000 bequest to Spencer himself, or Sarah's yearly pension of £400.[24] Another instance of a higher estimate of Cowper wealth than was merited came a little more than a year after Sir William's death, when an acquaintance told Sarah she was believed to have received £6,000 for her share of an investment made by Sir William. Sarah noted that the actual dividend was £164.[25]

If Sir William was without the landed estate commensurate to his baronetcy, Sarah was even more precariously perched. Considered from Sarah's perspective, regardless of how she felt about William personally, what is notable is how far up the social ladder she rose. For her the insecurities of being financially unable to support the style of the Cowper rank were added to by the uncertainties of personally having risen so far socially in the first place. Consequently, many of the comments in her diary about society in general and the Cowpers' position in particular demonstrate an intense concern with how best to spend her material and "symbolic capital"[26] in order to maintain her own status and that of her family. In 1700, very early in the diary, she wrote about both the family income and rank in the context of disparaging her husband's conceit, but at the same time she betrayed her anxiety over their financial inability to assert their prestige in her lamentations over the disunity that prevented an impressive family showing:

> At Even, S^r W fell to Magnify himself, boasting of the Riches in his ffamily (what have we that we did not receive?) and made it out that among 'em they are possess'd of 2500^l a year, besides what his Sons now gett which he says makes it above 4000 yearly. If this rais'd his Conceit, it gave me a low opinion of their Wisdome and Conduct, that with all this Estate we live in a despisable fashion, and are dispers'd into holes and Corners, whereas we might make a hansome figure in House, Table, Equipage and what not: did we unite in Love and ffriendship a thing w^c Common prudence wou'd have done, as a means to raise us out of that Contempt we are fallen under.[27]

The remedy for "contempt" (brought on generally by a poor social showing and specifically by Spencer's trial) that Sarah proposed was to marshal the assets of the entire family in order to put on a display of conspicuous consumption and hospitality. Instead of relying on political success, the family would reassert its status in society by exhibiting the normative attributes of high-ranking gentry. It is notable that William and Sarah counted as family assets the income of all the Cowper relations, when in reality, they belonged to each family member alone. And furthermore, it is a significant indication of William and Sarah's shaky financial situation that she felt it would require a reuniting of the family under one roof and pooling all its resources to achieve the necessary level of display.

A few months later, she reiterated her concern with the standing of the family, this time framing her anxieties about social contempt—loss of status—in terms of the family's rank rather than income. Here, however, Sarah contradicted the strategy she had previously advocated, disclaiming any interest in the very "exterior advantage" she had proposed augmenting earlier. She dissociated the risk of disgrace to herself or her family from the failure to sustain the appropriate material display, pointing instead to the other unstable buttress holding up the family honor (in the sense of rank)—their political activity:

> This day in the year 1641 S^r W: Cooper was Created Baronet of England. . . . To be almost at the Top of the Gentry is place Enough, yet I never felt any gratification from that matter. I was never proud of any Exteriour Advantage, and am sure I have no temptation to be so from any interiour Endowments. My pride Consists Cheifly in being not able to bear Contempt, or disgrace Cast on my Self or family, with that Submission and Humility as I ought. At this time I Experience somewhat of this fraillty, upon hearing how industrious the Malitious Quakers are to revive the Scandalous persecutions of my Son.[28]

Religion was a doubly effective strategy for seeking security in that it provided personal comfort and a system of explanation for the misfortunes of social life, as well as offering a means for Sarah to enhance both her own reputation and that of her family through a religious public persona. Patricia Crawford notes the attraction of godliness for women because it gave them public esteem and brought "honor to their kin."[29] Moreover, the godly element was crucial to Sarah's maintenance of an appropriate social circle in her approach to upholding her family's status. Unlike Sir William, who relied on his alliances with Whig patrons and the Dissenting community, Sarah chose to cultivate connections with people who were members of the establishment in both church and state, but especially church. With this approach to defending the family and her own reputation, it makes sense that Sarah frequently evaluated the social and moral quality of her acquaintances, recorded her diligence in going to church, gave account of her charitable activities, and recounted her efforts at bestowing patronage. All of these activities contributed to her presentation of her public identity as a pious gentlewoman, a construction that simultaneously allowed her a means of exercising some forms of authority in an arena theoretically closed to her, and that promised security in negotiating the social pitfalls of this world as well as in deserving a place in heaven.

In early modern England, visiting and receiving visits was a crucial means of maintaining social position and a "favorite diversion" of the social elite. It was an opportunity to keep up family reputation through conspicuous display and the provision of hospitality.[30] More broadly, historians have suggested that it helped to promote social cohesion, especially on the local level.[31] The middling and upper ranks and men and women alike seem to have shared this preoccupation, but Sharpe points out its particular importance for women, for whom visiting provided a potentially prestigious social role and means of accruing honor. Two social trends are especially relevant to the practice of visiting in this period. First, Norbert Elias, Philippe Ariès, and others have argued that across western Europe, the development of a new concern with manners and a code of civility meant that relations between state and citizen, and between individuals, were increasingly formalized and helped to reinforce the social hierarchy.[32] Books describing appropriate deportment began to appear in the sixteenth century, dealing with a range of situations, from basic table manners (as in Erasmus's *Manners for Children*) to interactions at court (as in Castiglione's *The Courtier*). This interest in new forms of behavior spread down the social scale, and became an important way to demonstrate relationships and assert identity.

Second, the seventeenth and eighteenth centuries are often seen as a period when women were increasingly marginalized in terms of their economic production, and consequently, in the case of the prosperous classes, relegated to an idle life in the private sphere within the confines of a new vision of domesticity.[33] Amanda Vickery, however, contests the conceptual framework of contrasting an Edenic agricultural age during which women made valued contributions to the economy with an industrializing period of increasing confinement to a restrictively defined private sphere.[34] To begin with, she notes historians' continued reliance on prescriptive literature to describe both the conception of and adherence to the ideology of separate spheres, regardless of their simultaneous acknowledgment that the men and women in public and private arenas could not and did not operate in reality without significant overlap and fluidity of boundaries. She also points out that recent scholarship has disqualified any period from being a "golden age" for women in terms of the conditions of their work and the ideology concerning their role, so that narratives that trace a decline in women's autonomy, mobility, and productive capacity do so from an idealized starting point. Rather than discarding the entire conceptual framework of public and private, however,[35] in this case it is worth using a much more rank-specific and at the same time looser definition of these terms. Rank was a vital factor determining interactions with the world outside the immediate family, and if middling women found themselves shut out of economic production and the marketplace, while their experience would have been more applicable to a large segment of the female population, it would not have applied to those at the top—elite women who would not have been involved in this sort of economic activity in the first place. Consequently, a definition of "public" and "private" spheres that refers primarily to public commercial space, and to women as producers within that space, is not relevant to all levels of society.

If instead the definition deals in the main with women's opportunity for participation in the political and legal arenas, then it is certainly true that public space for speech, especially from the authoritative position of a politician, lawyer, or other "professional" was not available to women of any social group. But even while admitting that elite women spoke in houses rather than in legal courts, banks, or Parliament, the extent to which that meant that they were unseen and unheard by people outside their family is arguable. If strictly private—domestic—meant interaction only with one's own family, inside one's own house, and strictly public meant speaking in commercial, professional, and political spaces, then much of these women's activities would fall outside of either category. Visiting, for example, is a private activity, in that the space involved is usually a house, but those who visit are very much on public display in a social sense, and their words are heard, repeated, and may have significant repercussions.[36] Similarly, while women may not have had voices of authority in churches, the law courts, and Westminster Hall, their attendance there on state or religious occasions can be acknowledged as public activity, because women present in those places signaled their social position, political affiliation, and by their attendance countenanced or even helped to legitimate that particular public ceremony.

The converse of this broad conception of public activity is the acknowledgment of the impact that private actions could have on public events and institutions. In many respects, the social and familial was the political, in that through visiting it was possible to build up a network of contacts that could be used for obtaining professional or political favors

for oneself and one's kin and friends. Patronage often worked through
these informal connections, and intertwined as it was with party allegiance, had a significant effect on the workings of government and the
church, political alliances, and actual legislation. The potential innate in
social interactions for a woman to exercise influence through arbitration
of status and particularly through the opportunities it gave her for acting
as a patron, have not been sufficiently recognized as means by which an
elite woman could take advantage of her rank to assert a public presence
in a way not possible if women are defined in solely domestic, gendered
terms. Sara Mendelson, for instance, assigns much more weight to differences in age and marital status than to rank in describing a woman's
daily routine. In her depiction, the case of married women with children
is typical, where they spent the day "running the household, educating
their children, supervising servants, sewing and reading, entertaining
friends and relations, visiting the neighboring poor, and performing a
lengthy devotional routine."[37] While I would not contest her general portrayal of home life, I would argue that certain parts of it deserve greater
emphasis and expansion for high-ranking women, in ways that allow
them to be seen as active in a broadly defined "public" sphere.

The importance of visiting (and the behavior that went with it) to social structure and interaction can be seen in the number of books that
prescribed social etiquette and sought to regulate public interaction according to religious and secular principles.[38] From Jeremy Taylor's work
on friendship, through Richard Allestree's conduct books, to Halifax's
advice to his daughter, and Richard Steele's essays, with varying degrees
of emphasis on religious duty, morality, and social propriety, numerous
authors catered to society's concern with status and relations between
ranks. Directed specifically to a female audience, *The Ladies' Calling*
and *The Lady's New Year's Gift* are both most concerned with women's
demeanor, and insist on the importance of modesty and the preservation
of a chaste reputation as their contribution to upholding family honor
especially when outside the home.[39] They advocate a posture of reserved
gravity in company, and Halifax in particular portrays the social world
as a hostile public space, warning: "It is time now to lead you out of
your house into the world. A dangerous step; where your vertue alone
will not serve you, except it is attended with a great deal of prudence:
you must have both for your guard."[40] They also assume women are
prone to frivolous chat, insincerity, and backbiting and warn against
these vices.[41] Related issues were choosing friends and the effective use of

censure, both of which were important for maintaining one's own standing. Taylor concentrated on the comforts of friendship, for those who chose companions with good dispositions, worthy morals, and the ability to keep secrets.[42] Halifax, on the other hand, was much less concerned with the spiritual benefits of friendship than with the risks of association with those of tarnished reputations, and he advised his daughter not to choose friends under social censure and immediately drop those who were even accused of misconduct.[43] He assumed there would be cases where it would be necessary to censure others, and though advising patience, discretion, and softness in doing so, made it clear that some behavior was to be greeted with disapproval, as if not doing so might reflect badly on the onlooker: "An aversion to what is criminal and a contempt of what is ridiculous, are the inseperable companions of understanding and vertue . . . " and furthermore, "humility is no doubt a great virtue, but it ceaseth to be so, when it is afraid to scorn an ill thing."[44]

Sarah, therefore, was part of a society where formal rules of social deportment were of increasing importance, disseminating down the social scale, and being written about in pieces directed at a mass audience, affirming the social hierarchy while trying to promote the moral virtues of this form of public interaction. Moreover, this public activity was encouraged for women as well as men, so that the attitudes Sarah expressed, the way she conducted her social life, and the character of her acquaintance all have implications for understanding the potential for mobility, autonomy, and power that upper-class women might have gained through public social interaction in this period.

Sarah's understanding of the social round and her worries about it often followed two of the main themes addressed in contemporary literature—how to choose appropriate company and how to converse properly with those chosen. If Jeremy Taylor and the marquess of Halifax represent opposite ends of the spectrum on the question of choosing friends, where Taylor focuses on the pleasures and rewards of friendship and Halifax emphasizes the dangers and drawbacks, Sarah leaned heavily in Halifax's direction. At one point she directly cited his eloquent advice on the pitfalls of choosing friends:

Use a Strict Care in the Choice of your Friends, perhaps the best are not without their Objections. The Leagues Offensive and Defensive Seldom hold in politicks and much less in Freind:ships. The Violent Intamacies when once broken, of which they scarce ever fail, make such a Noise; the

Bagg of Secrets untied they ffly about like Birds let loose from a Cage and become the Entertainment of the Town. If Formality is to be allow'd in any instance, it is to be put on to resist the intrusion of such forward persons as shall press themselves into your ffriendship, where if admitted, they will be either a Snare or an Incumbrance.[45]

More generally, Sarah often portrayed visiting as a public activity fraught with danger to one's own religious and social well-being, but necessary to avoid worse dangers:

I visit Some people for the Same Causes as the Indians Worship the Devil, least provoking them by neglect and dislike, they Shou'd do me Some mischeif. In our Converse in the world we must expect Temptations from the Devil, provocations from the ffolly or Malice, of Evil men, Vexations by unhappy Accidents, and they will be surpriz'd who do not forecast and Arm against 'em by the advantages of retirement and Secret Devotion; part of which is, to premeditate our Conversation, and So to forecast the Occurrences of life that we may Conduct our Selves to the best advantage of our Spiritual interests.[46]

It may be that one of the reasons Sarah echoed Halifax's characterization of the world as a hostile place populated by untrustworthy companions was because of her experience of social ostracism and betrayal during the trial and disgrace of her son Spencer. The treatment of her family by supposed friends during that period may have made her quick to take the most pessimistic view of the intentions of her acquaintances, a tendency she herself commented upon:

Beleive thy ffriends love thee is a precept I Some where mett with long Since, and never had more Need to use it than Now. the Coldness of Some, and the distrust of my Self makes me apt to doubt it. . . . I wou'd perswade my Self into a beleif of their kindness and good Will in order to loving them agen, ffor Certain in Nature ther's no such thing without it.[47]

Ironically, in recounting Halifax's advice, it seems that Sarah subscribed to the very philosophy of distancing oneself from potentially scandalous people that led these acquaintances to avoid her. Here, as elsewhere, she appropriated part of the text, using it to describe and condemn the dangers of society, yet she did not acknowledge the logical result of following the entirety of the advice, which was that she could expect that others would terminate their acquaintance with her on the basis of even a potential, indirect stain on her character through the actions of her son.

Part of this conflict stemmed from the fact that leading a pious life required choosing edifying company and conversing profitably. But if the ideal of associating as much as possible with fellow pious Christians was hard to attain, then the goal of conducting and sustaining (and being interested in) moral, worthwhile conversation was even more so. Selections abound in the diary on the need to work toward meaningful, pious visits,[48] and Sarah deplored her frequently unfruitful interactions: "My time wasts with unprofitable Company, yet since I am not Edify'd by them, I endeavor so to from my discourse as they may be the better for me."[49] She was, however, aware of the conflicting value placed on affability and the potential unpopularity of an upright manner, as her citation and comment on selections in the New Testament shows:

> I am much in Consulting and Contriving how to Carry on a Holy Life with most Advantage. Do not let Fail the Strictness and Majesty of your Conversation keep close to it, tho' for so doing wee must expect trouble from the world. I am sensible I incurr the displeasure of some ffor want of fflattering Compliance with them. But it must needs be good what Evill men hate, their approbation woud be a disgrace.[50]

This need for compliance in conversation was at odds not only with the requirement of edification, but with the exhortations of the church and Scripture to speak out against vice and sin. Sarah felt the pressure of the conflicting requirements, reminding herself,

> O that I cou'd imprint there what is to day I heard on this Text. I will Speak of thy Testimonies also before Kings and will not be asham'd. This is a Time to Assert Truth, and Defend Vertue with Courage and Constancy against Such as in Doctrine and practise, Boldly Attack both. All Shamefacedness is not good.[51]

In her treatment of texts on the relative merits of solitude and sociability, and of censure and affability, Sarah seems to have been uneasily aware of the conflicting pressures of prescription regarding these issues, but was willing to refer to both sides of this age-old philosophical and theological debate, depending on her mood and circumstances. Unlike her attitude toward many aspects of her domestic and social identity, here she seems to have been able to live reasonably comfortably without resolving the contradiction in ideologies of sociability, while still openly recognizing the existence of a conflict and her own difficulties in adhering to a strategy. Rather than suppress or subvert parts of the prescriptions, Sarah let them run concurrently, perhaps because whichever course she chose, or however often she alternated, neither choice reflected badly on her and both were useful for presenting an admirable image. If she could not entirely reconcile the models of interaction for a pious, thoughtful Christian and a gracious gentlewoman, they were still both commendable courses of action, reflecting in their inconsistencies only the basic divergence between secular, worldly life and the life of the soul.[52]

Sarah was perpetually poised between condemning and yearning for society—between isolation and overabundance of visitors. Her attraction to the admirable religious and intellectual model of a solitary contemplative life spent at reading and writing was at odds with her obvious interest in daily interaction and in hearing the latest news and gossip, however wearying. Occasionally she translated this praise of the contemplative life into a resolution to retire from the world, because visits were simply too risky to her personal ease and piety,[53] but she never actually carried out this resolution, perhaps feeling the demands of upholding family reputation or pressure from would-be visitors. Certainly her diary indicates one important reason, since the number of entries praising retirement is similar to the number of entries concerned with her loneliness when she is not in company. The theoretical pleasures of solitude are repeatedly belied by her experience of many hours alone, despite the dangers of insincerity, insult, and malice from enemies.[54] More than once, she ruefully reflected on her own ambivalence:

> I neither make nor Receive a Visitt without Reflecting on what I Hear, or Say. Which Seldome leaves me pleas'd or Sattisfy'd. Yet to be long without Society (to w^c Nature enclines) is Dull, but alwaies in Company Dissipates the Spirit.[55]

The whole experience may have contributed to the impression her diary gives that she was always uneasily aware of the need to uphold the family reputation in her role as emissary to the outside world through her visits. She was particularly proud of her discretion throughout Spencer's ordeal, and felt she had successfully avoided contributing to the aspersions cast on the family during that socially perilous time.[56] With such a suspicious and disapproving attitude toward social interaction (her condemnations of the behavior of acquaintances are constant), it is not surprising that Sarah vacillated between bewailing the troubles of keeping company and complaining about her solitude when she was alone.

In all these facets of social interaction, Sarah tended to select negative and pessimistic writing to express her views on the subject. The strategy she described for coping with the public life of visiting seems to have been to take very much to heart admonitions to be discreet and reserved—hoping that by withdrawing and acting with humility, she would be able to avoid unfavorable notice and thus preserve the reputation of her family and her own tenuous standing. Her feeling that the public world of society was a dangerous, unreliable place was, after all, reinforced by the experiences of her sons and husband. While it is impossible to know whether her acquaintances would have agreed with her presentation of herself as modest and discreet, it seems that she considered herself successful in presenting that image, thereby preventing dislike or social censure as much as possible.[57] While she counted hardly anyone a friend, she counted no one a personal enemy.

In some ways, Sarah's conception of her social role echoes her strategies for family life. She withdrew in both cases: in public, by means of frequent retreats to her books and writing, and by as careful a watch over her tongue as she could manage; and in private, by retreating from the wifely duties of conjugal relations and overseeing the servants. In the former arena she seems to have been reasonably satisfied with the results. Despite the vanity and insincerity of society, she had led an essentially blameless public life as demonstrated by her good reputation and the esteem in which people held her. But in private life, perhaps because it involved deliberate subversion of prevailing family ideology, the effectiveness of her strategy was seriously compromised by the conflict it caused with her husband. Self-righteousness over her dealings in public does not seem to have detracted significantly from her overall satisfaction with how her behavior was received, whereas in her family, the constant need to justify herself and her conception of the wifely role may have meant that her self-righteousness directly contributed to marital friction. All that went into being a pious woman in public—a grave, reserved manner and abstinence from sexual license—accorded well with Sarah's character in the first place, so that she was able to fulfill the prescriptive ideal without having to alter it significantly to meet her own requirements. This harmony between prescription and behavior may have been further aided by her high rank. For though she was required to show deference to superiors, and preserve a modest demeanor in general, there were many people from whom she in turn could expect a satisfying degree of deference. Within the family, however, the prescriptive ideal required constant, meek deference to her husband, whatever his faults and regardless of her social status. It is not surprising that in contrast to her disappointments in reworking domestic prescription to create a worthy personal identity, in the social world (despite bewailing its worthlessness) Sarah was generally able to live comfortably within the boundaries of its ideologies, successful in her presentation of herself as a pious gentlewoman.

From Sarah's diary it is possible not only to assess her attitudes toward visiting, but to use passing references to arrive at an approximate picture of her social milieu. There are enough clues over the course of the seven volumes of her diary to get a sense of the size and standing of her visiting circle.[58] She herself numbers and ranks her circle of acquaintances, commenting, "I hold acquaintance with about 40 persons, not of the meanest sort; yet scarce know whither to go where I may Spend an hour with Complacence."[59] That number corresponds very roughly to the number of people she mentioned more than once as having contacted, although over the entire diary there are over a hundred she specifically named and indicated that she had interaction with, rather than simply hearing news about them. Of course, a number of these people died or were referred to only in one section of the diary, so at any one time, it seems that the instances of named social interaction in her diary corroborate her own estimate of the size of her acquaintance.

From the titles she gives them and from further investigation of biographical details where possible, it seems that "not of the meanest sort" means a fairly solid majority from the gentry, an occasional aristocrat, and a number without any title.[60] Of those people mentioned more than once, the women outnumber the men, but only by about seventeen to twelve. Where it is possible to tell, the men are often involved in the legal profession and the House of Commons—hardly surprising, given her family's activities. But most notable in terms of profession is the predominance of clergy, and especially bishops. Equally unsurprisingly, her companions seem by and large to have been Whigs. Nonetheless, she seems to have disapproved of the more zealous Whigs she knew, and was especially condemnatory of Dissenters and other detractors from the Church of England.[61] Sarah was obliged to have contact with some of these people because Sir William had chosen to construct alliances with the heterodox and extra-establishment groups to further his political career, but her own preference and efforts were directed toward cultivation of orthodox members of the establishment. Sarah may have had no real choice in her contacts with Dissenters and skeptics if she were to carry out her responsibility to support her husband in his career and maintain his social status, but she actively pursued an alternate strategy as well. Her observations on the company she kept in Hertford suggest that she felt obligated, for the sake of her family, not to offend by shunning her husband's connections. But she was distinctly unhappy at having to do so and was willing to minimize contact as much as possible.[62] She mentioned arguments with them about the church and having to put up with their derogatory comments:

> At Dinner my zeal grew warm against some that methought talk'd irreverently about matters of Religion which to discourse of at all, I think may very well be Spared at Such times. It greives me to perceive any one offended with my reprimand but then agen I take Courage Since I am not inferior to any present, and think others ought to be tender of giving me so just offence.[63]

She seems particularly offended by the presumption implicit in Dissenting from the established church, and cast aspersions on the sincerity or intelligence of doubters.[64] The virulence of her comments may also have to do with the fact that it was in Hertford that she was most surrounded by Dissenters, especially Quakers, who had been Sir William's leading supporters in parliamentary elections, but had then betrayed the family by charging Spencer with murder. Dislike of Hertford and dislike of Dissenters may have been inseparable.[65] As well as being out of sympathy with the religious attitudes of her husband's acquaintances and affronted by their treatment of her son, she was displeased by their low social status, complaining that "we Scarce See the face of what's Calld Gentry once in a Moon, and then for want of Use we are scared like frighted Hares."[66] Here, as in her disapproval of Sir William's management of the servants, she thought he had failed in a family duty—in this case, to uphold the family reputation through making and keeping contacts with the most respectable and highest ranking members of local society. But in another strike against Sir William's political and social strategies (from Sarah's point of view), by connecting himself to Dissent and Whiggery Sir William had effectively barred himself from useful ties to many of the local gentry, since a prominent political and social group in Hertfordshire was the Royston Club, a Tory party organization that kept the two county parliamentary seats firmly in their hands.[67] Despite her disapproval, Sarah was on occasion willing to rejoice with her husband at the downfall of a political competitor, although only after she had recast self-interest as providential judgment:

> S^r W Came home full of glee with the News that Mr Philmer his Antagonist for the Election at Hartford was drop'd down Suddenly Dead. how litle thought he to Enter the Chamber of Death before the House of Comons. Never did any one Triumph more in his Acheivm^t. than by relation did this Man. Let such Examples put us in mind of the Admonition of our Saviour, Except ye Repent ye shall all likewise perish. and of this precept, Rejoice not over thy greatest Enemy being Dead, but remember that we dy all. We may not wish the death of another be it never so much our interest, but when God has declared his Will, if my family may receive Benefit by ye Consequence, sure I am not denied the Sattisfaction resulting therfrom. Besides, if I know some false Malicious knaves that may meet with trouble from it, I may take Content to see wickedness not prosper, but punished.[68]

A related area of friction with Sir William over the conduct of their social life came in displaying the household and hospitality to the visiting world. Reiterating her displeasure at the low rank of those with whom William chose to associate, Sarah also complained of his mismanagement of the occasions of interaction:

> S^r W hath so ordered Matters that at Table we see not the face of a Gentle:Man or Woman in an Age, but the most despicable people one Can imagine. . . . If I carve to these kind of people, he bids me let 'em help themselves. if I let alone he Calls on me to do it. If I put them upon Calling for a glass of Wine, he saith Sure they best know their own Time, and Commends the Small Beer, and so on in every the like instance. In very Solemn fashion I have desired him not to have me So perpetually under Correction, but to no purpose, he persists Even before my Sons, w^c makes me Shaggrin and uneasie that they Shou'd see us so Silly. It is impossible to be pleas'd with Such things, they Constrain one wither to Chafe, or be dogg'd which part I Chuse to act at this time and am willing though to beleive it is purely amusement, and Confusion in him for want of being used to good Company, and not any studied intention to be troublesome. Such fail in the entertaining part at their own house as hold their Visitants in Continual restraint.[69]

Sir William's behavior on these occasions was not only embarrassing in its public display of disrespect for Sarah as a person, but in its mortifying revelation of social ineptitude. Sarah did not want to be seen as part of a "silly" couple—a pair incompetent in the social graces—who failed to maintain their social standing by inviting people of the right rank for dinner. She did not want to be blamed in the presence of others for misunderstanding social distinctions and the corresponding cues that were to be followed in offering hospitality, especially since she felt it was Sir William who was oblivious to the appropriate etiquette in the first place. As a wife, the management of the symbolism of hospitality ought to have been her domain, and among the effects of Sir William usurping this role was that he chose both the wrong audience and wrong rituals for asserting status. Moreover, the infrequency of encountering the right audience made them less adept at the correct forms of display and deportment.

Despite William's assertion of control over finances and furnishings, Sarah seems to have had a significant level of autonomy in choosing her own friends, and she also seems to have had extensive physical mobility.[70] She conducted most of her visiting by herself, in the family coach, sometimes ranging quite far from central London.[71] She also seems to have walked extensively, both in London and in Hertford. And while she may have been obliged to receive or visit Sir William's connections, it is clear that much of her visiting was to people of her own choosing, with no accommodation to Sir William's tastes or preferences. In fact, her selection of friends may have been an implicit demonstration of an alternate (and therefore correct) method for accumulating the assets of social connection, as opposed to the strategy employed by Sir William. Perhaps her best friend had been Martin Clifford, master of the Charterhouse, and her neighbor from 1672 to 1677.[72] This friendship seems to have been entirely independent of Sir William, and one that she missed sorely. On more than one occasion she regrets his absence, and at one point described her sense of fellow-feeling for him in the warmest terms she ever used:

> In vain do I wish to meet with such another Old ffellow as Martin Clifford. In laughing at a Worthless World wee Shou'd agree more than ever. Upon Reflection and Experience I find the Same Notions and Sentiments about humane kind as appeard in him Because he treated Fools according to their Folly, it gott him the Charecter of ill Nature; but I never knew him other than Compassionate, Charitable, generous and Just nor did I ever hear him talk profanely or Obscen'ly at any time. He was an approver of Vertue in those that had it. No Contemner of Religion, or Such as maintain the principles of it but wou'd express great Veneration for

Bishop Wilkins Dr Tillot: Dr Barrow and the like—I hope his Sins are forgiven, and his Soul at Rest.[73]

The only other person receiving consistent praise was Lady Rachel Russell. In this case, however, praise was expressed in terms of admiration and gratitude, as Lady Russell was much higher up the social scale and did favors for Sarah as well as being part of her visiting circle. Her acts of kindness to Sarah were treated as the benevolence of a superior rather than the meeting of minds of equals.[74]

As mentioned above, the most striking overall characteristic of her social circle is the number of clergymen she knew, and particularly the number in the upper echelons of the church. Of those people she named more than four times, ten in all, half were or later became bishops. Similarly, two of the four acquaintances she named more than ten times were bishops. Of course, it is hard to tell how closely the number of mentions of these people in her diary corresponded to the extent of her contact and friendship and intimacy with them, but it does seem that in the case of the bishops, at least, that they (and often their wives) played an important part in her social life. It is also notable that these bishops held the comfortably middling sees as far as income went. While they were not in the top five wealthiest posts, neither were they in the notoriously poorly endowed bishoprics at the bottom of the episcopal scale.[75] Politically, they tended to be moderate Whigs.[76] High-flying Tory clergy, such as Thomas Hodgkin, rector of Hertingfordbury, Doctor Sherlock, and Sir John Trelawny, bishop of Winchester, came in for a good deal of scorn when Sarah mentioned them, and they were certainly not part of her normal social circle.[77]

In any case, Sarah's frequent association with the clergy certainly does not seem to be at William's instigation, though it may very well have been partially for the social benefit of the family he headed. He criticized her clerical friends but did not attempt to restrict her interaction with them, and his comments seem to be part of their larger conflict over temperament and piety, as far as can be seen from Sarah's complaints, such as: "I am Reproach'd for being of the Church wherin are a pack of Rogues among whom D^r M[anningha]m is said to be Notoriously so. It moves me to hear good people reviled meerly because I like them and vexes me so that I Cannot Sleep in my Bed."[78] It may also be that Sarah chose to spend time with the clergy because as well as bringing honor to the family, it was a means of setting herself apart from her husband and asserting her moral superiority.

Moreover, from the perspective of someone who was searching not only for ways to maintain the family status but also for avenues for personal authority, association with the clergy of the established church assisted in upholding her own reputation for piety and could provide an important window onto the political and professional world, both as informed observer and as indirect participant. Because political issues were often fundamentally bound up in religious questions, Sarah could legitimately show an interest, and through the bishops, had highly placed sources of information who actually affected government policy in the House of Lords. Equally important for assessing the extent of Sarah's access to information and power was the potential inherent in friendship with the upper clergy for exercising authority and extracting respect—in the visible realm through one's attendance at public religious events and invisibly by dispensing charity and exercising patronage.

Going to church was a religious duty—a public, civic counterpart to one's private devotion. In sermons and conduct books, the clergy insisted on the necessity of spiritual preparation for church attendance, especially for receiving communion, through self-examination, meditaion, and prayer. Regular, frequent attendance was also necessary, and authors warned in particular against using lack of preparation as merely an excuse for neglecting one's duty to participate in the Eucharist. Furthermore, numerous authorities prescribed the appropriate mental attitude and behavior of churchgoers; members of the congregation were to be sincere, reverent, solemn, and to pay devout attention to the prayers and sermon. But as well as being a Christian duty, churchgoing also provided a means of publicly displaying one's social standing, piety, and even allegiance to a particular religious stance or political party. Norman Sykes suggests that because of the reaction against seventeenth-century religious zeal, attendance at public prayers was for many people a social exercise—part of the routine of polite society—in which the fashionable, in London especially, attended Anglican services to see and be seen and to be entertained by the sermons of eminent divines.[79] But as Sykes also suggests, it is wrong to see the post-Restoration changes in religious practices in entirely negative terms. Part of one's practical training in earthly citizenship was preparation for heavenly citizenship, and sermons were consequently the main focus of a liturgy designed to praise God and to inculcate man's duty on earth.[80]

In evaluating Sarah's own experience with this particular form of public expression and her use of prescription relating to it, it is first of

all important to consider how her social links with the clergy might af-
fect her attitudes toward churchgoing. Sarah's home parish was Saint
Andrew's, Holborn, whose rector was Thomas Manningham, later bishop of Chichester. As noted above, aside from presiding at services attended every Sunday by Sarah, Manningham was also one of her most
frequent social contacts, at least as can be gathered from the number of
times he was specifically mentioned in that context in the diary. The fact
that Sarah knew him socially, and knew some of his religious and social
superiors as well, may very well have changed the power dynamic and
affected how Sarah viewed the man who preached to her as a religious
authority. Because of their relationship outside the pulpit and the pew,
Sarah may have felt entitled to evaluate his sermons, and not just on the
basis of doctrine, but in terms of his character and even his politics.
What is more, it is likely that Sarah's multifaceted relationship with a
churchman in which imparting and receiving religious dogma was only
one (admittedly important) of a number of interactions was replicated
by many of the elite, both on a personal level and also in their response
to prescriptive literature written by the clergy. And this multiplicity of
social and political elements in the relations between clergy, prescription,
and gentry does not even take into account the added complication of
patronage. Fierce competition for benefices also tended to put clergy in a
subservient position in relation to potential patrons, a position that
might carry with it social or political obligations as the price of success
in seeking preferment.[81] An additional problem for clerical independence
and moral authority was that a great many of the more lowly positions
in the church were very poorly paid, a fact that could lessen respect of
the poor parish priests and curates among the wealthier members of
their congregations and encouraged pluralism and nonresidency.[82] In
Sarah's case, and quite probably in the case of other members of the upper echelons, interactions with the clergy stemming from the act of
church attendance and reception of clerical ideas on how one should attend church, did not seem to be on a one-way track, from superior, religious authority, to inferior, lay receptor, but were in part colored by
social contact with these clergy and by the multiple purposes of churchgoing—personal, religious, social, and political.

As in her association with the clergy in general, one personal reason
Sarah may have had for going to church as she did was to assert her difference and autonomy from Sir William, not just in theological leanings,
but in deciding on the best strategy for making social connections and

declaring religious and correspondingly political allegiance. It is difficult to tell exactly how many times in a week she attended services, and how regular the pattern was, but in general, the frequency was high. It seems that she went twice on Sundays, at least once during the week, on all holy days, and more frequently during Lent. She also took communion on the last Sunday of the month and on high holy days.[83] It is not at all clear how regularly Sir William attended church, if at all. From an argument with him about servants that quickly expanded to take in friction over the church, it seems he did not attend and in fact distanced himself from the established church:

> S^r W affirm'd that all peoples servants were as proffligate as ours and he knew not where to gett better. I said if that were true which I hoped was not, it was a Sad instance that Masters were to blame in neglecting the Word and Worship of God in their ffamilies wherby they shou'd be taught their Duty. He replied we might thank the Church of England for that Neglect, in former daies such order was Observ'd but laid down since that Came in. I asked if he any where found the Church forbid it, sure all might do it that pleas'd, and if he wou'd come there he might meet with frequent Exhortations to the performance of it.[84]

Although in this episode she had to defend her allegiance to the Church of England, Sarah clearly felt she was doing so from a position of moral strength, in contrast to her husband's lack of attendance at church. She took church attendance even further in the domestic struggle with her husband, although we only see the tail end of a presumably long-running argument where she had to accept defeat over use of the coach but still made her point about needing it:

> I have a long time been disattisfy'd with my way of Spending the Sabaoth going to Church but once in the day by reason S^r W will dine so late that I Cannot have the Coach time enough to go any whither. . . . So I have found a place where Doctor Haley preaches, and the service begins at 3 a Clock, whither I go on foot.[85]

In both cases, it would have been hard for Sir William to forbid an activity that, while perhaps indirectly defiant, was a blameless independence exercised to fulfill her Christian duty.[86] Sarah most often cited prescriptive sources when reminding herself of her duty to attend services.

Sarah evaluated the clergy for the same reasons—ministers were supposed to conduct the act of public worship itself in the right spirit in order to please God, and they ought to help her own thoughts to an ap-

propriately spiritual state for the furthering of her own salvation. Citing
prescriptive sources and her own priorities, Sarah felt entitled to evaluate the way ministers led the service and the way they preached. For instance, disappointed in the Lent lecture, she reflected on the outward
qualifications needed to preach:

> Every man is not fitted for a pulpitt, a good voice and Comely person are
> necessary quallifications for those as appear there. and such as get up in
> great Churches before larg Auditories without 'em, it may justly be feared
> do want judgm' to Come off well in other performances. and so it hap-
> pen'd this Day.[87]

From the frequency with which this virtue was commended, however, it
would seem that for Sarah, earnestness, or sincerity, was the most important criterion for evaluating the clergy and their pronouncements.[88]

Moreover, based on her evaluations, she assumed the right to choose
where she worshiped, and therefore she is an important example of the
extent to which a practicing Anglican might exercise his or her own discretion in fashioning not only a personalized doctrine, but to a limited
extent, a personalized public practice. Ordinarily, she attended the morning Sunday service at her own parish church, Saint Andrew's, Holborn.
But she felt entitled to go elsewhere if she had a poor opinion of the presiding minister and especially of his sincerity:

> D' Manning: whom I beleive to be Sincerely good therfore wou'd not
> leave for any one. but being told he did not preach, and that his place
> was to be Supplied by M' W: whose sermons are Composed of much witt,
> so that every Sentence might be an Epigram which way I like not, but had
> rather dispence with dull Earnest, than hear a Man talk of Sacred Things
> as it were in jest. I went therfore to M' Crook a Man admirably quallify'd
> for a preacher, perticulerly endued with a great Memory to discourse
> without Notes (tho' I hope I despise not reading) which gives a great
> grace to the Delivery.[89]

She did not always need to shop around to discover the various preaching styles of the upper clergy, as guest preachers at Saint Andrew's included the bishops of Salisbury, Oxford, York, and Dublin.[90]

On other days and other occasions she went elsewhere. Generally,
though not always, on state-appointed holy days she went to churches
most closely associated with the state—often the Queen's chapel at St.
James's Palace.[91] She also attended the Boyle and Lent lectures at Saint
Paul's Cathedral, both of which had a revolving roster of preachers, and

she resolved to go to Dr. Stanhope's weekly lectures at Saint Lawrence's.[92] She knew how services were conducted at Saint Alphage and Saint Giles[93] and may have been to other places, since sermons were often mentioned in the context of who preached them rather than where they were preached. Over the whole of the diary, Sarah mentioned hearing sermons by a total of twenty-two ministers, including her own parish priest, during the time she was living in London.

Sarah's search for services that met her requirements was an exercise of consumer choice that has implications for our understanding of the relationship between the established church and its adherents. In a society where participation in the Church of England had recently become essentially voluntary, Anglican clergy needed to maintain membership not just by insisting on the obligation of Christians to attend services, but by offering public spaces that delivered an attractive liturgy and satisfactory sermons. In London, the frequency of services, the plethora of lecture series, the number of churches with prosperous, eminent divines holding the position at least partially because of their preaching skills, and the round of guest preaching or special-occasion preaching by bishops,[94] may have encouraged the pious or even just the sociable to think and move beyond the confines of Sunday morning services at their parish church. In any case, Sarah seemed to think she had a certain amount of discretion in choosing where to worship, based on her evaluation of the congregation and presiding clergy. Occasionally, she even acknowledged the entertainment value of such a large pool of talented speakers.[95]

For people like Sarah, from the upper and middling ranks of society, another fundamental component of belonging to the Church of England was the exercise of charity. The "philanthropy of piety"[96] was a large part of what religious duty was about, since in James's epistle and Anglican commentary, one of the guiding principles of Christianity was that its adherents were obligated to attempt to emulate divine charity.[97] But the act of giving had additional meanings: It established ties of obligation and could be motivated not only by benevolence, but by power-seeking, by the expectation of gratitude and respect, by the opportunity to demonstrate one's own righteousness (and perhaps derive a sense of moral superiority from doing so), and by the need to display philanthropy to assert and confirm one's social standing.[98] This multiplicity of motivations can be seen in Sarah's acts of giving directly to individuals and also in her benefactions through intermediaries, especially to institutions, by which she both worked to fulfill her Christian duty and to collect power and respect from many levels of society.

Although the Anglican church insisted on the obligation of charity, it also set out clear restrictions "as to the extent of giving which was religiously or morally obligatory or socially beneficial."[99] Just as on the larger scale of parish poor relief, only the "deserving poor"—those incapacitated by reason of illness or age rather than the unemployed in general, who, if able bodied but without work were presumed to be lazy—were to receive help, it was important to select the right beneficiaries, not the "idle poor" for personal charity. Worthy beneficiaries were to be industrious, humble, patient, and grateful.[100] Speck, among others, argues that this attitude toward the poor was hardening from the late 1600s onward as the paternalism of the propertied classes gave way to a more ruthless, condemnatory strategy for dealing with social problems, where "even discriminating charity was circumscribed."[101]

Sarah's experience of and attitudes toward charitable giving mirrors some aspects of both religious prescription and social trends. During the years of her marriage that are recorded in the diary, when Sarah was only in control of a £50-pound pension every year, she spent perhaps £10 of it per year on "charity and bounty,"[102] much of which was dispensed around Christmas time. It is very hard to tell what proportion of this total was given directly to individuals, but it is clear that some was because of Sarah's expression of discomfort over the question of whether she was discriminating enough in her choice of recipients:

> I am prompt by Nature to Acts of Charity, and give pensions to Some meerly because thay are poor, for otherwise they deserve not well; so that it abates the pleasure of doing good, because I give to the unworthy. Where I know no ill Charity Enclines me to beleive and hope the best, therfore am most sattisfy'd when I Cast my Bread upon the Waters.[103]

While this figure for cash charity is unremarkable in the absolute, at least as far as the fragmentary evidence goes, it is a very high proportion of her personal annual income—rather higher than Beckett's estimates of perhaps 4 to 7 percent of income among leading families and 1 to 2 percent among the gentry as a whole. While warning of the wide variety of amounts and occasions of dispensing cash charity, he uses Viscount Lonsdale's distribution of £5 at Christmas as a typical example of the pattern of giving among the propertied classes.[104] A contrasting example, showing the extent to which this might vary in form and amount, is that of Alice Brownlow, a gentlewoman who with money from her inheritance had a bede house built in 1659 for six aged women and supplied its running costs of £42 per year out of her husband's income.[105] Of course, Sarah's pension was all disposable income, since her basic living expenses, while contentious, were covered by Sir William's allotment of housekeeping money. Ordinarily she was expected to furnish her own clothing out of this money, but, having never been ostentatious in dress, by 1700 she said in reference to allocating a portion of her pension to charity, "I shall think much to bestow above half upon my person at this time of Life."[106]

At any rate, roughly £10 a year seems to be her average expenditure on charitable causes while Sir William was alive, part of which at least was dispensed on single, personal cases that she explicitly defended for their merit:

> The wants of two persons, a woman that lies In and a labouring man who hath wounded his hand that at present he Cannot work, Calls for some help. Those are ripe for Charity which are wasted by Age, or impotence Especially if maim'd in following their Calling. add to these, those that with diligence fight against poverty tho' neither Conquer till Death.[107]

Sarah had also been a regular contributor to charitable institutions since the beginning of her diary, and as such was a participant in the concurrent movements for moral reform and education in the early eighteenth century. In November 1700 she subscribed to the new girls' charity school at Saint Andrew's, Holborn, a project initiated under the auspices of the recently founded Society to Promote Christian Knowledge (SPCK).[108] Sarah seems to have taken the initiative (although her support may have been solicited earlier) in this first instance of her dispensing money to an institution by way of a clergyman. She recounted that she went to Dr. Manningham, her parish priest, and promised him £3 per year toward the operation of the school. Nothing further is specifically mentioned about this pledged sum, but it is initially interesting as an indication of Sarah's early interest in charity schools. She also specified that this donation came from her own pension, although it is unclear whether she counted it in her total reckoning of bounty distributed or not.

Among the motivating factors for the surge in the establishment of charity schools in this period were an interest in instilling social disci-

pline in the poor in the face of social unrest, pauperism, and growing ir-
religion through early training for the poor to perform the duties of their
station in life and to develop in them habits of industry and sobriety.
Another factor was an attempt to immunize poor children against popery by partly countering the setting up of Jesuit schools.[109] Subscribers
were mostly from the middling ranks, with some from higher levels of
society, and included laymen and clergy, men and women, and a wide
range of political and religious opinion.[110] The original members of the
SPCK included a number of bishops and bishops-to-be, and aside from
the £100 subscription of Francis, Lord Guilford, most pledged between
£3 and £5.[111] The SPCK itself did not, however, actually oversee the
founding and running of each charity school. It was up to the subscribers, usually the pastor and some members of the congregation in each
parish, to set up, fund, and run their own schools, though with help and
encouragement from the society.

By her gift, Sarah was associated with an early and unusually successful charity school endeavor. After seven months of collecting subscriptions, Dr. Manningham reported in January 1700 that Saint Andrew's
parish had enough money to run one charity school and was beginning
to collect money for a second school, this time for forty girls.[112] It may be
in this expansion phase that Sarah felt impelled to donate, especially to
her fellow females. In November of that year, the girls' school was up
and running, and by the end of the year, nearly £130 per annum had
been subscribed for the schools at Saint Andrew's.[113] By the time of the
first annual report in 1704, subscriptions for all fifty-four newly founded
London charity schools totaled £2,164 per annum, of which Saint Andrew's had the highest annual subscriptions for its three schools at £194
yearly.[114]

Sarah's support of the moral reform and Anglican reinvigoration
movement expanded when in 1705 she contributed money for catechisms to the Society for the Propagation of the Gospel in Foreign Parts
(SPG)—the offshoot of the SPCK founded in 1701 to assume entire responsibility for the first SPCK goal of spreading the gospel to the English
plantations abroad.[115] In contrast to her description of her donation to
the charity school, here Sarah was apparently solicited by the bishop of
Lichfield, who presented her with a sermon preached before the society,
and she responded by giving him 5 guineas.[116] Mention of an equivalent
donation recurs roughly annually in her diary for the next three years,
through either the bishop of Lichfield or on one occasion though Dr.

Manningham once he had been promoted to bishop of Chichester.[117] On the last of these occasions, Sarah noted that she had been reading the annual account of the society and that had prompted her gift. In contrast to the Saint Andrew's charity schools, the SPG had recurring financial problems. Set up to furnish books, pamphlets, and ministers to help in the conversion of the Indians and to acquire the allegiance of Christian settlers in North America, they sent out a number of clergymen on salaries of £50 per annum, to counter the influence of French missionaries and to assert the presence, liturgy, and organization of the Anglican church in the colonies.[118] Despite this support, news from America was often discouraging, and members fell into arrears with their subscriptions.[119]

As with the charity schools, subscription amounts were not very large; on the first subscription list they were generally between £2 and £5.[120] Interestingly, and perhaps because the charity school accounts were dealing with aggregate figures for a large number of parishes, instead of the more limited number of contributions to the SPG, the charity school accounts make no mention of individual donations, while the SPG lists a number of contributors specifically, and several others indirectly, as having contributed anonymously through named intermediaries.[121] Of the twenty-one named contributors in the 1706 account, two were women,[122] but it may be that more were included in the phrase "Many persons have sent in their generous contributions with a modest concealment of their names; as several sums of 20 or 30 pounds have been delivered by [society members serving as intermediaries]."[123] This modesty held true for one woman at least, Dame Jane Holman, who made an extraordinarily large donation of £1,000, but wanted her name concealed. Her identity was revealed only after her death, by her intermediary, Reverend Maplecroft.[124] The wording of this report, where anonymity was described as laudable, parallels the plaudits of divines in funeral sermons in which the deceased was praised for relieving the poor secretly.[125] Sarah herself on the occasion of one of her donations to the SPG echoed this sentiment: "Alms given by the Sound of a Trumpet make a great Noise on the Earth, but reap litle fruit in Heaven. What need we any Spectators of our good Works?"[126]

If religious writers put a premium on hidden bounty, sometimes in a more general recommendation of an unostentatious life,[127] there seems to have been a contrary impulse from the social side of charity to advertise one's benevolence. Even in the SPG accounts, the very act of listing certain contributions is a sort of public acknowledgment, and the opportunity to attend public catechisms, or annual sermons and ceremonies affiliated with the charity schools, also implied financial support of the endeavor among those who attended. Subscription lists as a general tactic as well as minutes of charity movement meetings imply publicity, at least for those in the inner circle of the movements. Peter Borsay in fact suggests that in the whole category of philanthropic endeavor, gifts were rarely anonymous, since subscription was "one of the most effective devices for self-advertisement" and conveyed prestige through the image of "selfless benefactor," and through association with other elite contributors.[128] Although Borsay acknowledges that contributors believed in the value of philanthropy as a civilizing, educational influence, he asserts that it also "provided an altruistic facade behind which to pursue self-centered ambition."[129]

If there was a conflict between motivations for charity in general, for women it may have been a special bind, since they were enjoined in particular to practice the virtue of modesty and to avoid public comment. As may have happened with other women, Sarah availed herself of what may have been a very attractive strategy for donation that combined ostensible modesty and piety with private acknowledgment, at least from those whose opinion might have mattered most, of her bounty. In the arena of charity, then, Sarah found a means of displaying her piety in a socially acceptable, discreet, yet powerful way. While all and sundry may not have known of her generosity, and while she did not contradict the idea that women should give anonymously in keeping with their modesty, the fact that eminent clergymen acted as agents in her benevolence afforded her an admiring, if limited, audience for her good deeds.

CHAPTER 5

The Angry Years: Intellectual Life, 1700–1704

Perhaps in consequence of this wholesale withdrawal from what she may have considered unworkable roles of wife, mother, and mistress, Sarah was a prodigious reader. It also may be as a consequence of her advancing age that Sarah was particularly interested in charting her progress toward deserving salvation. Certainly, she was concerned with the approach of death for much of the diary and with what she ought to be doing in whatever time was left to her. Even early on in her entries, it is clear that she had her increasing age and the prospect of death firmly before her and explicitly related her chosen activities of reading and writing to that which was appropriate for her advanced years:

> Perhaps some may think my writing so much, a very dull drudgery. But it sufficeth to sattisfy me in the practise, that I find it otherwise. At worst, it may be allow'd an employment as significant as any sort of work I can do, and if for every stitch that others prick in a clout, I with pen set a letter upon paper that, as long may remain a witness to purg me from the scandal of idleness . . . sure then gameing and plays is yet a more wretched amusemt. than unecessary work, for such as are advanc'd in years and draw near the end.[1]

Furthermore, Sarah specifically distanced herself from the family duties of earlier stages in her life. Part of this "vigorous" stage of Sarah's fifties and sixties was a certain degree of freedom from responsibility; in her view: "I am under no obligation but to live for my self and to spend the remainder of my life as agreeably as I can."[2]

The first significant milestone in the diary in terms of changes in Sarah's experience of aging was when she fell seriously ill in the winter of 1702 with an ailment that started as a cold but progressed into a lengthy fever and resulted in permanent blindness in one eye by the end of March.[3] The gravity of her illness and her long recovery also seem to have caused new concentration on the urgency of preparing for death and its priority as the weightiest business of the aging:

> Are wee grown old, wee have then less time to spare from our most important business. Our forces being diminish'd, our industry shou'd be encreas'd. We shall grow more indispos'd, it will be too late when dotage hath seiz'd upon us. . . . There is no care, no employment proper for old age, but to prepare for dissolution.[4]

Sarah's extensive reading and her personal contact with the shapers of political and social discourse were important factors in the fashioning of her outlook. Although as a woman she was denied political participation in any formal sense, she had the advantage of being able to base her opinions on the "inside" knowledge available to someone in her privileged position. Sarah presented an image of herself as a contemplative sage—a mature woman who with the benefit of study and experience could claim an elevated perspective. With such a suspicious and disapproving attitude toward social interaction (her condemnations of the behavior of acquaintances are constant) it is not surprising that Sarah vacillated between bewailing the troubles of keeping company and complaining about her solitude when she was alone. She reflected on the pleasures of retirement, describing the admirability, especially for the pious, of the solitary life of meditation: "One true end of Retirement may be Self Defense. The World is a Hostile Country therfore wee have Reason not to Expose our Selves but Choose retirement not as a State of perfection, but of Safety. . . . the family of the Contemplative ought to give him no Disturbance but if possible Animated to suitable inclinations to his own."[5] Her diary and commonplace books specifically refer to at least 150 separate works, slightly over half of which are listed in her "Catalogue of Books at London 1701."[6] And this total does not take into account the plethora of letters, addresses, single sermons, satires, topical verses, ballads, and other short printed pieces, selections from which she collected in commonplace books and at the back of most of the volumes of her diary. At a very rough estimate, there are notes on something like 200 of these pamphlets and tracts. In addition, she was a regular reader of the broadsheets and literary periodicals. Moreover, it is likely that many of the quotations in her diary are from works not included in those totals, since as discussed above, she quoted Mary Chudleigh, Mary Astell, William Gouge, and others without attribution.

Sarah favored the writings of those clergy she knew and admired both for their theology and for the conduct of their own lives. Here again, personal contact with the writers of these works was important for enabling her to feel qualified to judge their argument. It demystified the printed text, and it gave her more than one set of criteria on which to make her evaluation. Often, she knew the man behind the divinity, the extent to which he himself followed his admonitions and line of reasoning as well as his more personal failings. Nonetheless, she prided herself on being able to separate the man from the message and judge accordingly, as in the case of her approbation of the bishop of Exeter's sermon, which she praised despite her dislike of him on personal and political grounds:

> I have heard y[e] Bishop of Exon writ to the Corporation of Tottness that they were going to Choose a Man [Spencer] who Drowned the Quaker. If he did so 'twas a twofold Lie . . . I have Newly read the Sermon he preached at the late Te Deum and tho' from the Character of the Man (with the Reason aforesaid) I began it with prejudice enough, yet it must needs be allowed whoever made the Sermon wanted not Sense and parts, it being excellently fitted to the Time and Occasion. and I feel Some pleasure to find my Nature so just, that no prepossession can make me so partial as not to own what is well done, tho' by One I otherwise like not.[7]

This self-congratulatory passage also points out that in addition to having a social as well as an intellectual opinion of a clergyman, Sarah might also have reason to judge on the basis of political involvement and corresponding contact with or relevance to her family.

Sarah's religious thinking is in many respects the implementation on an individual level of much of the doctrine characteristic of the moderate Anglicanism promoted in this period.[8] Like the leading divines who produced such a huge amount of material on right belief and right practice, Sarah emphasized practical morality over doctrinal adherence, the congruence of reason and revelation, the need to eschew controversy and speculation, and the benevolent rather than the judgmental aspect of God's nature. Her outlook exemplifies the shift historians have seen in Anglican thought in the later seventeenth century away from the Calvinist insistence on predestination, reprobation, and election toward salvation through personal virtue, with the necessary help of God's grace.[9] While Sarah did not apply the label to herself, there is a very strong latitudinarian strain in her choice of authors and selection of material, a preference that can also be seen in whom she singled out for approbation of their sermons or characters.[10] One of Sarah's main tactics for asserting the legitimacy of her intellectual endeavor was to base the authority of her evaluations not on claims to expertise in theoretical abstractions, which as a woman barred from the universities she lacked, but on her personal knowledge of clergy and politicians through social contact. In basing her judgments on a reading of character, she reflected the common practice in this period of evaluating historical figures or events on ethical grounds, but Sarah took the technique further by exploiting this moral yardstick to compensate for her lack of formal education.

If the number of books by any one author listed in her catalogue are taken as a measure of popularity, Simon Patrick comes out as the clear favorite. She owned at least a dozen of his works, far more than those of any other writer. Not only did Sarah quote Patrick in her diary, but her approval of his writing can be seen in the preface to her own scriptural commentary, where she noted that she would skip Ecclesiastes, the Proverbs, and Song of Solomon because Patrick's exposition had been so masterly.[11] Of course, many churchmen were not as prolific as Patrick, so the relatively high number of his titles in the booklist can be a misleading measure of his influence on her religious outlook. In her diary, Sarah referred to John Tillotson, Isaac Barrow, and John Wilkins in terms of highest praise for their preaching and principles, and she frequently quoted Tillotson especially. Their collected sermons are listed in her catalogue, but as single items, they do not hint at the high estimation she had of the authors.[12] If Tillotson was the epitome of a venerable latitudinarian, Wilkins was the embodiment of those principles of moderation and irenicism in the previous generation. The association of the two prelates was more than just intellectual; Wilkins was Tillotson's father-in-law. As part of the previous generation, Isaac Barrow was associated with the same principles, though not with the group. Aside from these divines, the rest of Sarah's book catalogue is also heavy on the side of humanism, moderation, virtue, and reason. Representing the ancients are translations of Plutarch, Seneca, Cicero, and Epictetus; authors from the more recent past include Erasmus and Hooker. Also on the list are works by the Cambridge Platonists Ralph Cudworth, Benjamin Whichcote and Henry More and by the Latitudinarians Edward Stillingfleet and William Wake, as well as other works dedicated to defending Christianity from a rational standpoint, such as Robert Boyle's *The Excellence of Theology Compared with Natural Philosophy* and Hugo Grotius's *Of the Truth of the Christian Religion.*

This is not to say that Sarah's bookshelf consisted only of this section of the Church of England. She also listed works by Jeremy Collier and John Kettlewell, both Non-Jurors, and she asserted her broadmindedness and discretion in choosing what to read:

> In reading such Authors as treat of Divine Things my business is with an equal mind to search after Christianity without following either Sect, party, or faction. I light the Candle Sweep the House to Seek the lost groat and when or wherever I find it, I greatly Rejoice. Some in Searching have set the house on fire, but I wou'd take Care to proceed Safely. I am for the peace of all parties, not for the humours of any. . . . I do read Bishop Hall and Doctor Manton with the like Affection, believing both to be pious good Christians.[13]

Unsurprisingly, given her relatively advanced age, Sarah was acutely aware of her approaching death and consequently concerned with ensuring her salvation. She sought to reassure herself that through discovering and fulfilling her Christian duties she could expect an eternal reward. She often borrowed from those writers who conceived of Christianity in those terms, as when she encouraged herself by commenting:

> Sure the late D' Tillot:n had Considered the point and Understood the Matter So well as not to be in a Mistake when he Constantly prayed, God wou'd give us Grace So to Live, as we Shall Wish we had done When We Come to Die.[14]

She repeatedly reminded herself of the admonition in Ecclesiastes: "Fear God and keep his commandments. For that is the whole duty of man."[15] This was not an uncontroversial passage; it would have been highly contentious in the Dissenting view of man's place in the world and relationship to God.[16] In quoting it, Sarah was acquiescing in the trend toward making the individual active in his or her own salvation, out of which came conduct manuals such as Allestree's *The Whole Duty of Man.* But as John Spurr and C. F. Allison have pointed out, the rigorous demands of this vision of a holy life could be far from reassuring.[17] The responsibility (though not the credit) for gaining eternal life was on the shoulders of each individual through a program of self-examination, repentance, and working to correct faults, and such a burden might be as anxiety-producing as the Calvinist question of whether one was, in fact, one of the elect. Sarah did indicate anxiety about the sufficiency of her efforts at self-improvement:

> Every day I make Resolutions and am forming Rules to a better; but Alas! I find not the desired Effect. O Lord I pray thee favour my good Purposes with the Constant Assistance of thy Holy Spirit that I may be able to accomplish my intentions and perfect Holiness in thy Fear. Help me to Redeem the Time lost with Extraordinary Diligence for the future, and to Walk exceeding Circumspectly, and improve every Minute to ye best Advantage, as the only way to make some amends for my former great Neglects, and wasting So much of the precious Opportunity given for working out my Salvation.
> . . . What Shall I say in Excuse for my Sloth; and even Worse, much Worse, how unaccountably have I trifled away abundance of my days, and Spent them Idly in the Market, rather than my Closet or the Temple, in Vain and Worldly rather than Heavenly pursuits, and Stupidly took but very litle care about the One thing Needful. O my Compassionate Redeemer look upon me, and tho' it be the Evening of my life, yet Call me So powerfully by thy Grace, that I may at last Receive that inestimable Reward w^c thou art pleas'd to Promise to Sincere tho' imperfect Obedience.[18]

Nonetheless, although Spurr wonders how likely it was that individuals would embark on the rigorous course prescribed, Sarah certainly attempted it. Moreover, in her case, the effort to live well offered some productive, attractive earthly rewards, aside from the presumably ultimate prize of eternal bliss. First of all, it was very compatible with one of her personality traits, her tendency to create tasks to accomplish. Sarah herself remarked on this habit, once even reminding herself it could be carried too far. But the program of living well offered the hope that this habit could be set to good and eventually effective use—that with enough effort, and with God's assistance, it was possible to progress and to overcome faults. Second, the possibility of successful self-improvement and the methodical working toward that goal offered Sarah a sense of control and a potential for praiseworthiness, despite the emphasis in the literature on shouldering responsibility for self-reformation and not expecting praise for it. It is because of her adherence to this concept of the requirement of constant effort that Sarah expended so much energy trying to find remedies for what she considered her main failing—anger:

> It may be Observed I Muster up whatever I read or hear said against Anger, the predominant passion in mee. It not only disturbs our Selves but draws on the hatred of Others. It is a great Deformity of the Mind, and is apt to breed a Secret Contempt of Us. and to bring our prudence into question, because 'tis a Sign of a Weak and Impotent Mind that either hath lost or never had the Government of it Self. It is esteemed a perfection to be able to restrain our passion. To be impatient is to be overcome, but patience is power and Wisdom, and Victory. Yet after all so hourly provocations do Assault me, as leaves me no hope totally to Subdue it; or to find other Remedy for this Evil but daily Repentance.[19]

Sarah recognized her own responsibility to control her emotion—in the terms current at the time, to restrain her passions—as part of the larger Christian effort to subdue all bodily passions and within the context of the philosophical and religious rhetoric of rational man. The strategies she employed for doing so included attempting to follow the example of people who were notable for self-restraint; reminding herself of the need for a sense of proportion (since all afflictions and annoyances of this world were trivial and ephemeral in comparison to eternity); remembering her own blessings in comparison to the lot of others;[20] and continually repenting her outbursts of anger and resolving to improve. But despite accepting the blame for failure to govern her anger entirely and failure to maintain her patience, Sarah refused to shoulder the entire responsibility for her loss of control. Moreover, she was aware of both the impossibility of attaining the ideal of perfect meekness and the disadvantages such an ideal entailed. She noted the lapses in this regard of even the most admirable:

> My lesson this day [Acts 23:2, marginated] gave me no small Comfort to see the Saints of God when unjustly used may be surprised with passionate Expressions. Let thy Mercy Come also unto me O Lord so shall I have herewith to answer him that reproacheth mee psal:119.41.[21]

More important, she described herself as at fault more in the unguarded response to attacks rather than in the feeling and expression of anger in general. The fault really lay with her husband, servants, and children: She described her outbursts in terms of their provocation, or the tempta-

tions and surprising assaults they put her under rather than in terms of
her own bad temper:

> I affect but few things, finding business enough within my Self. To Swal-
> low[?] passions is not to oppose, for that inflames, but to divert and gent-
> ly lead the Mind to other Matters, if one cannot vanquish, turn the
> Thought to Somewhat else; Escape by going out of the way, yet Some-
> times all those means avail mee Nothing. but I am surprised at last into
> Some impatient thought or peevish behavior, by Continual provocation
> to Anger.[22]

She also noted the bad effects of adhering to the ideal of total self-
suppression:

> It is a great provocation to Anger and discontent to See my Self perpetu-
> ally abused by—[Sir William]. I resolved with my Self not to be vexed at
> it, but rather take Care to be inoffensive in all my Actions, and especially
> to watch over my Tongue that no undecent Complaint nor intemperate
> Speech Should break from me. And this purpose I kept for some time so
> that I remained Silent tho' while I thus denied all vent to my resentment it
> was the more increased. For tho' I said nothing I Could not Choose but
> have Sad thoughts of the injuries I suffered.[23]

In her reading, responsibility was at least partially transferred to the
causes of her annoyance and consequently in her restraint, she was attempting the silent suffering of affliction and injury rather than the subduing of an irritable personality.

Another way of distancing herself from fault and pointing out who
was really to blame was to make the distinction between indignation, a
reasonable emotion to experience in the case of injustice, and passion,
the ungoverned impulses of the body. Indignation had behind it the virtue of justice and righteousness:

> Now I examine whither my anger be directed against the person, or
> against the offence; (because there is a vindicative anger against offenders
> which is our Duty) and do hope, it is altogether against the last. . . . tho'
> Love Cannot hate it may be justly angry, and abate all Concern which is
> more than reasonable and enough.[24]

By using the term "wrath" to describe her own emotion, Sarah even implied an analogy between God's anger at sinners and her righteous anger
at servants:

> So Wretched are the Circumstances of our Domestic Affairs as they un-
> avoidably Stir up Wrath which in may Texts of Scripture is Attributed to

God, therefore not Evil in it Self. It is Certain that there is no passion in God, and it is Certain also that if Anger were a Vice it Shou'd not be Attributed to God. Be Angry and Sin not, whence it follows that one may be angry and not Sin. Yet remember that Anger troubles the Serenity of our Mind.[25]

Sarah's other self-acknowledged fault was fear—fear of dying in particular, a fear that was often occasioned by the sudden deaths of others. This failing was on the one hand less reproachable than anger, but on the other a potential measure of the distance to the goal of achieving tranquility through living well, being assured of salvation, and thus not being afraid to die.

> It happened that upon hearing a relation was well and six hours after Dead of the Colic, I was struck with a Sudden and painful fright, ye Effect of a disturbed Spleen, or the infirmity of humane Nature, and not (I hope) a terror of mind proceeding from the weakness of reason, or Want of Faith.Being Good:Friday providence (I think) led me to hear a sermon on Heb: 2.14. And deliver them who through' fear of Death were all their life time Subject to Bondage. Tho' Nature doth decline Death, as that which hath a Natural Horrour and Contradiction to the present interest of preservation yet no good Christian that duly Considers the Efficacy and End of the Death of Christ, Can be overcome or remain under the Fears of Death. Grant O Lord that the Words I heard on this Subject may be inwardly grafted in my Heart, that they may bring forth the fruit of good living, the only way to remove the fear of Dying.[26]

It was also bound up in Sarah's rueful deprecation of a tendency to superstition: the other occasion on which she had most thoughts of dying was June 29, the date on which, many years before beginning the diary, she had a dream that seemed to her to presage her death.

> I must be Confessed that neither Reason or Religion doth rid me of the Superstitious fancy that for near 30 year hath haunted me about this time of the year. . . . If formerly I perceived my Self to be in bodily health it Sufficed to abate the Conceit I had taken of dying of this Day. But of late I meet with so many Stories of unforeseen Accidents, and so frequently hear of Sudden Deaths, that it causes many twinges and pangs of fear which I endeavor to Conceal, but by no means Can totally Expel.[27]

In discussing this annually recurring fear, Sarah referred to the current concept of the mutual reinforcement of reason and religion in a way that simultaneously displays her acceptance of this pervasive idea of rational religion,[28] yet it also suggests one of the difficulties with this notion: that is, that the mysterious, irrational side of belief was not addressed entirely satisfactorily. Sarah's reading of almanacs and other works of prophecy and astrology, as well as her recurring unease on Saint Peter's day, indicates that this brand of Anglicanism did not offer a system of thought that could encompass the irrational but powerfully present fears that Sarah put down to a superstitious tendency. It also indicates that the tendency toward secularization in eighteenth-century society, which is a standard historical construct,[29] had not yet happened in Sarah's mental world to the extent that it would later in the century. Sarah's language of reason and interest in astrology place her at the transitional stages of this development.

Interestingly, Sarah visibly affirmed her membership in the company of the pious and her rejection of what she considered the prevailing irreligious attitude in a manner that reworked a badge of another theological and moral danger, Roman Catholicism:

> It hath been in my Thoughts for some time to place in my Closet a Cross, meaning to Signify in this degenerate Age (in which Christianity Seems to decline) I desire to be of the Number of those who are not ashamed of the Cross of Christ. For the same Reason, I bow at the name of Jesus when the Creed is Rehearsed, thinking it needful at this time when the Socinians Spread their Doctrine, and dispute that Article of the Christian Faith, the Divinity of our Saviour.[30]

> A Roman Catholic gave me a Cross and Crucifix. The one, I place in my Closet, the other I wear, not with popish Superstition, but a desire to distinguish my Self all manner of ways from the Infidelity that abounds in this Age, be it Deism, Socinianism, or Enthusiasm, and openly declare my Self a follower of † [Christ].[31]

The debates over ecclesiology seem to have been "things indifferent" in both senses for Sarah; government by bishops was not at issue in her diary. Displaying the common distaste of those who remembered the excesses of religious zeal in the Civil War and Commonwealth, she derided Dissenters, Quakers especially, for "enthusiasm" and fanaticism, but the fact of their separation did not particularly exercise her. It may be that there was an element of personal hostility to Dissenters (quite apart from their actual religious principles) because of their political and perhaps temperamental association with Sir William and consequent unwelcome presence in her house. Equally, she was not terribly concerned with Roman Catholic dogma, apart from the occasional deprecations of idolatry inherent both in her comments on how to understand saints and saints' days and in her general condemnations of superstition.[32]

This direct association of the writer's character with the worth of his argument comes up in Sarah's response to the challenge Socinianism presented to the Church of England.[33] Socinian ideas had implications for not just how believers were to understand Jesus the man, but how they were to understand his crucifixion, resurrection, and redemption of sinners, and his relation to God in the Trinity. In doubting the divinity of Christ, Socinianism questioned two crucial elements of Anglican belief. First, that Jesus's death, which Christians were commanded to commemorate in the sacrament of the Eucharist, was entire propitiation for the sins of the world (on the condition that people believed, repented, and obeyed God),[34] and second, that that sacrifice was effectual because Christ was coequal and coeternal with God the Father and God the Holy Ghost in the Trinity. Sarah expressed this orthodox view of Christ's nature and the meaning of his sacrifice in the words of eminent divines, often on appropriate days in the liturgical calendar,[35] or when events prompted her to think about these questions. In one case, for instance, commenting on Convocation's censure of William Whiston and Samuel Clarke's writings, she paraphrased Tillotson's assertion of scriptural authority and simplicity regarding the Trinity:

> Go Teach All Nations Baptizing them in the Name of The Father, and of the Son, and of The Holy Ghost. [Matthew 28 verse 19 marginated] Upon this Form in Baptism appointed by our Savior, Compared with what is Elsewhere Said in Scripture Concerning The Divinity of The Son and The Holy Ghost; is principally Founded the Doctrine of The Blessed Trinity. I [Bishop Tillotson, marginated] mean in that Simplicity in which The Scripture hath Deliver'd it; and not as it hath been Since Confounded and Entangled in the Cobwebs and Niceties of The Schools.[36]

Spurr and Griffin both note that in claiming the simplicity, rationality, and comprehensibility of the minimalist doctrine Christians needed to know for salvation, Anglicans of this tenor staked out for themselves the territory of reasonableness, of common sense, from which position they dismissed other ideas or scruples as stubborn illogic and willful blindness.[37]

As well as facing intellectual threats from writers nominally within its fold, the Church of England faced the challenges of both Dissent and Catholicism in a state in which for the first time membership in the national church was voluntary.[38] Anglicans had to counter not only the theological but the ecclesiological arguments of other organized religions. The clergy of the established church frequently addressed the issues of church government and unity. One the one hand, they labeled as schismatic the nonconformists' refusal to accept an episcopal structure and Anglican liturgy as things "indifferent," and on the other, attacked the concept of papal supremacy and infallibility and defended their own church from the Roman Catholics' charge of schism. In their arguments for unity there were differences in the extent to which clergy argued that it was practicable or desirable to compel allegiance to the Anglican church, and some historians think that latitudinarian portrayals of comprehension, while sounding more moderate than coercion, actually still meant the Dissenters should do all the accommodating,[39] but all condemned the Catholic persecution of Protestants, in France especially.

Sarah does not seem to have been as interested in the intellectual challenges presented by Dissent and Catholicism as she was in the threats of atheism and Socinianism. It is certainly true that she constantly reiterated the importance of "living well" for salvation—an assertion which by implication rejects the Calvinistic view of redemption—but the emphasis is not on the doctrinal difference between faith and works so much as on the importance of good deeds, not good (or doctrinally precise) words. Here again the point was that the valid measure of a person's worth was moral standing, whether it was in judging the value of their writing or their likelihood of reaching heaven. In insisting upon the Christian responsibility to act charitably and obediently, she implicitly but not explicitly warned against the potential in predestinarian thought for abandoning upright morality as irrelevant to salvation.

The other problem with the elevation of human rationality, and the one that seems to have concerned Sarah the most, was its potential to be taken to excess, to devalue revelation and by extension Christianity in its entirety.[40] She therefore echoed the attempts of contemporary divines to demonstrate on the one hand that religion and faith were entirely consistent with the use of reason, while on the other hand not diminishing the distance between God and man, the importance of the workings of Providence, and the incomprehensibility of the mysteries of religion. She quoted Tillotson on the nature of God to that effect:

> It is not Repugnant to Reason to beleive Some Things which are Incomprehensible by o[r] Reason; provided that wee have Sufficient ground and Reason for the Belief of them; Especially if they be Concerning God who

is in His Nature Incomprehensible; and we be well assured that He hath Revealed them. And therefore it ought not to offend us that these Differences in the Deity are incomprehensible by our Finite Understandings; because the Divine Nature it Self is So, and yet the Belief of that is the Foundation of all Religion.[41]

This potential problem with estimating too highly the importance and usefulness of human reason and natural as opposed to divine law was manifested in contemporary alarm about "atheism." Defenders of orthodoxy defined the term in its broadest sense—not a declared disbelief in the existence of God (an assertion that did not occur in print in this period) but heterodox ideas of God, man, and the natural world that tended to undermine revealed religion. Moreover, the attackers of atheistic ideas often connected them with immoral conduct by their advocates, so that theoretical skepticism was often tarred with the brush of libertinism even though examples of the conjunction of these two qualities, such as in the earl of Rochester, were rare.[42] The association suggests that Sarah was not alone in considering both the content of an argument and the moral character of its propounder when she decided on its validity. Her criticism of Socinianism and Deism echoed the general alarm at the perceived growth in vice and immorality in this period, its attribution to the prevalence of a skeptical, scoffing attitude in fashionable society among the "wits," and the assumption that the questioning of Christian doctrine on the nature of God and Christ led inevitably to the rejection of all but basic "natural" morality, a position that hid the sinister ulterior motive of abandoning altogether religion and the moral restraint it carried with it.

> By a Degeneracy Peculiar to these Dregs of Time; a Set of Christianity falsely So Called, though to their Shame Baptized and Educated in the Faith; Do yet with Boldness lessen and Detract from the inestimable Benefits by the Manifestation of Christ Jesus; turn Advocates for, and wou'd gladly Reduce us to, the Conduct of Reason, and Natural Religion. But Sure we have not So learned Christ, as to quit His unsearchable Riches, for so wretched a Voluntary Poverty. . . . these Teachers give us too just Cause to Suspect, that while they bend their Forces against Revealed, their real Design is to Subvert All Religion, as Knowing, that if the former be once given Up, The Natural, for which they now profess so heartily to Contend, Cannot long Stand its Ground.[43]

One of the atheistical ideas in circulation in this period to which Sarah devoted particular attention was doubt about the immortality of the soul. It was obviously crucial to Sarah's whole religious universe to believe that her soul would live beyond the death of her body and would be rewarded in another life for her good behavior in this world. In this issue especially there was a congruence of public debate and private concern; her intellectual search grew out of her personal situation as an aging woman preparing for death and the relevant controversies in the public domain. Apparently, Sarah had to confront this threat to her peace of mind not just on a general level from its existence in the intellectual discourse of the period, but was specifically faced with it in her social life, through the borrowing, lending, and giving of books:

> An Acquaintance lent me a Book Writ by Doctor Coward a Phisitian. denying 'tis Said the immortality of the Soul. I Set about reading it not without Fear least I Shou'd find something Said might infest my Imagination and Disquiet the most Comfortable persuasion wee Mortals are Capable to Receive and without which this Life wou'd be insupportable to the Most of humane kind. But I Came in View of no danger Wither the Notions therein advanced are So Abstruse (except to the learned) or so Shallow is my Understanding that after turning o're every page, Cou'd fix on nothing I understood and must Needs Say I Cannot tell what the Author means.[44]

In her efforts to reaffirm the fundamental tenet of the immortality of the soul, Sarah used whatever ammunition she could find, from the devotional to the political. The breadth of her literary resources on this issue illustrates the fact that literary output in this period, even when ostensibly secular, was applicable to and indeed directly addressed religious ideas. While J. C. D. Clark's argument that eighteenth-century England was still a confessional state in which the Church of England was omnipresent is taking the point too far, it is worthwhile to note that Sarah could draw on social essays and even party political propaganda to reinforce what would now be considered an exclusively religious belief.[45]

In her response to the challenge of Socinianism, Sarah most vividly employed the tactic of associating the writer's character with the worth of his argument. By doubting the divinity of Christ, Socinianism questioned both the efficacy and the sufficiency of Jesus's death as propitiation for the sins of the world. Sarah used the words of eminent divines to express the orthodox view of Christ's nature and the meaning of his sacrifice; however, her opinion of the most infamous exponent of Socinian ideas, John Toland, was based not on the value of his arguments, but on the very unfavorable impression she had of him as a person:

> Toland the Author of this, and that, and what not; is Come back . . .
> from Hanover. I was with Company where he did Vent such incredible
> Stuff that he seems to out lie the Devil, who 'tis like would have more
> Wit and Manners than this impudent pragmatical Irish Teag, who goes
> about to impose on people's sense and understanding Such ridiculous sto-
> ries. Had he address'd 'em to my beleif I Shou'd have been hugely Urged
> to ha' given him a Box i' the Ear. For a Sample; he tells how that talking
> to the Mistress of the prince who was then Coming in, one of the Guard
> told him it were best to withdraw. . . . he was Sturdy and would not Stirr,
> but when the prince Came in Sight, this Hero bravely laid his Arm on the
> Lady's Shoulder; the prince you must think dare not take Notice of this;
> nor many other such insolencies did not procure him so much as a kick if
> you Can believe our Celebrated Author, who by Some is thought able
> and fit to be guide of their Faith.[46]

In this passage Sarah rejected Toland's claim to intellectual prominence and the validity of his theological ideas because of her outrage at his offensive social comportment—his attempts in polite company to garner admiration through stories of sexual and hierarchical transgression.

Sarah also used this technique of conflation of the person and the idea in her approbation of John Locke, an approval based on his behavior in society, not on the strength or implications of his theories. On the occasion of his death she quoted a eulogy that focused on his intellectual capability and affability rather than on what it had produced, remarking, "He knew how to write controversie and differ in conversations with equal strength and manners."[47] Similarly, Sarah defended Locke from charges of atheism not on the basis of the content of his writing, but on a report of his expression of conventionally pious sentiments:

> I mett with this Fragment of a Letter Writt by the justly fam'd Mr John
> Lock to his Friend . . ."May you live long and Happy in the Enjoyment
> of Health, Freedom, Content, and all those Blessings which Providence
> has bestowed on you, and your Virtue Entitles you to. All the Use to be
> made of it is, that this Life is a Scene of Vanity that Soon passes away,
> and affords no Solid Sattisfaction but in the Consciousness of doing Well
> and in the Hopes of another Life. . . . " Methinks the Man who writes
> thus Ought not to be term'd either Atheist, or Infidel; as some take Lib-
> erty to do.[48]

In the realm of politics, not only personal assessments of character, but extensive reading in history made her feel competent to judge current events. Reading history was recommended by contemporary prescriptive literature as a virtuous exercise that provided lessons on the nature of humanity. Sarah's diary and commonplace books indicate a long-standing strong interest in history. In 1686 she had compiled a 600-page extract from an even more massive *History of the World*[49] and there are frequent notes in her diary on numerous histories and memoirs and on references to historical examples in observing current affairs. Sarah, however, in implementing this understanding of history in her own reading, interpreted past and present politics as a struggle for place and power that was not guided by any admirable principle. She expressed this view for instance in her assessment of the Civil War itself and the parallel she drew with the driving force behind contemporary politics: Her conclusions in reading more recent history, of the Civil War especially, were similarly uncomplimentary to the personages involved. They mirrored her negative opinion of human nature in general, and more specifically and importantly, in them she articulated her conception of past and present politics.

> In Colliers Dictionary I mett with an Abstract of our late Civil War and read the Story without being affected for either party Since both Seem to me a pack of Self ended Knaves that disturb'd honest people who gladly wou'd ha' been quiet. The same Sentiment have I of persons and Things in these present Times, and Cannot feel the least glow of zeal for either of the now pretending Patriots of their Country, nor know how to imagine they so much as mean the publick good. Interest and Faction is all I can perceive guides 'em, and they devise deceitfull matters against them that are quiet in the Land.[50]

Sarah expressed similar sentiments, this time emphasizing the deceit and hypocrisy that she presumed accompanied ignoble motives, when reflecting on her reading of the earl of Clarendon's history of the Civil War:

> The Declarations that pass'd between King and Parlim[r] Seem to Want Sincerity, neither Side meaning what they Said, but Saying what was ffitt the better to Conceal what they did intend to do. The progress of Affairs Shew mee the Irreligion Perfidy, Ingratitude, and base Designs of the Undertakers in each partie, as hugley encreases my Contempt of Humankind; apt to be (perhaps) too much before. . . .[51]

It was this universalizing judgment of men's motives at any time and place that helps to explain Sarah's distancing of herself from avowed allegiance to either party in her own political world, despite her family's Whig identity. She asserted her own nonalignment, pointing to the vanity and ignominy of political ambition. Her assertion implied that she, at least, had the public good in mind in her own political ruminations, from which moral high ground she could portray herself as an independent, objective observer. In this depiction, her ineligibility to actually participate in politics because of her gender became an affirmation of the worth of her judgment—an affidavit of her impartiality. Moreover, it may have been a useful way for Sarah to think of herself because her political sentiments were distinctly divided. On the one hand, she was attracted to what the Tories stood for in terms of a conservative, ordered society and adherence to the Church of England, although she abhorred the high church element of Toryism that tended toward coercion in religion and Jacobitism in government. On the other, she was a staunch supporter of the Revolution Settlement and Toleration and had her family's ambitions to think of, but she deplored the disorder and laxity she saw in the Whigs.[52] It may also be that the association of Sir William and the Whigs reinforced in Sarah's own mind the connection between Whiggery and licentiousness. The fault of looseness in her husband's government of the family on the domestic scale may have magnified her impression of disorderly Whig government nationally.

Consequently, Sarah's commentary on contemporary party politics paralleled her assessment of events in history, reiterating frequently that principle and virtue had little to do with the workings of government. She was generally critical of whichever side was in power and thus had untrammeled opportunity to do their worst. In the case of her passing criticisms of the Whigs, there may also be an element of unspoken reply to her husband in disparaging the pretensions to moral worth of his party:

> The Whiggs go down apace, it may be not for the Worse. I cou'd never
> yet see more Religion or Vertue among them than other people.
> Self:interest, power and place is all this generation Contend for.[53]

Interestingly, while it is obvious from her collections and from comments in her diary that Sarah read a great deal of political satire, astrology, newspapers, and other relatively lowbrow topical material, early on in the diary she denied reading such things altogether: "After many

Traverses of thought I am grown to know what I must Trust to, I know the world and Care not for it, therfore never read any printed news."[54] Her interest in history was easily justifiable, but keeping up with the popular prints much less so, and perhaps to maintain her position as a morally elevated political observer, Sarah repudiated her more scurrilous sources of information. It is also possible that this passage was a direct quote from another author speaking in the first person and was meant to signal Sarah's correct grasp of priorities and superiority to the vanity of this world rather than a complete disavowal of popular literature. It is certainly true that works of fiction are notably absent from her booklist and diary citations. If her reported excursions into fiction were as rare as she asserted, they were rare indeed and always resulted in disappointment and turning back to her more typical choices.[55]

For Sarah, as for the rest of English society, political and religious outlook were inseparable.[56] Party affiliation and religious affiliation were intertwined, and church and state met most controversially in political debate over toleration, comprehension, occasional conformity, divine right, passive obedience, and the threat of popery. Understandably then, these were also the issues that concerned Sarah the most. Like her contemporaries, Sarah assumed a fundamental interdependence of religion and politics, but she was very critical of excesses in politicization of the church, perhaps a natural consequence of her suspicion that the motives of men of state did not spring from a genuine desire for the good of the church and the nation. Her general feelings about religious unity and the validity of toleration of Dissenters can be seen in comments like the following:

> Unity, and Uniformity are two Things. The Coat of Christ had no Seam, But the Churches Vesture was of Divers Coulers. Men must beware that in procuring Religious Unity, they do not dissolve and deface the Laws of Charity and Humane Society. Peace is not the Matter which they Seem to aim att, but Following, and Party.[57]

More specifically, she was interested in and commented on legislation that had to do with uniformity. The first Test Act (1673) had required government officeholders to take oaths of supremacy and allegiance, repudiate transubstantiation, and receive the sacrament of communion within the Church of England. The practice of "occasional conformity"— that is, attendance at an Anglican communion service once annually— enabled Dissenters to hold office despite their usual nonconformity. This circumvention of the law infuriated many high churchmen, and four bills were introduced in Parliament between 1702 and 1711 to prevent the practice. The last, least punitive bill finally became law in 1711 and was repealed in 1719. Sarah discussed her opinions on uniformity and its enforcement in the context of the debates on the first bill against occasional conformity in the parliamentary session of 1702–1703. This bill would have imposed stringent fines on officials who attended conventicles and disbarred them from office unless they took Anglican communion three times within a year.[58] Sarah consistently voiced her opposition to coercion (again suspecting the motives of the legislators) and deplored the lack of charity and the hypocrisy in the use of religion for political purposes.

> With all my Heart I wish the Act of Sacramental Test were Repeal'd. I abhorr to See the Sacred Mysteries of our Holy Religion prostitute to Secular interests and Ends. But the Lords have done the Next best, by So altering the Bill about occasional Communion Sent up by the Commons, as will Effectually throw it out to the Shame of those who talk high for the Church yet never Come in to it unless for a place or office in the State.[59]

She also combined her assumption of self-interest as the engine behind politics with an assumption of absolute right and wrong, accessible by the proper application of reason, in her assessment of the voting on the bill:

> The AntiChristian Bill (so I take it to be) about occasional Conformity has made great Stirr among Men. Many of the Bishops Dissented from it. and the Judges in other Cases Divide as much. It must be the interest and Faction of parties, which makes them thus differ, Sure the Consciences of Men Cannot be So various Since Truth and Right Reason are One and alwaies the Same.[60]

By virtue of her age, rank, knowledge, and piety, Sarah claimed the right to consider and judge matters of theology and political philosophy. Moreover, her emphasis on character enabled her to declare her allegiance to the ideals advocated by latitudinarian churchmen whom she personally admired, and to claim political nonalignment while rejecting challenges to church and state because of the moral deficiencies of their authors. This use of this strategy did not mean, however, that Sarah engaged in rigorously logical or profound mental wrestling with the issues. Rather, Sarah's claim to an elevated and informed perspective based on the use of an alternative set of evaluative criteria indicates ways in which high-ranking women could redefine the terms of political and religious debates in order to assert the validity of their opinions and thus claim a degree of participation in the intellectual realm.

CHAPTER 6

Riding the Crest? 1705–1706

The future probably did not look bright in 1700 to the Cowper family.
The Stout trial had been a serious threat to their standing. Sir William
suffered defeat in the 1701 election on account of the political fallout
from the trial, and that loss proved to be the end of his political career.
Despite the scandal, however, in the early years of the new century the
younger generation of Cowpers managed to continue building up their
law practices to quite lucrative levels.[1] Moreover, for the elder son William the Stout affair proved to be only a mild setback in a spectacularly
successful career in politics and the law that culminated in the lord
chancellorship and an earldom. Sarah observed her sons' career fortunes
from the perspective of a proud but fearful and resentful mother who
expected but often did not receive the marks of respect and the opportunities for wielding power that she regarded as rightfully owed to parents
from prosperous grown children. In addition, William's extraordinary
leap in status exacerbated Sarah's difficulties with social interaction at
the same time as it brought rewards in residual prestige. She had to
worry not only about keeping up the family honor among the gentry,
but about comporting herself and displaying a household commensurate
with the mother of a high government official and member of the peerage. Thus William's spectacular rise actually produced further insecurity
and tension with regard to its benefit to Sarah and William's status by
increasing the discrepancy between their social and economic standing.

In the period from 1701 to 1704, William's prospects grew ever brighter both in politics and in finance because of his talents, temperament, and resourcefulness. In response to the collapse of the Cowper political interest at Hertford, he looked outside his family connections for sponsorship in Parliament. William first secured the help of the powerful leader of the Whig Junto, Lord Somers, who convinced the duke of Bolton to sponsor William for a seat at Totness. While in the end the competing political interest of the mayor of Totness won out, William managed to gain a seat at a by-election in Bere Alston through the recommendations of Whig politicians Lord Stamford and Sir Francis Drake.[2] Once safely returned to the House of Commons, William put his considerable oratorical skills to work on behalf of his patrons, that year speaking against Lord Somers's impeachment over the commission to Captain Kidd,[3] and defending Lord Stamford's management of the woods of the Duchy of Lancaster against attacks by other members of Parliament. As well as demonstrating himself as a reliable supporter of his patrons, he was reinforcing his growing reputation as a speaker. Even a Tory opponent, Sir Edward Seymour, "commended his great parts and oratory and said he could make a bad cause a good one."[4]

With his wife Judith's substantial dowry and his own earnings, William had begun buying scattered pieces of land in Hertfordshire in the 1690s.[5] In the summer of 1704 William apparently felt prosperous enough to build a country seat outside Hertford, at Cole Green. But even this most successful Cowper did not in his standard of living and public display live up to the social code. The new house was small and inexpensive, costing only £1,720 when it was originally constructed.[6] Nonetheless, it apparently afforded Sir William great satisfaction. As in his counting of his sons' income when adding up the family's financial assets, here too he seems to have adopted William's signal of prosperity and social merit as his own:

> Our Son is Set about Building a Seat near Hartford, and S' W. has Sett his Heart So much upon the Matter that he talks as if he Thought on Nothing else. It brings to my Mind the parable of the Rich Man, [Luke 12: 15, marginated] and makes me Sometimes afraid—[Jeremiah 9:23–24 marginated] The Whole Employment of most mens Lives is to improve their Fortune, and yet the Title by which they hold All is no more than the Fancy of the Legislators. But their possession is Still more precarious than their Right and at the Mercy of a Thousand Accidents.[7]

Despite having earlier advocated housing display and appropriation of the assets of all the Cowper kin, here Sarah pointed out how insubstantial and transitory success could be, and cited Scripture affirming her depiction of its instability and redirected attention to what should be the highest human priority.[8] Perhaps because of a desire to distance herself from Sir William and from his method of reliance on the accomplishments of the next generation for honor, and perhaps because of a very acute sense of how unreliable their success could be, given Spencer's experience, Sarah instead explicitly focused on the support of religion and the acknowledgment of God's providence as a bulwark against the inconstancy of social place. Indeed, that very autumn offered Sarah a good example of the perils of politics to support her attitude:

> The Malice and Envy of our Hartfordshire Enemies agen is att Work till it foams so much in the Mouth as to move in the House of Comons to Send My Son Cooper to the Tower for being Councill to L[d]. Hallifax (tho' the Queen gave him Liscence) without their leave, w[c] they Say ought to ha' askt as he is a Member of Parlim[t].[9]

While this attack by the two Tory MPs for Hertford (Charles Caesar and Ralph Freeman) went nowhere, it reinforced Sarah's perception of the shaky foundation of political good fortune and the dangers of championing the causes of preeminent nobles such as Halifax. The matter was resolved the next day:

> The Comons did Debate about y[e] aforesaid Matter, but after all, tho' the Fiery Old Dragon (S[r] Ed: Seymour) with other litle dragons (Freeman, Cesar t.C.) had Spew'd up Some of their innate Venome, The Delinquents Came off Triumphantly with fflying Coulers; there being on their party 154 and 111 agst them, forty wherof wou'd never have Voted that Way, had not the Business of L[d] Halli: been Mix'd with it.[10]

It is no wonder then that given her pattern of fluctuations between advocating solitude and sociability, in this period of political uncertainty she asserted, "One true end of Retirement may be Self Defense. The World is a Hostile Country therfore wee have Reason not to Expose our Selves but Choose retirement not as a State of perfection, but of Safety."[11]

This whole proceeding may also suggest that by the end of 1704 William's political standing was high enough to be considered threatening by the Tories, who saw him both as an effective Whig in the House of Commons and as a potential candidate for government office. Ordinarily, the advancement ladder for a rising lawyer serving the Crown would

involve holding the job of attorney general and then perhaps solicitor
general before having even a faint chance to head the legal system as
lord keeper of the great seal. But in the wake of the dismissal of the incompetent, corrupt, and unpopular lord keeper Nathan Wright in October 1704,[12] and the Whig gains in the elections of 1705, the Whigs were
casting about for likely candidates for this critical office. One plausible
person for the job in terms of professional qualification and standing
was Lord Somers, who had served as lord keeper and then lord chancellor under William III from 1693 to 1700. But Queen Anne was determined to keep as far as possible to her aim of nonparty government
and found the Whig Junto led by Lord Somers particularly obnoxious in
their aggressive partisan and ambitious demands.[13] Wishing not to con-
cede too much to the Whigs in general and to the Junto in particular,
Queen Anne wrote to Godolphin on July 11, 1705: "I wish very much
that there may be a moderate tory found for this employment, for I must
own to you I dread the fayvours shewed them [the Whigs] of late, that I
feare a very few more will pull me insensibly into theire power . . . " and
that it would be "an unexpressible uneasyness and mortification to me"
to have "one of the heads [Somers] of them in possession of the Seale."[14]

In view of the queen's resistance to Somers, William might well have
appeared a good second choice. He was held in high regard by much of
the political world as an eloquent speaker ("Much the finest speaker of
all the lawyers if not of all others in England," said James Lowther in
1705[15]) and the modern assessment is glowingly positive: "From a pack
of more or less corrupt politicians, William Cowper stands out as unique
in his acceptance by both parties as an honest man. . . . an eminent lawyer and orator, charming, modest, and fairminded. . . . "[16] Nonetheless,
obtaining the position of lord keeper turned out to be a very difficult
project, for a number of reasons. First of all, although William's name
was put forward by some of the key players in Queen Anne's court, including the duumvirs Lord Godolphin and the duke of Marlborough,
and the duchess of Marlborough,[17] his Whig allegiance, his connection to
the Junto,[18] and his personal history made him suspect in Queen Anne's
eyes. Tories, not Whigs, were the party identified with the defense of the
Church of England, an important qualification for a job that had so
much to do with selecting clergy for ecclesiastical appointments. Anne's
current advisors on filling benefices, the Tories Robert Harley (her secretary of state) and the archbishop of York, John Sharp, insisted on this
point, perhaps as much to preserve their influence as to further the Tory

cause. There is also some suggestion that his affair with Elizabeth Culling came back to haunt William; Swift asserts in his *History of the Last Four Years of Queen Anne* that "Some former passages of his life were thought to disqualify him for that office by which he was to be the guardian of the Queen's conscience."[19]

Whatever the relative weight of these factors, the queen held out the whole summer, despite letters from Godolphin urging the appointment. Finally in September, the duke of Marlborough wrote to the queen and pointed out that if she refused to appoint William Cowper, her only recourse was to return to the high Tories for a candidate and risk alienating broad-based political support: "I see no remedy under heaven, but that of sending for Lord Rochester and Lord Nottingham. . . . I think they have neither courage nor temper enough to serve your Majesty and the nation in this difficult time, nor have they any support in England, but what they have from being thought violently at the head of a party, which will have the consequence of the other party's opposing them with all their strength."[20] The queen reluctantly agreed at the end of September to appoint William, but she imposed a significant limitation on his powers as a condition of offering the seals. In order to keep control of important church preferments, and also to continue the roles of Harley and Sharp in advising her, Anne insisted that William agree that "all ecclesiastical livings with an annual value above 40 pounds which were at the disposal of the Lord Chancellor were actually to be given by the Queen."[21]

During these weeks of negotiation before William actually received the seals, the theme of the transitory, uncertain nature of such honors resurfaced frequently in Sarah's diary, as this gratified mother contemplated her son's potential good fortune yet feared for its permanency. Her first comment on the matter, in July 1705, hints at some notable drawbacks to the whole enterprise: "Here hath for some time run a Rumour, that our Son is to have the Great Seal; and I feel no Elevation of Thought when I hear 'em Talk on that Theam; ffor I pretend not to know w^t is best in ye Case. Sure I am the Business he now is in, brings him Esteem and profitt enough, without depending on the pleasure of fickle Mortal Man."[22] If William became lord keeper, he would have to give up his thriving law practice yet had no guarantee as to how long he would fill the post. Accordingly, following Lord Somers' precedent, William bargained for an annual pension of £2,000 as some sort of compensation for the "impermanent nature of high office" and the loss of income from his private practice.[23] Moreover, as a commoner, though Speaker of the House of Lords, he could only put the question, not participate in debate, so at the level of political influence in legislative debate, he was sacrificing political power.[24] What is more, the office, while powerful and prestigious, was an immense burden, combining as it did the job of presiding judge, legislative functionary, personnel director for thousands, royal advisor, and administrator.[25] Lastly, becoming lord keeper meant standing out as a target for political attack and professional jealousy both on matters of government policy and because of the patronage aspects of the job. One could make powerful enemies, as Sarah worriedly reflected while considering the dangers of rising too far too fast:

> Here is much talk at this time, of great Matters intended for my Son. . . . He Councell'd well who said, Observe a Gradation, ffor tthe Slowest Steps to Greatness are most Secure. Swift Rises are often attended with precipitate Falls. What is soonest gott is generally Short in the Possession, and He that Monopolizes Honors or Wealth is most times Envyed to his Ruin. Be Content and Strive not to out:run thy Fate.[26]

In the end, despite the problems on both sides, on October 11, 1705, William received the great seal from the queen. He was only forty-one; "'tis said the youngest Lord Keeper that had ever been."[27] William thus became one of the "great officers of the crown"—the half dozen or so men at the top of government, alongside the lord privy seal, lord president, lord treasurer, and two secretaries of state. "In matters of precedence he was second only to the archbishop of Canterbury."[28] The lord keeper of the great seals was immensely powerful in all the major aspects of government. He presided over the chancery court and over the House of Lords when it acted as a court of appeals in cases from the common law and equity courts, acted as speaker of the House of Lords, and served on the monarch's privy council, and he acted as the conduit of appointment, supervision, and dismissal for England's judges, justices of the peace, and clergy of the Church of England.[29] As representative of the crown he also was guardian of the legally incapacitated, superintendent of charitable trusts, and inspector of royal hospitals and colleges.[30] Furthermore, William became lord keeper at a moment when the House of Lords "was at the very peak of its prestige and influence" and so he, more than many previous and succeeding men, held this office at a high point in the authority of the body over which he presided.[31]

During the negotiations, William had apparently stipulated that he receive a peerage whenever the next occasion arose for a round of promotions.[32] Accordingly, as part of a slate of concessions to the Whigs at the convening of a new session of Parliament in 1706, Queen Anne elevated William to the title of Baron Cowper of Wingham.[33] Once ennobled, William could not only guide business through the House more aggressively, but actively participate in debate.[34] Moreover, as a legal expert, his opinion was of particular weight in the House of Lords in the appeals cases that body heard.[35] At the elevation of William to the peerage Sarah breathed a figurative sigh of relief, saying:

> I must own this brings me Some Sattisfaction because if Things Change he is plac'd above the reach or Violence of a Angry Party in the House of Commons who Usually pott most at Such as Serve the Prince and Government Best. Besides the Place of Lord Keeper being so Precarious it seem'd to mee not So much as Lord Mayor that thing being Certain for a Year, this not for a Day.[36]

Even so, social elevation carried in and of itself an additional burden—the obligation to support the appearance of living up to noble rank— but no commensurate additional funding to ensure that this form of correct social display was possible.[37] William's appointment as lord keeper of the great seal brought him a substantial salary,[38] two-thirds of which he invested in stock and securities instead of land, because the interest rates were better.[39] Despite his emphasis on stocks, by 1721 he had spent a total of £25,821 on 2,214 acres in Hertfordshire, and another £6,847 on land in Kent.[40] Even so, he still lived modestly for a peer, only adding wings on his original building at Cole Green for an extra £1,300 in 1710. In the next generation, an acquaintance of the second Earl Cowper called it "more by way of a villa near the town than a country family seat."[41] His London residences were equally unimpressive; he was the original renter of the house Sarah and William moved into in 1706, lived in Great Russell Street for four or five years, and finally bought land in 1718 for a "modest" house off Hanover Square.[42]

By the time of William's spectacular career jump, Sarah had a history of marshaling evidence to justify her assertions of authority as a parent (and sometimes more specifically as a mother) and to validate her condemnation of William and Spencer's "negligent" behavior toward her. Characteristic is the blame she assigned to Sir William for the lack of respect she and he received as parents from their children, saying: "neither of us have Power or Interest with our Sons; ffor the truth is, S^r W: hath Order'd things So; They Both despise Us Both."[43] Because of the circumstances of her marriage, while Sir William was alive, her claims for authority as a parent did not usually involve an alliance with the other parent, but instead special emphasis was placed on the sufferings of and duty owed to the deserving mother. She understood the Commandment to "honor thy father and mother" as encompassing for adult children a multitude of demonstrations of filial respect and gratitude, including sociability, solicitation of parental advice, recognition of financial links, and material expressions of honor and obligation. It is not surprising then, that the peak of Sarah's frustrations at what she perceived to be her sons' insufficient fulfillment of their Fifth Commandment duties was when William made this dramatic political and economic advance yet did not accord Sarah what she considered to be her rightful share in his rewards of honor and wealth.

Sarah's depiction of herself as a patient mother was seriously put to the test by William's appointment and its substantial salary. Since sons were by this time doing well,[44] Sarah expected that they would begin to "recompense the pains and cost" of their parents. In the cycle of dependencies, Sir William and Sarah had established the financial links with the next generation in paying for their sons' education, setting them up in a profession, making a settlement for them at marriage, and, of course, in the end, by giving all the rest of their belongings to their children through inheritance. In exchange, it was now up to the rising generation to at least symbolically acknowledge these ties and the debt of familial obligation they created through giving gifts. A few months after William was appointed lord keeper, Spencer's son started university. This reaffirmation of financial ties, this time between the second and third generation of Cowpers, was an occasion for Sarah to express her discontent at her sons' failure to acknowledge their corollary obligation to their elders. Sarah was tempted to retaliate in kind. They had not performed their part of the exchange to their parents, so she would withhold a gesture of support to the next generation:

> My GrandSon W[illiam] C[owper]. going to the University at Oxford I thought my Self Resolv'd not to bestow any Gift upon him at parting. Because neither of my Sons have made mee a Present out of their Plenty. Yet so Bashfull was I when it came to the Push (tho' all Shamefac'dness is not good) that I cou'd not forbear but gave him a Guinnea. There is a

Sattisfaction and Pleasure in Bounty and Liberality that none understand
but those that have Minds great enough to Excercise it.[45]

Her natural generosity and embarrassment at so contravening the dictates of expressing family feeling won out, in implicit contrast to her selfishly individualistic sons.

A few days later, Sarah renewed her hopes that her sons would accord her a symbolic share of their good fortune upon the occasion of the queen's birthday, but again to no avail. This time, Sarah explicitly referred to scriptural example to justify her expectations:

The Queens:Birthday is past, and I looked for The Purse and Two: or
Tup:pence in't. but now my Expectation is quite baulk'd and Worn out
of all Date.—To his Father he Sent after this Manner. Ten Asses laden
with the good Things of Egypt—Do this Carry down the Man a present.
Spices, and Myrrh, Nuts. . . .[46]

But in a sleight of hand and reordering reminiscent of her use of Halifax's commentary on avarice, in her version of the Genesis story of Joseph, the implication is that a dutiful son (Joseph) sent goods from Egypt, including spices and myrrh and nuts, as a present to honor his father (Jacob). In the actual text, however, the second half about a present of spices comes earlier in the narrative than the first half, and more importantly, Jacob, the father, was ordering spices sent to Joseph in order to appease him, knowing him not as his own son, but as the powerful controller of grain in Egypt.[47]

The next month Sir William and Sarah moved into a larger house in London that had previously been occupied by their son William.[48] There is no evidence to indicate the circumstances of that transaction, but it is possible that by inhabiting the previous residence of the lord keeper they felt they were in some sense moving along with him, if several steps behind, as he rose in status. Sarah, however, was displeased at William's failure to further support the status his parents were "borrowing" from him by leaving behind household amenities, especially considering she expected Sir William to provide only sparse accoutrements. Moreover, she coupled her complaint of his ungenerous behavior in vacating the house with a description of his inappropriate performance of gift-giving on another occasion when he intimated he would give Sarah a present that in actuality was a loan, and not even an entertaining loan, at that:

My Son Keeper hath Gutted the House and left me no kind of Thing behind him; tho' He knows full well his Father's Spareing Humour. Yet he
lately told mee he had gott a play:thing for mee Which Cost him 18.
Guinneas. I prickt up my Ears and Cou'd Scarce trust they inform'd me
right. But at length the Wonder Came to no more than that it was a Very
Antient Book of Curious Painting with Popish Devotion which I Shou'd
have the favour to See. But alas! My Eies Cannot Discern the fineness of
its Work, and being Compos'd for the most part in Latine, with very litle
English and that so Obsolete 'tis Scarce Intelligible to mee, I return'd it
without being Edify'd att all, unless it be to know, He Can be Free to
Part with his Mony when he has a Mind so to Do.[49]

For William to spend a large sum of money on an antique book instead of on his mother and then expect her to treat the loan of it as a gift
was unacceptable to Sarah on a number of counts. In her view, William
was bestowing his largesse capriciously, distorting the ritual of the exchange of gifts and gratitude and refusing to recognize the correct priorities in the distribution of his new wealth.

This new house in Bedford Row continued to present problems directly connected with William's elevated status and with the family's
uncomfortably tight finances, social unease, and marital tension. Having clearly moved up the scale of physical ostentation, Sir William made
an effort to display gracious living in the decoration and furnishing of
the house. In doing so, however, he was again usurping a role that ought
to have belonged to Sarah[50] and demonstrating both his own ignorance
and his consequent failure to educate his wife in the knowledge of
proper decor:

S^r W: intending to Hang a Drawing Room with Damask Condescended
to ask me Whither One or Two Coulers woud Do best. But he hath Bred
me so Ignorant in Such Matters that I cou'd not Resolve him till I have
Enquir'd of the Skillfull. yet after this he allows me not the priviledg to
place a Table or a Stool but where he Fancies.[51]

Sarah was uncomfortably aware that her own upbringing did not
qualify her to decide such things. Her husband's social station should
have meant that he would know, except, of course, this was a feminine
activity. Sarah's only recourse was to consult someone else, but despite
this proof of Sir William's unfitness to govern in this area, he continued
to insist on his own prerogative to arrange the furniture. But to top it
off, after suitable decor had finally been accomplished, Sir William

balked at providing a basic requirement for carrying off the demonstration of family stature:

> Wee have now gott a Drawing: Room hung with Damask and furnish'd well enough, So I propos'd there might a Billet be kindled every afternoon and if no Visitants Come by 4 a Clock the Usual time I go forth the fire wou'd be soon laid by. but Sir W: Said No, that was very expensive 'twere better light it when Company Came in being Soon done. to which my reply was I wou'd not Expose my Self So as to be Calling Out Fire when La: were there who 'twas like wou'd be gone to save mee that trouble. and if that was to be his way I chose rather to Sit by a Coal:fire in the Parlor.[52]

Sarah might have had the appropriate surroundings in her new house, but having to call to have the fire lit was a revealing admission of straitened circumstances and of the nonhabitual use of that room. From her very proposal to kindle a fire in the drawing room for just a few hours every afternoon it is clear Sarah knew Sir William would be reluctant to heat the room for more than the minimum amount of time necessary to preserve appearances, and that she agreed with that general principle. In addition, it may be that the interaction with servants in front of guests that lighting the fire would entail was also perilous in the opportunity it presented for demonstrating Sarah's lack of control over her staff.

The high point of Sarah's anger at her son's approach to spending came when she discovered through Pennington Cowper that William was contributing £40 a year toward the university expenses of his nephew, yet another William:

> Came P[ennington] C[owper] and told me (I beleive unaware of the Effects) that the Lord Keeper had send W[illiam] Ten Guinneas more with a promise to Continue the Same every Quarter added to his Fathers allowance. O Jesus! how it Struck me with a Pang not to be express'd; tho' Sure there lives not a Soul more free than Mine from Envious grudging at the good fortune of another. Yet I must own a Pinching Sense of the unkindness to mee his tender Mother who never has the least Benefitt from all His Affluence, tho' he knows his Father Can deny mee Sixpence. It much aggravates the Matter to mee, that upon the Strictest Scrutiny I cannot find the Cause of this Cruelty either from my Own Demeritt, or Defect of right Understanding in him what is just and fitt Behavior toward mee.[53]

In the margin she added a quote that she cited as being from Psalm 119:78: "They have dealt perversly with me without a Cause." Here

Sarah accused William of willfully ignoring the precedence of her claim on a share of his prosperity to that of his nephew. According to Sarah's understanding of the hierarchy of family dependencies and obligations, as mother she ought to have had priority over any other generation when it came to circulating money within the family, especially since she was already suffering the injustice of being denied her fair share of the income by her husband. In helping his brother and nephew financially, particularly since Spencer was wealthier than Sir William by this time, William was favoring what Sarah considered lesser ties of obligation in a way that had the effect of redirecting money within the family to where it was not only least needed, but least due.

That summer, after giving William one last opportunity to acknowledge his duty, Sarah let fly with a recriminating letter itemizing his offenses, using the very same phrase she had in her diary to comment on the lack of a gift on the queen's birthday:

> if on your Birth:day or the like, you had sent, The Purse and Tuppence in't might have been Seasonable enough. Perhaps to ha' Spoke out my Resentment wou'd ha' Seem'd Querulous, but no Mortal could forbear Thinking. Now 'tis wondrous how the Complaint Dropt from my Pen; Sure it was provok'd by hearing you gave 20 l for a Musty Book, 20 Guinneas to a Fulsome poetical priest, and allow 40 l per Annum to Ease your Brother who 'tis said gets 3000 l a year with other such like superfluous things—I am too Bashful to bear any Talk on this Subject, therfore Choose this way to tell you, as I did not Expect, so I utterly refuse any thing in way of Pension, but Shall leave that and all matter Else to your better Judgment not doubting but it will direct you to what is Best and fit.[54]

Sarah was clearly uneasy being so direct about her monetary demands; the passage is filled with attempts to deny and distance herself from them. Nevertheless, they are there, and Sarah justified them by pointing out the "superfluous things" upon which William was (mis)spending his money, in incorrect preference to her more fundamental deserts. By emphatically refusing a pension, she made clear that that scale of remuneration was, in fact, what was owing; and that it was up to William to come up with a graceful means of offering that would allow her to accept a large gift as a token of filial gratitude rather than a payment to a mercenary relative.

Sarah's demands and William's refusals to comply with them also need to be seen in light of his concurrent efforts to reform the most flagrant financial abuses in chancery. He signaled his intentions to run an upright and honorable operation in this law court early, and by personal example. It was the practice of chancery appointees at the beginning of the year to offer their boss the lord keeper a "gift" of money. The payoff was called the "New Years Gifts" and considered part of the perquisites of the office. Sums collected in this manner are variously estimated at £1,500 or £3,000.[55] At the very first opportunity, William refused the New Year's Gifts, making rather a stir with his self-sacrificing move against undue influence.[56] While Sarah knew and highly approved of her son's actions in this regard (and William made sure she saw his letter to his father explaining the reasons for his actions), she apparently did not conclude that she consequently ought to sacrifice her own claims to financial perquisites.

Even given a certain amount of reshaping of prescriptive sources, in the role of mother Sarah had the weight of a hierarchical, deferential ideology on her side when claiming power and authority as a parent. When asserting her demand for authority as a mother, vis-à-vis a father, there were sources available that did not require too much distortion to make her case. The ideal in this particular relationship, while still not attainable in reality as Sarah experienced it, required much less subversion for reasons of gender than did the role of wife.

In contrast to her earlier experience garnering support for William's appointment as king's counsel, when Sarah attempted to act as a patronage broker herself, in her capacity as mother of the lord chancellor, she was not nearly as effective, partly because here again she was erroneously counting William's assets as her own by virtue of her conception of the ideology of family ties and obligations. Sarah managed to construct an active role for herself in the patronage system in her interaction with female friends for the benefit of kin, but much less so in her interaction with kin for the benefit of friends.

In her efforts for clients through her relationship to her son William, Sarah found herself confronting the problem of differing priorities in the use and cultivation of connections. Her attempt to garner personal power through the benefits she obtained for others foundered on another aspect of the issue that had arisen when William became lord keeper—that is, how he was going to dispense the largesse in money and offices that came with his post. As lord keeper, William was in a position to fill over seventy places in the courts of chancery, from masters through ushers,[57] and to commission anywhere from thirty to one hundred justices of the peace per year[58] and hundreds of clerical livings. Sarah expected to receive some share in his ability to bestow places, an expectation that was not entirely unreasonable, given the frequent solicitations she received from acquaintances who assumed she had influence with her son. But William rejected these claims to his intangible assets in favor of his own priorities for maintaining his honor—favoring those whom he needed to please in order to maintain his own position. To begin with, the obligations of patronage networks required William to return favors to those who had been instrumental in his promotion and would remain vital allies in politics and government administration. Apparently, William viewed the duke of Marlborough as his most important advocate and ally, since immediately after receiving the seals, William sent the duke a letter of thanks that ascribed to him credit for the appointment. Moreover, this letter expressed William's strategy for future conduct on the levels of both policy and patronage. He explicitly declared his independence from the Junto, asserting that his political successes were "wholly owing to my own industry, so that I was found free from all engagements to any one."[59] This rejection of obligation, while disingenuous in not acknowledging Somers's support, signaled William's choice of a course of Whiggery close to but not in invariable alliance with the Junto, and correspondingly relegated Junto claims to patronage favors to a lower priority.[60]

Indeed, this letter suggests William anticipated the multitude of solicitations he would receive for places, not only from the Whig Junto, but also partisan women who did end up attempting to apply pressure over commissions for justices of the peace, notably William's own sister-in-law Anne Clavering, and female friends whom he would be reluctant to disappoint, such as the duchess of Marlborough, all of whom aimed at replacing enemy Tories with Whigs in the counties.[61] However, from his record of dismissals and replacements of justices of the peace, it seems William was determined to follow a gradual, cautious process of replacement of Tories by Whigs in the counties, rather than wholesale purges, both for the sake of political prudence in being reluctant to needlessly infuriate country Tories, and being perfectly willing to let competent, moderate Tories remain in their positions while going for a long-term strategy of aiming for a majority of justices being Whig.[62] In her sarcastic disclaimer of activity in this realm, Sarah indirectly recognized the priority William was giving to the networks of rank and political obligation over the presumed rewards of family ties: "I have been

Worried and Still am like to be with Solicitations about places, by Acquaintance and Strangers, Friends and Foes, but I presume not to Meddle in Things too high for mee."[63]

Initially, William's appointment as lord keeper must have seemed a fortunate convergence of interest and means to Sarah, given her ties to the clergy and her son's ministerial capacity to grant a large number of clerical livings delegated to him by the Crown.[64] But upon attempting to capitalize on William's new powers, Sarah ran first into the problem of conflicting visions of the claims of family relationships and then the related difficulty of the nature and extent of the demands made on William by other solicitors for places within the church. In the best of circumstances, demand for these livings consistently outpaced supply,[65] and so the competition for benefices placed numerous conflicting pressures on government ministers and the monarch, who had difficulties trying to satisfy kin, patrons, supporters, and political obligations with insufficient vacancies.[66] In William's case, he faced the even more restrictive limitation of his agreement to leave to the queen's discretion all ecclesiastical appointments worth over £40 per year.[67]

Without any discernible regard for these restrictions, immediately after William's appointment, Sarah began to attempt to use the presumed ties of family obligation to obtain a place for one of her own distant kin as William's chaplain. When she ran into difficulties, she reported the congratulations of a bishop side by side with the precedent of sons in classical Greece to validate her claim to part of her son's "prize" by demonstrating that both contemporaries and classical authors assumed mothers partook of their children's successes:

> [The bishop of Sarum] . . . Complemented me with the Saying of Solon who being ask'd whom he Thought the most Happy person in Greece, replied the Woman whose Son Won the Prize at the Olympick Games. Sure these Mothers had Some Share in the Prize, but what mine is may be seen as follows."[68]

What followed was a transcript of five recommendations for her candidate Mr. Brown (three from bishops and two from chaplains), proving, as Sarah said, "that my attempt was not rash and unfit." Her other comments on the matter, however, indicate some of the pressures William was under in granting places: There was at least one rival candidate for the position,[69] and an important factor was probably party affiliation, or at least the rumor of it. In an indignant response to Sir William's dismissal of the letters ("Pah, quoth S^r W: what's this to the Purpose here's nothing bespeaks him a ffriend to ye Governm:'"[70]), Sarah pointed out that the two recommending chaplains' patrons (the duke of Somerset and the countess of Falconbridge) were hardly likely to employ Tories. Perhaps the deciding factor in the unsuccessful outcome of this solicitation was the information supplied by the very same person who was encouraging Sarah to think of herself as deserving prizes in the patronage game. As William noted in his diary, the bishop of Sarum

> advised me to beware that I was not imposed on by Dr. Browne, who was a knave, a man used to talk against his judgement according to his company, and who had formerly cheated him so far as to obtain a certificate from him very much in his favour. I had seen this, and several other certificates and was doing my best to get him a very good Prebend, in obedience to my mother's commands, and thus against my own judgement . . . I set this down here, to excuse the ill effects of this man's rising, if he takes his first rise by my hand.[71]

In this small glimpse into William's perspective on the matter, it would appear he felt the pressure to defer to his mother's wishes even above his own judgment, but in the end, political and moral considerations prevailed. Even Sarah, in the same breath as she called the successful applicant an atheist, had to admit that "few men preach better."[72]

Twice Sarah counted up the number of solicitations she made to her son; the first time in the week after his appointment, when she asked for two places and succeeded in one, grumbling, "And I am poorly come off, having only gotten in the train:bearer."[73] Three months later, frustrated and stung by her husband's criticism that she was bothering her son too often, she itemized the number of solicitations as seven in all, with only one success (she did not mention the trainbearer), a charity case.

> S^r W: had provok'd and Teaz'd me with an Ugly Air. . . . I was under Reprimand for puting a poor Woman who is ready to Perish in a Way to gett Some Box:Mony given last Term. This was my Fault. He told me I had been troublesome to my Son about 20 Such like Impertinencies; but upon the Strictest Scrutiny they prove but Seven in all. Three Parsons that are akin to mee, Mr Brown, t c: but by the way nothing is gott for any of 'em Unless 40:$^{sh:}$ for one Poor Woman. So Potent is the Interest of Lord Keeper's Mother.[74]

In this passage, rather than presenting an image of a powerful, benevolent mother effectively using the legitimate influence accrued by obligation and gratitude from her son, Sarah was confronted with a competing derogatory image supplied by her husband, in which attempts to participate in the social system of favor and reward were denigrated using the language of rank. Her attempt to increase her personal power and prestige in dispensing benefits to her own clients were greeted by deflating derision from her husband, who classed her solicitations as "troublesome impertinencies."

Unfortunately, even when Sarah was effective in her brokerage (though it must be noted that here it was more a question of canny political advice than direct patronage) she could not term it a success:

> By Accident I have been too instrumental in getting a good Place for the Son of M^{rs} L: by giving him the hint that he Shou'd apply to Lord Somers who I guess'd my Son wou'd be ready to Please. And now She tells me that instead of allowing her any Share in the Acquisition, he is att Law with her for the litle She has left and Shews his good Will to Starve her.[75]

As with her unfruitful efforts for Mr. Brown, not only were questions of the rightful strength of maternal influence at issue, so were there doubts about the moral qualifications of Sarah's candidates. Ironically, this woman who so insisted on her own righteousness was repeatedly associated with unrighteous petitioners. Nonetheless, despite her complaints that people pestered her for favors without realizing her unjust lack of influence with her son, she seems to have persisted in her efforts. Half a year after his appointment, she again defensively denied being meddlesome and described a current project:

> I alwaies Thought a Woman of Business or a Busie Woman a most Impertinent Troublesome Creature. Now of late I am in danger to fall under the like Denomination and perhaps others think the Same of mee; but I purpose to decline that Charecter, ffor; Some I can Perceive look coyly at my Request who Can put on a Different Air when they Ask of mee. I mainly Solicite for the Worthy Mr Clark to be Lecturer att St Andrews; ffor a Scandal to our Church it is that a Man of His Meritt hath yet gott no more preferment than Chaplain to the Bishop of Norwich. It is not fitt he Shou'd be pass'd off to a Country Parish and So Obscure that Light which Shou'd Shine before Men—[76]

In this case she implied that there was in fact a reciprocal relationship in place with her son, or at least that it ought to be reciprocal, since she

had fulfilled her part of the ideology of "mutual benefit." Sarah never
referred to this particular project again, so it is unclear what the outcome of her solicitations was.

Sarah's experience with the patronage system illustrates both societal
expectations of the rewards of motherhood, and the reality that motherly influence varied, depending on a mother's relationship with her
son and his acknowledgment of her claims to influence. Although it was
possible to reshape the image of motherhood in such a way as to turn
an ideology that restricted women to the home into one that allowed for
intervention in public matters for the benefit of family, as Sarah found,
the potential offered by social and religious prescription for authority in
the role of mother, while important for valorizing and validating a
woman's positive construction of both domestic and public identity, did
not necessarily mean that she would be able to exercise her theoretical
power effectively, or with optimal results for the good of church and
state.

CHAPTER 7

Widow's Heyday, 1706–1710

On November 20, 1706, Sir William had a stroke, and six days later he died. Sarah did not record the stroke the day it happened, or the day after, but then there is a gap in the diary until December 1, when she related the facts of his death. Rather than put up even an appearance of mourning him, she described the event as astonishing, since unexpected, and reflected on the transitory nature of human life, the suddenness of death, and the necessity of being prepared for it spiritually.

Interestingly, Sarah also began a new diary volume with the December 1 entry, as if to mark her entrance into her new condition—the "third estate of womankind"—that of widowhood.

In a period when marital status was the fundamental descriptive category for women, prescriptive literature and women themselves considered daughter, wife, and widow to be the three basic stages in the female life cycle. Young unmarried women, while owing obedience to their parents and absolutely required to preserve their virginity, were otherwise in the most carefree condition of a woman's life. Marriage was the first and foremost turning point. It could produce a great deal of anxiety beforehand about the loss of freedom it entailed in the legal and personal subjection of wives and in the potential for bad treatment from the superior member of the partnership. Furthermore, upon entering this new state, married women had to face the responsibilities, worries, and traumas of childbearing and childrearing in a period when surviving either pregnancy or childhood was not at all assured.[1] In the third stage of life, as widows, women experienced financial, legal, and personal autonomy, often for the first time. Anomalies in the patriarchal scheme, they were the heads of their own households. For some, the loss of husbands could be overwhelming financially as well as emotionally, so that widowhood was both sorrowful and impoverishing. Others "came into their own" as widows and relished their independence and control.[2]

Sarah Cowper certainly fell into this latter category of widows; her first two years in that state seem to have been the heyday of the diary and perhaps of her adult life. She clearly regarded herself as having escaped from an unpleasant, oppressive situation, and never once expressed regret at Sir William's death. Two months after she had been widowed, in her contemplation of a long-dead friend, Martin Clifford, she wrote wistfully, "I then found complaisance in his conversation, and shou'd now be glad of such another companion if I knew how to find him." In the very next entry she hastened to add:

> But I meant not for a Spouse. Wear not a Straight Ring. Lead your Life in Freedom and Liberty, and throw not your Self into Slavery Since it may be truly Said I have outdone Anna the Prophetess in Chastity; tho' not in piety and Devotion. ffor She liv'd wth an Husband Seven year from her Virginity; wheras I scarce five in that Sense, tho' in a Matrimonial State near 43. So that doubtless there Can be no such temptation befall mee now I am grown Old, yet wee have Some Examples of Widdows that have Married at fourscore and four.[3]

Prompted by her repudiation of remarriage to compare herself to a biblical paragon of widowhood, here again, six years after her first declaration of her sexual righteousness (now with more direct but equally suspect reference to Scripture) she repeated her reshaping of chastity into celibacy and her valorization of the redefined term as a wifely virtue. In the original text, however, the context of Anna's "chastity" is clearer: "She was of a great age, and had lived with an husband seven years from her virginity; and she was a widow of about fourscore and four years. . . . "[4] That is, while married she had been "from her virginity"—a sexual partner for her husband—and then she resumed her virginity/celibacy as a widow, whereas Sarah had resumed her virginity while her husband was living and maintained her celibate state throughout thirty-eight years of marriage.

Six months later, reflecting on her married life she was bitter, not nostalgic:

I have observ'd enough to make me approve my past Conduct of Affairs, and must needs think it deserves a thousand pittys for that it was my hard Fate to Live with Such as Understood it no better. Do Thou O Lord Translate all my Affections from these lower Objects that so I may Delight to meditate on Thee.[5]

On the first anniversary of her widowhood, Sarah again meditated on the need to always be spiritually prepared for death. Indirectly, she also acknowledged her initial relish of her newfound power, as she bewailed her unreformed household:

I have now been a Year in a State of Liberty wherin I thought to have order'd my Way of Living So as to attain more peace and quiet of Mind than formerly I had known. But alas! by Sad Experience I find that Things without us will not give it, but that it Springs from What's Within Us.[6]

After Sarah's husband died, the tone and content of the diary changed noticeably. It was less concerned with family life, less indignant and complaining, but also less lively, and a smaller proportion of its entries were in Sarah's own words. Part of this difference may be attributed to a more gradual experience of increasing ill health and infirmity as Sarah aged, but in large part, the shift seems to come from the loss of that daily friction in her married life that furnished her with material and motivation for her entries. In general, the diary volumes written in the years of her widowhood are much less a litany of complaint than a collection of memorable or edifying extracts from her experience and reading. In addition, in these years there is a shift in her construction of her remaining domestic roles, those of mother and mistress, for a number of reasons: First of all, Sarah no longer had to contend with an intervening authority in her domestic relationships; second, the family itself changed in composition in these years with the addition of William's second wife and four new grandchildren, and the new personnel necessarily altered family interactions; finally, Sarah's increasing physical infirmity affected how she saw her servants and her sons. Sarah continued to complain that she was not treated properly as a parent and to portray herself as a long-suffering mother, but these protests decreased in frequency and were refocused on Spencer alone.

Relations between mother and sons continued to be tense in the first two months after Sir William's death, particularly because there seems to have been a problem realizing the capital to pay Sarah the annuity settled upon her.[7] When William married Judith in 1686, Sarah gave up her dower rights to any of the lands or tenements owned by Sir William (and passed directly on to William) in return for a £400 annuity, payable "without any deduction, defalcation or abatement whatsoever" in quarterly installments.[8] Even before Sir William's death Sarah had been troubled by the issue of financing her own independent life should her husband die before her. She apparently had little expectation of this happening—Sir William, while slightly older, was in excellent health—but because of her chats with a female acquaintance about ten days after Sir William's sixty-sixth birthday, the possibility arose that her jointure was insufficient to support her as a widow:

> Visiting Lady Holt we chanc'd to talk about rent charg. Pah, quoth she thats a word devis'd by husbands to cheat their wives. Penny:rent is the thing. I askt what difference? She answer'd the last was free of all abatements; the other liable to taxes. So home came I with a flea in my ear; and enquir'd of Sir W[illiam] how the matter stood in my case? who told me he cou'd not remember so long; which reply makes it very suspitious that I have been these 20 years under a great mistake.[9]

Her anxiety about her financial solvency as a widow, even when there was no immediate prospect of losing her husband, and the suspicion both she and Lady Holt had of the mechanism of jointure, indicate the perilous nature of widowhood even in the upper ranks of society. If provision were inadequate, and had been made so by the very people who were supposed to protect these women's interests, even elite women might be reduced to straitened circumstances.[10] At the time this concern surfaced, in 1705, Sarah took the jointure documents to a legal expert— her son Spencer—who reassured her she was due £400 per year as a pension plus the house in Hertford for life.[11] Not only is it worth noting Sarah's lack of trust in her husband's benevolence, it is also remarkable that she was both uniquely protected and uniquely vulnerable because of her sons' legal expertise. She might either benefit from excellent advice if her sons were so inclined, or she could be handily deprived of her legal due should her sons prioritize other family interests, including their own.

The question of solvency in widowhood continued to bother Sarah, especially when Sir William took a lease on a larger house in London and the couple moved there at the end of March 1706. In contemplating the expense, Sarah was again worried that if she should survive Sir William, she would be left in financial straits. Telling Sir William so, he agreed, and promised "he woud leave order with those to whom he gave his mony that they shou'd pay the rent for my life"[12]—a relief to Sarah, but also extraordinary in that until she brought it up, this possibility had not occurred to Sir William, even though both of them were unlikely to survive the entire length of the lease.

As it turned out, Sarah's concern was only too pertinent. At the time of Sir William's death, she was initially comforted by Spencer telling her William had told him to assure her that "that he wou'd be not only Just in my Concerns, but also very kind to mee, and he wou'd Advance the Next Quarter:Rent."[13] Right after Christmas, William gave her the £50 bequeathed to her to buy mourning, but the next week,

> he Came again without a Ragg more of Mony, only hinted that in a litle while he would make even the Account of last Quarter, but not a Word of Advance. So I pray'd him to Explain his meaning. Wherupon he Seem'd to Insinuate that if he quarterly paid mee a Whole 100. without abatement 'twas more then I could Claim, it being Chargable with the Terms laid on Since the Settlement, but however it shou'd be done so long as he was Able and then proceeded to talk of a Scanty Condition near to Poverty, saying the Estate left by the Death of his Father wou'd not afford to pay yearly 450.' Dry Mony till after Michalmas Next when Some Leases Came out to make an Improvment.[14]

Alarmed, Sarah checked the settlement documents to make sure she was in fact due the annuity without abatement, clearly suspicious that she was being cheated, and in her diary she reproduced the entire text of the jointure settlement.[15] While this was a symbolic act of inscription that validated her interpretation of what was due her as inheritance, it had no legal weight and would not help her enforce her rights. Her distrust and resentment again rose when William sent a tradesman to her for payment of the bills for the thirty-five days of the preceding quarter after Sir William's death. Without William or Spencer's side of this story, it is difficult to decide whether there was miscommunication about what had been promised, and whether Sarah was justified in her suspicion and anger. She certainly was in an unpleasant situation had she wanted to take legal advice against her sons, prominent men of law, about her legal rights to her annuities. Worse yet, her son William as lord keeper and then in 1707 lord chancellor was head of the very court that had jurisdiction in these matters. It must have been very alarming to think she might be deprived of her inheritance as a widow, without any real recourse to law. If William really did promise an advance on her quarterly allowance and then retract the promise and instead suggest she was not really entitled to the full annuity, she would be forced to depend on the sense of justice and duty of the very man who was cheating her to deliver her income regularly.

Cash may actually have been short: By the terms of Sir William's will, £80 had to be distributed immediately for mourning, and Spencer was to receive £1,000 within six months. An accounting of Sir William's estate to the beginning of August 1707 reckoned the disposable balance at that point, but not before, to be £694, 1 shilling, 5 pence.[16] The matter was shortly settled, however, when the very next week, William paid her the full annuity installment due for the previous quarter, plus an additional £7 pounds, 10 shillings. While he did not advance her the current quarter, Sarah hoped the additional £7 would continue to be paid, a supplement that would be preferable to the advance, because despite Sir William's assurance, she ended up paying the house rent herself.[17] As Sarah never complained again about the settlement, it seems she was satisfied with this arrangement.

Once this initial conflict was settled after Sir William's death, the next effect on Sarah's relationship with her children came when William broke the news to her (by letter) that he had secretly married Mary Clavering some months before. Her initial response was to comment that "'twas high time to let me know it; when Some while before Mad: the House:Keeper cou'd tell it to who She pleas'd."[18] This suggestion that she had some inkling of the marriage previous to being told is reinforced by an entry the previous November, where Sarah noted, "The Town Rings that Somebody is Weded and Beded with somebody. Use not much the Company of a Woman that is a Singer (or playeth upon Instruments)."[19] Mary was an excellent musician. In their first personal encounter, Mary asked Sarah's blessing. Showing Sarah appropriate marks of respect due a parent was perhaps especially easy, since Mary was more than forty years younger than her mother-in-law, unlike William's first wife, Judith, who had entered the family in her late teens, when Sarah was only in her early forties herself.

While Sarah did not stop complaining entirely about the lack of visits or respect from her sons, the incidence of complaints, by far the most frequent in the first volume from 1700 to 1701, dropped significantly after Sarah was widowed in 1706.[20] In all but one of the six summers following Sir William's death, Sarah spent at least a month in the country, dividing her time fairly evenly between Spencer's family at Hertford Castle and William's family at Cole Green. Other than those summer visits, by Sarah's count, William visited her about once a month and Spencer about once every two months,[21] a frequency that, as far as can be determined, is not fundamentally different from their earlier standard. From this point, Sarah's interaction with her two sons diverged. On the one hand, she became much less critical of William and interacted with him and his family more and more frequently; on the other, actual contact with Spencer and his family became more constrained all the time. The general tone of her comments about William and his visits softened considerably. Slightly less than four years after she was widowed, Sarah used the words of *The Tatler* to depict a visit from William as a form of socially approved homage to the deserving elderly—a tone completely different from her earlier complaints about his coldness:

> My Son Lord Chancellor (for So I may Call Him) came to Dine with mee Alone. There is not a greater Pleasure to Old Age than Seeing that wee are Not quite laid aside in the World; but that we are either Used with Gratitude for what we Were, or Honor'd for what wee Are.[22]

As William's mother, she was, of course, deserving of gratitude for her past care of her son, and, as this prescriptive text indicated, could rightfully claim continuing honor as a mother in her old age.

During those four years, her daughter-in-law Mary had impressed her very favorably by her consideration and dutiful behavior. The few letters surviving from this period show a dramatic contrast to the discontented, complaining letters Sarah wrote to her son in the years when her husband was alive. When Mary wrote and invited Sarah to stay at Cole Green the summer immediately after her marriage and Sir William's death, Sarah was clearly pleased.[23] On the second day of her stay there, Sarah delivered her verdict on her new daughter-in-law, saying, "It is the general Vogue that La[dy] C[owper] is a great Beauty and a Great Wit. My Vote is, I think her Neither, but very much Better than Either."[24] In contrast to Judith, who Sarah complained had consistently failed to observe the formalities of presenting her duty to or asking after her mother-in-law, Mary seems to have used both the language of deference and the currency of gifts to please Sarah. Interestingly, Mary's demeanor as a daughter-in-law apparently helped to outweigh her commission of the same fault that had so outraged Sarah regarding Pennington—that is, the failure to obtain consent for the marriage in the first place. Of course, the circumstances were significantly changed by this time: among other things, William was not the very young, untried, financially dependent son he had been at his first marriage. But in any case, when Sarah had returned to London from her visit, she was equally happy to receive letters quite soon from both William and Mary—and sounded the picture of benevolence in her reply.[25]

Even more important was the birth of a granddaughter in December 1707, and Mary and William's decision to name her Sarah and to ask Sarah to stand as godmother.[26] A letter from Mary to William immediately after the birth of their next child (William) in 1709 depicts a harmonious, joking relationship between Sarah and Mary, and also portrays Sarah as a doting grandmother to her granddaughter, recounting that "She and I have had a loving dispute this afternoon for she is so partial to her Granddaughter to fancy you were never quite so handsome as she, and I can't allow it her."[27] For the rest of Sarah's life, her letters asked especially after her granddaughter, "Sall," and indicated by gifts and special instructions that this was the grandchild closest to her heart.

Patricia Crawford points out that many women in this period particularly looked forward to the role of grandmother, "and wrote with pleasure of their grandchildren's activities." She notes the example of Lady Joan Barrington to suggest that as grandmothers, women may have gained in social respect and in familial power.[28] The later life of Lady Rachel Russell, a friend of Sarah's, supports this image of a loving, powerful grandmother: Having spent a good portion of her life as a mother raising her children, arranging their marriages, and exercising political influence for their benefit, she also was involved in arranging the education of her grandchildren, and overseeing their upbringing.[29] While it is doubtful that William's children helped Sarah become a family matriarch, they (and to a limited extent, Spencer's older children) allowed her the role of benevolent dispenser of affection, advice, and gifts, for which she received gratifying letters of thanks from her grandchildren.[30]

In contrast to this changed relationship between mother and son after the death of Sir William, Sarah's relationship with her servants changed little. As a widow and thus sole governor of her household, Sarah's status had been transformed, but her actual power to extract what she considered acceptable behavior was only augmented in the sense that she was in control of the penalties for misbehavior, including the supreme penalty of dismissal. Although she could rid herself more easily of servants who provoked her repeatedly, her intentions to reform the servants

morally and behaviorally and thus to achieve a well-ordered and harmonious household failed utterly.

As soon as Sir William died, Sarah immediately began to implement
her vision of household governance. With the aid of precepts she had
collected, she tried to institute a regime of religious education and discipline, as her complaint two months after Sir William's death indicates:

> It is deplorable that Humane Creatures living under the instruction of
> Christian Religion Shou'd be so Brutify'd. In the most Serious manner I
> reprove them, but from Experience it is good advice To those who are
> not Capable to Penetrate into the Reasons of Things, give only a Plain
> and Positive Precept.[31]

The extremity of her concept of control can be seen in an entry from just
a few days later:

> Both the fellows Staid out this Night, and Came home so Drunk that no
> Noise cou'd wake one of 'em till near Noon. To prevent the like, Barrs
> are Set Cross their Windows, and a Padlock on the Door to keep them.

The remedy does not seem to have been effective, as the coachman again
stayed out all night the next month. When Sarah chastised him for it,
"he Huff'd and bid me provide my self agen his year was Up; So I turn'd
him out the Same Day."[33] This was the first of a string of dismissals, for
offenses that she had had to tolerate (or at least work very hard to punish) while Sir William was alive, particularly insolence and theft. Three
years later, this rapid turnover was still in evidence, as Sarah mentioned
in relating the occasion of her dismissal of another coachman: "So I
turn'd him off, and now in Nine Months have Cast out Nine Such, as
without any Breach of Charity may be Call'd Rogues and Whores."[34]

Despite her new power to hire, fire, and govern servants, Sarah found
it extremely difficult to impose the degree of order that she had in mind
for her domestic life. Her servants persisted in their misbehavior and did
not seem to benefit from religious guidance. After a year and a half of
reading morning and evening prayers and Scripture to her family, Sarah
lamented that at least one of them "Cannot Read, nor Rehearse the
Creed, Ten Commandments or the Lords Prayer; tho' all the Time afore-
said he heard it Repeated by mee, besides on Sundays at Church."[35]
Sarah continued nonetheless—after all, her daily reading and what she
heard in church reiterated the duty of godly, careful governance and
held up patterns and precepts to follow. Her New Year's resolution for
1709 was to reform her servants, and in that entry she cited Scripture

and sermons that demonstrated the necessity for masters "to train up those of their familys in the knowledg of the True God, and the Excercises of true Religion."[36]

One of the biggest difficulties with managing servants was determining how best to treat them and speak to them: Sarah collected conflicting advice and reported her success (or lack thereof) with a number of methods. She followed William Gouge's advice to first incite diligence in servants by promising rewards,[37] telling her coachman he could expect an annual raise of 10 shillings if he continued to perform well. This strategy was ineffective in this case, as the coachman soon asked her for three weeks' holiday and quit when she refused.[38] Isaac Barrow advocated meekness and sweetness in reproof,[39] Simon Patrick spoke of harsher, more stinging language to stir up a servant's repentance,[40] but Sarah concluded, "I have try'd both and by Sad Experience have found that either way avails but litle to their amendment."[41] Several years after the death of Sir William, she seems, by her own report, to have settled into a general pattern of unemotional insult:

> I am grown to hate Scolding att Servants when they do a fault I only say Ah! Thou hast a Head and so has a Pin, or some Such merry Expression which they hate worse than a Slap on the Face.[42]

And about two years later (suggesting she may not have been consistent in this tactic):

> I have taken up a Humor to Settle in a Profound Taciturnity with Servants, having found them to be Stupid Animals; and that to Instruct, Reprove, and Expostulate with them, is altogather Vain and to no purpose, but to Distract my Thoughts, and Disturb my Self; So as when I am under Some Apprehension of being forc'd to Argue with Them; I Retire from it.[43]

In keeping with her response to other domestic situations that she considered intolerable, here too Sarah withdrew from the conflict. However, her lack of enforcing power was not a result so much of the restrictions placed on her by a theoretical superior—her husband—but because of the resistance of those social inferiors on whom she was attempting to impose a household order that would reflect the theory of interaction between master and servant. As her harsh description above suggests, by this time she despaired of improving her servants in the ways advocated by prescriptive literature and firmly placed the blame on their stupidity and incorrigibility rather than on herself as governor. In a neatly phrased entry, she declared the hopelessness of correcting servants because of their idiocy and wickedness, acknowledged her expectation of managing better than Sir William could have, and yet denied her husband any claim to being right after all:

> Before I was a Widdow I used to Think that were I in Power I Shou'd Manage Servants to my Content. But so wicked and proffligate is this Age, that I find it Impracticable by any Means or Method. They Ease themselves entirely of the Fatigue of Thinking.[44]

Like many other masters in this period, Sarah fought an unsuccessful battle to impose a household order that mirrored fairly directly the structure set out by moralists. Faced with the pressure to govern well and to provide religious education for her servants, Sarah tried a number of methods advocated by the clergy and other writers to reform her household and make her servants act as they were supposed to. In this venture, however, prescriptive sources were probably only a comfort in the sense that they backed up her claims to superiority and deference and sanctioned her casting out the unregenerate.[45] She did not find effectual their suggestions for practical management, in the end relying on her own experience to determine what tone to take and despairing of affecting their thinking substantially. Her lack of success in enforcing a deferential code of behavior meant that she condemned this stratum of society generally (as did many of her contemporaries) as irredeemably vicious.[46] This view was not necessarily in accordance with reminders to social superiors to acknowledge the equal humanity and potential for salvation of their inferiors (a discrepancy Sarah herself recognized), but made it possible for Sarah to deny responsibility for failing to govern and educate her servants in the manner that she claimed to be her right.

Widowhood improved some aspects, at least, of Sarah's family life; it also afforded greater opportunities for wielding social influence, though again with mixed results. Whether it is simply a matter of Sarah's selective reporting, whether once her eldest son only had one parent to please he could afford to be more accommodating, or whether the initial rush for places once William was lord keeper had abated somewhat by the time of Sir William's death, Sarah seems to have had a better success rate as a widow in obtaining patronage favors from her son. In the early years of her widowhood she mentioned two cases in which she had been effectual in obtaining benefits for supplicants. In both these instances, however, the eventual outcome was nonetheless highly unsatisfactory to her. In 1707, Sarah lamented the behavior of a priest she had helped:

> A Parson who gott Drunk in the Morning Came to Dine with mee. This Worthless Wretch his Wife and family had lived for 30 year on 40.¹ per Ann: So to make his Age more Easy I had been Instrumental to gett him an Augmentation of a 100.¹ yearly more. But now I have lost the Pleasure of thinking I had done Well when it Calls to Mind what I heard a Doctor of Divinity Say, That Lord Keeper Wright had put more Dirt in the Church than wou'd be Swept out this Seven year. I Resolve it Shall make mee Cautious for the future that I add not to the Rubbich ffor being akin to me Shall be no Merit where it is Wanting.[47]

Much worse was the eventual outcome of her assistance to the Leighs, in January 1709:

> Sad Tideings have arriv'd to mee from Leicester of One I have known ever Since She was Born, and alwaies esteem'd Her as a Vertuous and Religious Woman But now Major Leigh for whom I was too much an Instrument in getting him the Best place about my Son; going down with a Commission of Bankrupt against her Aged Father; did so Insult and Threaten them, more like a Devil Incarnate than a Man; which Terrify'd Her so much that she lost Her Reason; and being Distracted (as the Coroners Jury found it) threw herself into a Deep Well and So Ended Her Life. This Deplorable Fact with all its Circumstances Amazes and Disturbs me more than Words Can Express.[48]

A few months later, Sarah implied a certain hesitation and hard-learned caution in attempting to involve herself in the patronage game:

> Being counted a good Church:Woman the Parsons haunt me to get 'em Livings. But I am aware that if a Clergy:Man be loose and Scandalous he must not be patroniz'd and Winkt att, the Example of few Such Corrupt Many, they will Share deeply in their faults who are the Instruments of their preferment. I likewise learn, that next to Obtaining the Suit, a Speedy and gentle Denial is the most acceptable to Suitors; they will gain by the Dispatch wheras else they Spend theire Time and Perhaps Mony in attending, and you will gain Ease in being rid of their Importunity. But if they Obtain what they reasonably desired, it Multiplys the Courtesie to do it with good Words and Speedily.[49]

On the one hand, this passage emphasizes Sarah's new visibility as an autonomous model of piety—a "good churchwoman"—who clergy believed (perhaps in this period with more reason) could deliver preferments and pensions. On the other, Sarah had come to this potential role as patronage broker late in life, with little previous scope for practicing the art of bestowing favors, given her husband's obstruction and the family's tenuous hold on status. The dramatically bad outcomes of her few ventures in this field may have added to her sense of social insecurity and thus encouraged her to retreat from this form of manipulation of power. In this entry she was reviewing the knowledge she had gained, though significantly, much of it had to do with learning how to say no. Perhaps in her diary she was testing out methods for giving an impression of refusal based on dispassionate evaluation rather than on inability to draw upon the source of power she was assumed to possess. At any rate, there is no further mention of specific attempts to use her influence with her son to gain places for clients, probably mainly because the next year was the trial of Dr. Sacheverell and the fall of the Whig ministry. William resigned and did not return to office until 1715, by which time Sarah was disillusioned with all things political and, moreover, too infirm to involve herself much in any form of public activity.

In some respects, Sarah's experience as a widow with bestowing charity parallels her experience with patronage. Although widowhood allowed her more scope in both areas, as with patronage, the results of her charitable activity were not always what she had intended. For the first two years after Sir William had died, out of her annual income of £400, Sarah gave away between £10 and £20 per quarter (usually closer to £10) to what she hoped, but often suspected, were not worthy causes:

> This last Quarter I have given, or thrown away, 15.¹ 17.ˢ Every Day expect to meet with unthankfull people, therfore Think a day before you promise. I must prefix a Law of Living Beneficial least inconsiderate and Easie Giving grow in favour under the Couler of Benignity.⁵⁰

The dissatisfaction she expressed with the results of her personal almsgiving seems to have increased in 1709 to the point that her contributions per quarter were halved, and their notation in her diary was accompanied by prescriptive justifications for prudence in giving:

> I have given away this Quarter less than in many before yet perhaps more than enough. It dos Bounty [two illegible words] to Shew Her so much as to make her be laugh'd att. Who gives and Spends too much must fall, or Else Desist with Shame. To Live well of a litle is a great Deal more Honour than to Spend a great deal Vainly. To know both when and What to part withal is a Knowledg that befits the Greatest. The Best Object of

Bounty is either Necessity or Desert; The Best Motive thy own Goodness; and the Limit is the Safety of thy Estate. It is not good to make our Kindness to Others to be Cruelty to our Selves.[51]

While these sums were not inconsiderable, it was really after the final settlement of Sir William's estate that Sarah could make more flamboyant gestures and move from fulfilling her everyday duty as a pious Christian to developing a more impressive image as a benevolent widow and benefactor on a large scale and then capitalizing upon the ties of obligation created by those gestures. Sarah made three major gifts in the period from early 1708 to early 1709, motivated by a combination of piety, seasonable opportunity, access to much larger sums of money than had been possible when she was married, and a desire to create a new identity as a morally upright widow—separate from, and clearly superior to her deceased husband. The first of those donations seems to have been prompted when Sarah received her share of an investment Sir William had made. From her return of £164, she entrusted £100 to Sir William Ashurst (prosperous city tycoon, member of Parliament, and long-time family friend) for the use of Christ's Hospital. This action seems in part to have been an act of differentiation between herself and Sir William, emphasizing that she knew what was required both ethically and socially of a family of his rank, and that Sir William had not known. Accordingly, with her more developed sense of right and wrong, she would remedy an outstanding inequity her husband had allowed:

Not only charity, but Justice requires it Shou'd be so, by reason S.ʳ W. C. was 30 year past Chose a Governer therof, put in Several Children as it Came to his turn, yet left 'em nothing in Return which Methinks is to Robb the Spittle, ffor Sure when They Choose Men of Estate 'tis Expected that Shou'd be Done. Consider what Degrees of Liberality are Suitable to your Ability and Station What becomes you as a Christian as a Promoter of every Good Work.[52]

At the end of 1708, she also gave £100 to Saint Andrew's, Holborn, for the charity schools, perhaps through Dr. Manningham, though she did not specify the method. In recounting this donation she alluded to more conventional religious ideology as far as her reasons for doing so, echoing sermons that insisted that it served to prove one's love to God, assisted in one's duty to glorify Him, and was comforting to the donor as an act of generosity and a means to more certain salvation.[53] Equally conventional was the rationale she expressed for donating to this good work in particular, that is, that through early training in piety, the young and poor might grow up virtuous and avoid the taint of evil example in this world. Here again, though, it may be that her reasons for the donation also included asserting her new identity as pious widow and church supporter of substance. Not only did she agree with the premise of charity schools, but this was an opportunity to demonstrate her new standing as an independent member of the parish, separate and autonomous from the restrictions of a husband or the taint of his bad example with newly available resources to back her standing.

And a very substantial gift it was, too: The SPCK account calculated that it cost about £75 per year to run a charity school for fifty boys, including paying for the schoolroom, heat, a master's salary, books, and clothing for each child, and that equivalent expenses for fifty girls amounted to about £60 per year.[54] While it is clear that there is some inconsistency in the accounts, it appears that Sarah's donation accounted for nearly a quarter of the total gifts the schools had received in the eight years since establishment.[55] Saint Andrew's was a particularly prosperous, large parish, with what seems to have been especially strong support for its schools: Its enrollments were significantly higher than all but six of the twenty-four total parishes for which it is possible to make some estimate. Annual income from sermon collections was much higher than all but five parishes, and it had the fourth highest total for gifts since establishment.[56] Nonetheless, Sarah's contribution was notably generous—the equivalent of nearly half the running costs for a year at Saint Andrew's and a gift that in many parishes would have kept their schools running for one or more years.[57] Dr. Manningham, the main instigator of the Saint Andrew's schools, was her intermediary in this donation, and so even if her name did not feature in subscription lists or minute books, the person in charge knew of her benevolence, may have told others, and could hardly help acknowledging her eminent piety, expressing gratitude and incurring some level of obligation.

Very shortly after this episode, Sarah made a third donation of £100 through the bishop of Lichfield to the Society for the Propagation of the Gospel. The reasons she mentioned were similarly reiterated in the annual sermons for this society—that Christians were called to aid in converting heathens, and that so doing helped them to have a "more abundant entrance into the Everlasting Kingdome."[58] A further reward was much more immediate, and while still in the arena of pious activity, points out the potential such charitable giving had for establishing reciprocal ties of obligation that enabled a very satisfying exercise of power on some occasions. Two months after bestowing her gift, Sarah observed:

> Nothing is more pleasant than to meet with the Eies of them wee have lately Oblidg'd. I found Double pleasure in Doing Good. One from the Oblidging Manner of the B.ᴾ of Litch:, and A:B:ᴾ of York to Assist by helping me to the Means and Oppertunity of getting a poor yong Woman Touch'd by the Queen for The Evil; the Other from the pleasing Hopes of Benefit Done to the Afflicted Person by the Hands of the Pious Operator.[59]

By means of one impressive donation, then, she reaped satisfaction on several fronts: First, she was performing her Christian duty with laudable zeal and so was simultaneously benefiting the souls of others and her own soul. Second, she was raising the esteem in which she was held by a section of society whose opinion she valued and was putting them in a position of indebtedness to her. Third, she was positioning herself to repeat the process, through calling in the bishops' debt in order to assist someone else. She was again gratified by the results of this further pious action: "Came the Girl whom I gott Touch'd by the Queen, to Shew me how very Well her Eies are Now; So that I mervell'd, and Glorify'd God wᶜ had given Such power unto Men. This sight brought Joy to my Heart."[60]

Sarah's donation, however, ran into problems. During the previous two years, many subscribers to the SPG had fallen into arrears while expenditures had not been similarly cut back, forcing the society to suspend sending further missionaries and to consider other ways of raising money.[61] There may have been a connection between the falling subscriptions and the increased politicization of the organization. Since its inception there had been potential for factionalism, as the two competing missionary interests already present in North America were the French Roman Catholics and the New England Company, the Dissenters's missionary society.[62] It has been suggested that the whole reform movement, beginning with the establishment of the societies for the Reformation of Manners and especially in the establishment of both the SPCK and the SPG, was fatally embroiled in the politics of religion and that the base of support increasingly narrowed and became "ever more Anglican," as Tories objected to the involvement of dissenters and Whigs correspondingly suspected the societies of increasingly high-flying tendencies and even Jacobitism.[63] In response, the SPCK shifted its em-

phasis somewhat from charity schools to missionary work, eventually
hiving off the SPG as a separate organization in order to counteract
charges of factionalism.[64] While Sarah never specifically mentioned
problems with factions in the charity schools, her experience with the
supposed supporters of the SPG indicates that attempts to keep it free
from politicization were a failure. Shortly after Sarah had the woman
touched by the queen, her original act of bounty was diverted:

> The Bishop of Lichfield with whom I had Deposited one 100.[l] for propa-
> gation of the Gospel in fforreign parts; Came and told me He had Con-
> sulted with Archbishop of Canterbury and they Both Concluded; Since
> that Affair is so ill Manag'd by parties and Factions; Some for Settling
> Our Church Government and Others Opposing it, 'twere better Dispose
> of it Some Other Way: So They agreed to bestow it on the Charity
> Schools of S:[r] Giles Parish Thus I gave a 100.[l] to Christs Hospital because
> S:[r] W: Should have Done it. And now have Given this because my Son
> Dwelling in That Parish, Shou'd Do it.[65]

It is very difficult to determine exactly what went on here, as there are
several confusing and potentially contradictory factors: The bishop of
Lichfield was not listed as an original subscriber to either the SPCK or
SPG, nor does he show up as an active member later. He did, however,
preach the SPG anniversary sermon in 1705[66] and was Sarah's channel
for donating to the society. The archbishop of Canterbury, on the other
hand, was a subscribing member of both societies from their inception
and provided space in his library for SPG meetings to be held.[67] It sounds
as if debates were raging at the time about the dissenting influence in the
missionary work, but it is remarkable that two ostensible supporters of
the endeavor would actively discourage contributions, even if they were
to be diverted into an equally good cause. Apparently, for Sarah at least,
there was no taint of high-flying Toryism in Saint Giles's charity school,
and as she herself explained, it was a satisfactorily symmetrical gesture
of fulfilling duties neglected by the male members of her family. It is interesting, too, to wonder to what extent Sarah had a veto on this change
in recipient. She does not seem to have been displeased with the new
choice, perhaps because the bishops involved had actively tried to present her with an attractive alternative, or it may be that the gesture of
benevolence itself and its high-ranking audience were as important as its
precise target.

Sarah Cowper's widowhood offered additional opportunities to exercise patronage and charity, yet impediments still remained. It was her

misfortune to be in a position to act in the public arena and to attempt to exercise power through money and connections at the same time as party politics and animosity were at their height. In both areas, Sarah was ultimately unsatisfied with the outcome of her efforts—in the case of charity, because of lack of gratitude from individuals and politicization of charitable institutions; in the case of patronage, because of her son's lack of cooperation, but also because of the dangers of favoring those who might turn out to be bad choices.

As with charity and patronage, in her married years Sarah had already employed churchgoing and visiting to garner respect and to differentiate herself from her husband. In going out in society and to church once widowed, two themes surface in her writing. First, more often than previously, Sarah depicted herself as an arbiter of the correct deportment of fellow worshipers, sometimes with brief biblical quotes on the necessity for gravity and silence during the service[68] and occasionally with more lengthy condemnations, as when after having not been able to hear the sermon for the noise of two women chatting, she let loose this diatribe:

> The Want of Reverence in the Church begets the Contempt of God; they cannot have Jesus in their Heart when they Affront him in his Temple. to do any thing in an Holy Place that is unseemly or uncomely Shall not pass unpunish'd. Where God is Specially present, and his Holy Angels do frequent, there for Certain thou dost very foolishly to intermeddle at all with Temporal Matters. Nor Make any Noise with your Voice—They were not to talk to one another as they went along but in a profound Silence wait on the Lord.[69]

Her disapproval of misbehavior in church was partly based on the idea that other people's lack of reverence ruined both the proper performance of the public, communal act of worship, and also the efficacy and full concentration of her own devotion. It may also have included an element of social discomfort if Sarah was excluded from those conversations of which she so disapproved. In addition, this censoriousness may be linked to her increasing age, her sense of pious widowhood, or perhaps even to a real increase in inappropriate socializing in church. Essays in *The Spectator* and other periodicals voiced similar criticisms, so the phenomenon of inattentive churchgoers seems to be a theme of some general concern[70]—whether Sarah would have been so vocal about it if she had not been reading this periodical is unclear.

The second, related theme is the result of her new position as the widowed mother of the lord chancellor. A sign of her warmer relations with her elder son in this new single role were regular summer visits to his estate outside Hertford. In the environment of her son's home ground, Sarah needed to help uphold the family honor, not just at the level of a backbench baronet, as her husband had been, but now at the level of a noble family whose head was an extremely visible and powerful member of government. Already anxious about sociability, ironically, Sarah found her family's good fortune worrisome. She was obligated to live up to her son's elevation with its attendant jealousy, expectations of patronage, and the hypocrisy of self-serving acquaintances.

Sarah's roles as arbiter of religious decorum and supporter of family honor combined in her disapproval of the offensive behavior of both clergy and congregation in Hertford when she attended services there while staying with her sons. She had been critical of the performance of the service and the sermon at Hertford for a long time,[71] but now was particularly scathing about the pastor of Hertingfordbury, a violent Tory who used his pulpit and pen for political attacks, sometimes against the Cowper family. When Sarah attended her son William's parish church in August 1707, she complained:

> To mee the worst of this Place is, I am bound to Sitt out the Preachment of Parson Hodskin who from the pulpit I heard profess that at the Time when the Laws were put in Vigorous Execution against Dissenters he never was for Such proceedings, but alwaies perswaded by gentle Methods to Convince Men of their Errours. Which I take to be utterly false having by me two inveterate Libels against the Party writ by him it was said and in those Days he did not deny it. Therin S.ʳ W: and his Son are in most Scurrilous Manner Severely dealt with; tho' it must be remembred S.ʳ W: had ffreed him from a perrilous Action brought ag.ˢᵗ him by yᵉ Earl of Shaftesbury for Scandalum Magnatum and by his Interception obtain'd his pardon. This Shews his Gratitude and no less Hypocrisie.[72]

She reiterated her disapproval of the conduct of services in Hertford churches in general (having apparently investigated all the options) the next summer:

> I have Now gone to both Parishes in this Town and may Say as did an ArchBishop of our own before the House of Lords; That Men now aday's Come into a Church with no more Reverence than a Tinker and his Dog enter an Ale:House. The Comparison is too Homely; But my just Indignation (Said He) at the prophaness of the Times makes me Speak it.[73]

In attending church Sarah was asserting high social and religious standing for herself as well as supporting the family honor at their country seat, but at the cost of tolerating impiety and sanctioning the hypocritical moralizing of a political enemy.

Sarah also detected hypocrisy in the friendliness of those who had previously shunned her, now that family fortunes had risen so precipitously, and her newfound popularity did nothing to improve her opinion of the loyalty of those with whom she was acquainted:

> Since my Son was Lord Chan: my Dear Friends and Acquaintances Encrease or Return Wonderfully, having not heard of Some in Many years before. Under a Course of good Fortune the Noise and Splender of Friendship Shall be Egregious; but wee can tast the true Joys of it only under Adversity for that is the true Test of Friendship; (then it was Wanting to mee).[74]

In this sarcastic commentary on the unreliability of friends, Sarah diverged considerably from one of her favorite sources on social comportment—contemporary periodical literature. In *The Tatler* and *The Spectator*, Richard Steele and Joseph Addison's satirical, amusing, sometimes even sermonizing essays advanced a less suspicious view of social interaction,[75] emphasizing an amiable, easy disposition and courteous listening when in company, rather than strict moral watch and disapproval. In fact, Sarah acknowledged the risk of being too censorious:

> Some Say a good Man Shou'd be displeas'd with the Wicked. But if he Shou'd be Offended att the Dissolute Behavior and Wickedness of Others, there's no Man more Miserable than He; and must Needs Spend the whole Course of his Life in Anger and Sadness; ffor what Moment Shall tthere be wherin he shall not See Some Matters that are to be disallow'd; He cannot Live if he be Incens'd as often as Cause requires.[76]

Moreover, she pointed to *The Spectator* itself on the connection between easy and open conversation, good breeding, and elite status, quoting this admonition against too much attention to the niceties of rank:

> There is more to Do about Place and Precedency, in a Meeting of Justices Wives, than in an Assembly of Dutchesses. Wee may Observe a great Revolution in good Breeding. Several Obliging Deferences, Condescentions and Submissions, with Forms and Ceremonies of Conversation by Degrees Multiply'd, and grew to be Troublesome Civility. The Modish World found too great a Constraint in them, and have therfore thrown most of 'em aside. An unconstraind Carriage, and a Certain Openness of

Behavior are the Heigth of good Breeding The Fashionable World is grown Free and Easie; Nothing is so Modish as an Agreeable Negligence.[77]

Sarah appears to have been particularly worried about this issue of deference, since dealing appropriately with social superiors and inferiors was crucial for someone who was relying on her social relationships to further family eminence and buttress her own newly acquired high status. Accordingly, she collected commentary on the difficulties of interaction between people of different ranks:

It is very hard to hit a Certain Temper of Freedom with persons Above us; So to be Easie as to become an Instrument of their Entertainment without being any way Offensive or Breaking in upon the Honour and Respect Due to their Quality.[78]

Sarah's interpretation of deportment advice was actually explicitly challenged on one occasion, when Gilbert Burnet, bishop of Salisbury, criticized her for acting with too much humility for her rank. She responded by using the same sort of strategy she employed in defending her understanding and performance of her domestic roles, transforming the meaning of a prescriptive commentary to back up the validity of her behavior. Sarah took a satire in *The Spectator* on a city woman disgruntled in the country because the provincials did not realize she was a wit, and made it part of an extended defense of her own demeanor. In the original, the woman from London was advised:

The best course Emilia can take is, to have less Humility, for if she could have as good an Opinion of her self for having every Quality, as some of her Neighbors have of yourselves with one, she would inspire even them with a sense of her Merit, and make that carriage (which is now the subject of their Derision) the sole object of their Imulation. Till she has arrived at this value of her self, she must be contented with the Fate of that uncommon creature, a woman too humble.[79]

Far from the spirit in which it was intended in this passage, Sarah used the last phrase to introduce a lengthy self-vindication:

I must be Content with the Fate of that uncommon Creature, A woman too Humble, as the Bishop of Sarum once told mee I was. Yet Submission in us to Others, many times (not alwaies) begets Submission in Others to Us. Civility and Candor Calms and Captivates the Rugged Temper of the Rude and Boisterous. Humility is ever found to dwell most with them that are most Brave. Shew me a Man thats humble out of Judgment, and

I can find him full of all good Parts. . . . I will never think my self dis-
parag'd either by preserving peace or Doing Good. I had rather be accounted too much Humble, than Esteem'd a litle Proud.[80]

As a result of the insecurities of deportment, continued ambivalence regarding solitude versus company, and with added emphasis on age and
widowhood, Sarah began to incline herself more frequently toward "retirement."

To Seek Company or to ffly it are two Extreams to be blamed; To Shun
all Company savors of disdain and Contempt, and to Seek after them is a
Sign of Idleness. ffor the most part Seek to be Solitary and Choose Meditation. Wee are in our Selves when Alone; Converse with thine own
Heart.[81]

But even in the years of widowhood and increasing age, Sarah could not
maintain that posture entirely. As she noted,

We are apt to grow into Discontent if wee be too much Retir'd, We are
apt to be Morose, Cynical and Sowr. It is a Thousand to One No Man
will Live Well alone, Neither as to himself, Nor as to God. Converse
tends to Dispose to Friendship and great Benevolence as well as to polish
and Cultivate the Nature of Man.[82]

Despite Sarah's uneasy ambivalence about her level and style of sociability, her new state presented the opportunity for carrying on what
she considered the proper business of her latter years, and her pleasure
at this aspect of her widowhood produced entries displaying the highest
degree of contentment to be found over the entire course of the diary:

Now I have leisure both to examine the errours of my life past, and prepare for that great day wherin all flesh must make an account of their actions. And after a kind of tempestuous life; I have the advantage from my
God whom I will daily magnify for this perticuler mercy of an exemption
from business, a quiet mind, and a liberal maintainance in this part of my
life. When age sounds a retreat from this world and invites mee to contemplation which I take to be the greatest felicity.[83]

Here too she returned to the theme of retirement into a life of contemplation as befitting her age, but this time with the added advantages of
financial comfort, autonomy, and domestic peace. Furthermore, quoting
Montaigne, she asserted her continuing mental activity:

Altho' I have one foot in the grave yet I desire to learn. . . . I toss over
books for an honest recreation to please and delight my self. I only en-

deavor to find out the knowledg which may instruct me how to live and dy well. ffor difficult points I fret not my self about 'em. But after I have given 'em a charg or two I leave 'em as I found them. I seek for good and solid reasons that may instruct me how to sustain the assaults of unruly Passions, and the approaches of death.[84]

While Sarah was following standard social and moral prescription here, this reflection should not be taken as a banal or insincere mouthing of conventional platitudes about the correct activities for living in the last stages of life. The scholarship on prescriptive literature and aging tends to discount the significance of this religious and moral perception of the duties and nature of old age, devaluing both the force of these ideas, and their importance in people's lives in this period.[85] Piety in general and mental preparation for death with the onset of old age in particular were sources of comfort, support, authority, and intellectual and moral nourishment for Sarah throughout the volumes of her diary, and they are inescapably pervasive themes in her writing. As she said in 1707 about the centrality of reading to her pursuit of a tranquil mind,

> Books every way assist mee, they comfort me in age, and solace me in solitariness. They ease me of the burden of wearisome idleness; they abate the edge of fretting sorrow and divert me from my importunate imagination. They help to bear the provocations of a servant; the importunity of years, the unwelcomness of wrinkles and such like mind troubling accidents.[86]

Although the years 1707 and 1708 were a relatively happy time for Sarah in which she was free to pursue her own pleasures, enjoyed her family interactions, and exercised the authority of an independent widow of means, by 1709 there are an increasing number of references to old age in her diary and a change in the nature of those references. It appears that Sarah's health was slowly declining and, moreover, that her mental condition suffered as well. Rather than achieving a detachment that was sublime, she often experienced depressing listlessness.

> Blessed be God I came Safe and Well to Hartford; but ye least Remove is a Fatigue to mee. . . . what Joy Can a Man have, or what Misery Can he be without when the Natural Heat and Vigour is quite Spent, and all the Powers and faculties of Soul and Body in a languishing Condition; when one trouble is no sooner gone but the like or a New One Comes in its Room, A Succession of Misery greif pain or weakness drawing on One another. The Mind grows feeble in all its Powers, the Understanding

Dim, The Memory forgetfull, The Reason Weak, The Will listless, Dull about our greatest Concerns, Inconstant in all its Resolutions.[87]

Moreover, while she was still keeping a distance between herself and the furthest extent of old age, the gap was narrowing, and she was contemplating increasing debility and decay at the doorstep of such experience, not from a safe remove: "I see objects abroad which plainly shew mee I am not yet arriv'd to the worst condition of old age by much. I mett Mr. W. G. who labors under it I beleive with patience; yet sure it must be very tedious if not terrible."[88]

In these years, when she wrote down exhortations to read, the theme of reading to find help in old age, from a position of being beyond worldly ambitions and focusing more intently on preparation for death, surfaces even more frequently than in earlier years of the diary:

> Books every way assist mee, they Comfort me in Age, and Solace me in Solitariness. they Ease me of the burden of wearisome Idleness; they abate the Edge of fretting Sorrow and divert me from my importunate Imagination. they help to bear the provocations of a Servant; the Importunity of Years the unwelcomness of Wrinkles and such like mind troubling Accidents.[89]

or:

> My Design is to pass over easily the Remainder of my Life; I Seek in Reading only to Please my Self by Diversion and Study no other Science but the Knowledg of my Self and how to Live and Dy Well.[90]

There were, however, drawbacks to such extensive reading. Though Sarah often spent seven to eight hours a day at her books, and frequently called it her best pleasure, it could be wearisome. Here too, as with the larger question of distaste for solitude versus enervation from conversation in company, a surfeit of reading was excessive as well. There was also the danger in reading that her faith might be tested or her beliefs confused by controversial or speculative works. In any case, those books that were not immediately edifying distracted her from the true pursuit of knowledge in the service of self-improvement. Sarah generally disavowed them:

> My best Hours are those which I pass alone with a Book, and of those I Choose the most Intelligible and Plain, avoiding Controversy about Abstruse Matters as altogether Vain and to no purpose unless increasing of Doubts more than Resolving them.[91]

In the case of history books, she explicitly connected her choice of reading material to old age, noting: "I read history because old folks live more by Memory than by Hope."[92] She also reiterated the value of reading history as affirmed by prescriptive literature that recommended its study for the edification furnished by exemplary lives and for the appreciation of the workings of Providence in human affairs:

> The Reading of History brings Pleasures and Profit. It Enriches the Mind with Observation and gives us a Veiw of the Actions and Contrivances, and the Over:Ruling Providences that have Sway'd the Affairs of the World. It is the Resurrection of the Age past. It gives us the Scenes of Humane Life, That, by their Actings we may learn to improve and amend; and the Errours that the Weak have fallen into are Mark'd out as Rocks that we ought to avoid. 'Tis learning Wisdom at the Cost of Others; and which is Rare, it dos make a Man Better by being pleas'd.[93]

This kind of virtuous reading was a source of lessons on the nature of humanity and how the world worked—lessons that were valid and applicable to the present political situation, both in the exemplary (or cautionary) "lives" this reading furnished and in the demonstration it gave of Providence in action. In her commentary, Sarah reflected the current historical emphasis on universal truths and the cyclical nature of human society over time. The record of the past was to be understood as a set of recurring events and patterns from which readers ought to learn, or at least be warned, and which confirmed the validity of the idea in Ecclesiastes that nothing was new under the sun. Moreover, the lessons of history were moral and intimately bound up with God, whose providence directed and whose judgments raised up or cast down nations because of the behavior of their citizens.[94]

In 1701, in the context of Spencer's recent trial and Sir William's defeat at elections, when reading about the English Civil War she had focused on the historical continuity of self-interest and party politics as explanatory devices for events—the Ecclesiastes aspect of history. In 1708, however, in the context of England's lengthy involvement in the War of Spanish Succession, the embarrassing Tory attacks on the Whig ministry's management of the Almanza campaign in Spain, the later throes of the power struggle between Lord Treasurer Godolphin and Robert Harley, and especially the French-assisted Jacobite invasion that threatened from Dunkirk,[95] Sarah took a history of the early ages of the British Isles as warning that the rise and downfall of peoples was because of their cyclical descent into corruption and vice. Caesar's con-

quest, aided and abetted by some of the natives through faction and ambition, was an example of the timeless danger of disunity and immorality:

> Thus for about a 100 year the Brittains Continu'd till the inward parts of
> the Isle Broken by Civil Warrs and Faction more than the power of the
> Romans fell under the Subjection of that Empire. They were So Violently
> Set upon Each Others Destruction that they were insensible of an Univer-
> sal Danger. Nay So powerfull was the Ambition and Resentments of
> Some that they were therby Corrupted and drawn Over to the Enemies
> Side and Made Solicitous for the Roman Interest to the Ruin of their own
> Country. Thus it was Then, And So it Is Now.[96]

And the same thing occurred time and again:

> The like Vices which had procur'd Slavery to the English were now Come
> to the Heigth in the Danes, and as in all Changes of State caus'd their
> Ruin in this Nation, and made Way for Another Revolution. For Some
> years before the Arrival of the Normans Piety and all good Literature be-
> came So unfashonable even among the Clergy that Contenting themselves
> with a Very Small Share of Devotion as well as Learning they Cou'd
> Scarce Read Divine Service. . . . Which brought Calamity upon them-
> selves and Country. Since Divisions and Factions, Immorality and Impi-
> ety Occasioned such great Miseries to our Ancestors; We Ought Carefully
> to Remember this One Maxim. That the Same Causes do ordinarily Pro-
> duce the Same Effects.[97]

Here too, however, despite the didactic value of history, Sarah found
much of it anything but uplifting:

> I take it to be very Necessary for Information and Direction of Life to be
> frequently Reading Antient History, wherin with little Labour we find
> what Others with great Pains have laid together. There we have a Veiw of
> the Vertues of Good Men, and the Vices of Bad . . . the Vicissitude of Af-
> fairs and instability of all Worldly Things. . . . Yet I find upon the whole
> Such knowledge hugely enclines me to much Contempt of Humankind,
> and I therby feel my Self in danger of becoming a fastidious person. . . . [98]

This inclination would only grow stronger over the next few years, as
Sarah Cowper experienced the increasing debility of advanced old age
and observed with increasingly heightened indignation the political di-
sasters of the Sacheverell trial and the consequent Tory resurgence in
government.

CHAPTER 8

Disillusionment and Decline, 1710–1716

The trial of Doctor Henry Sacheverell in February and March of 1710 marks the emergence of a new strain of disillusionment in Sarah Cowper's diary as she entered into later old age. As her health declined, Sarah observed first with outrage and then increasing cynicism the repercussions of the Sacheverell trial for her family and for national politics. Henry Sacheverell was impeached before the House of Lords at Westminster Hall—in front of an audience of something like two thousand peers, MPs, gentry, and commoners lucky enough to obtain tickets—for "high crimes and misdemeanors" associated with preaching a seditious sermon on "the perils of false bretheren in church and state" the previous November 5, the date of the Gunpowder Plot commemoration and the anniversary of William III's landing in England. Dr. Sacheverell had compounded the offense by having the sermon printed without the consent of the aldermen of the city of London, an action that might have gone unremarked if the sermon had not become an instant and huge bestseller.[1] Two days after the trial commenced, mobs rioted and destroyed or damaged several Dissenting meeting houses. The evening of mayhem was only finally subdued when the queen's guard was taken off duty at Saint James's palace and sent out to suppress the rioters. While there were no further disturbances of that magnitude because of the presence of militia and guard patrols, tensions were still high through the rest of the trial.[2] Although Sacheverell was convicted, the sentence was ludicrously lenient, indicating the weakening power of the Whigs, who were subsequently overwhelmingly defeated in the general election forced on them that autumn by the strength of popular feeling.[3]

The trial and its consequences encapsulated many of the hottest political issues of the day, and certainly those that Sarah considered most important. Moreover, both of her sons were intimately involved: William as lord chancellor presided at the trial, and Spencer was one of the managers for the prosecution. Most significantly for the Cowper family, in the aftermath of the trial Queen Anne began replacing the Whigs in her ministry with Tories, beginning with her dismissal of Lord Treasurer Godolphin in August 1710. She was advised in her cabinet reshuffle by her new right-hand man Robert Harley, who, like Anne, initially hoped to retain William in what they aimed to construct as a nonparty government. Queen Anne had developed a very cordial relationship with William by this time, and Harley entertained hopes of keeping him and a few other moderate Whigs on board to counterbalance the high church Tories.[4] When Anne dissolved Parliament in September 1710, however, the remaining Whigs resigned, including, eventually, William.[5] The Whigs remained out of government until the succession of George I in 1714. Despite this loss of power and prestige, his recent elevation to the peerage meant that William was still active in politics as a leader of the opposition in the House of Lords. Moreover, he retained his friendship with the Queen, acting as an adviser and intermediary although admittedly relations cooled during touchy political moments, as for instance when he was opposing the government's negotiation of the Peace of Utrecht.[6]

As well as being the cause of her elder son's political fall, Henry Sacheverell encroached on Sarah's physical territory. Not only did the riots of March 1 take place in the vicinity of her and her son's houses (and even threatened William's home with burning),[7] but while waiting for the verdict, Sacheverell himself, accompanied by a mob, was feasted at the house of his counselor, Constantine Phipps, who was Sarah's neighbor. To make matters worse, after the meal Sacheverell went out to promenade in Gray's Inn Walks—one of Sarah's favorite places for a stroll. It was just across from her London house.[8]

From the start of the trial on February 27, Sarah wrote about it directly or indirectly for the next twenty-five days, except for a single entry. Her unprecedented and sustained interest in this single topic reflected the preoccupation of the nation as a whole with events in Westminster Hall. On the day the trial began, in tones of mockery, Sarah took up what was to become a recurring theme in her commentary—the inequity and hypocrisy of the doctrine of nonresistance:

> This Day begins the Tryal of Sacheverel who is become the Toast of Such Ladys as Strenuously adhere to the Doctrine of Non:Resistance. . . . Also a plentifull Mobb attended him with Acclamations. Stupid Creatures, for according to His Doctrines Shou'd the Queen ha' Sett Her Guards to Knock 'em on the Head, they must not have Resisted.

> The Notion of unlimited Submission runs Men to Declare for a Doctrine that puts it into the power of the Prince if it be in His Intention to Destroy the Subject. But Certainly Men may be Taught to abhorr Rebellion without being told that they have not so much as a Right to preserve the Society from Destruction Shou'd their Governers Prove so unnatural as to Attempt it. David thought it not unlawfull to Stand upon the Defensive; and is farr enough from being an Instance of Passive Obedience. Wee know by Experience the Assertors of this Doctrin if themselves had not Confess'd; that Men of very Passive Notions have Natures that can upon some Certain Occasions Rebel against Principle.[9]

When mob violence became a serious threat, Sarah took note of its contradiction to nonresistance doctrine, suspected sinister direction from higher up behind the mob's actions, and voiced her fears for national stability:

> A Tumultuous Mobb has gutted the Meeting House of Daniel Burgess the Non:Conformist, and Burnt the Materials att Lincolns Inn:Feilds. The Same they have Done in other like places. Now is not this Insulting the Queen, Her Laws, and Government with the Ministers therof. The Lords and Commons having thought fitt to Call this Incendiary to Account for His Seditious Preachment att the Citty Cathedral. Are these the Effects of Passive Obedience? Sure this is Resistance with a witness[?]. No Doubt the Rabble are well paid by His Party for their Pains. And wee may Conclude whoever Stirrs up the Mobb, wou'd Raise an Army to Oppose when they Can. God Save The Queen.[10]

Interestingly, she recorded the March 1 riots on the third, not the second of the month, as might be expected given their newsworthiness, and did not mention any threat to her son's house. It may be that he did not inform her of his own fears, though they were apparently what impelled him to go to Lord Sunderland to have the guard dispatched.[11]

The end of the trial brought its own disillusionments, first of all in the sentence:

> The Majority in the House of Lords having pronounc'd D[r] Boutefeu Guilty of High Crimes and Misdemeanors They post a Mild and gentle Sentence upon it. To suspend Him for Three year from Preaching; but permit him to Read Prayers, Marry, Christen and Bury So as his Clients may make the Profits of that Exceed most Livings in the Land . . . However glad am I 'tis Over; ffor it Grates Ones Ears, and Galls Ones Toung to Hear and Talk of Nothing Else.[12]

Sarah was not the only one disgusted at the sentence. The Whigs were shocked and then appalled to find they were forced to abandon plans for a far harsher sentence, which apparently would have included a lengthier preaching suspension and a ban on preferment during that period, plus a short term of imprisonment.[13] More personally, Sarah was disappointed and offended at the behavior of two of her friends, Thomas Manningham, the bishop of Chichester, and John Hough, bishop of Lichfield, who absented themselves from the final vote:

> I have lately been Scandaliz'd att the Conduct of two Bishops who went Daily to the Tryal of Sacheverel and after withdrew from giving their Vote wither to Acquit or Condemn Him; ffor which Cause they are Call'd Sneakers. I am not Causuist Sufficient to Determine whither the Reasons they give for so Doing are good, they Seem not So to mee.[14]

The emotional pull of this episode is indicated in that Sarah actually confronted Bishop Manningham about his presumed failure of nerves:

> 'Tis Said that in the Cathedral att Chichester Stands This Motto, Trust Men according to their Deeds—I Slily ask'd the B.[p] if it were So, and Fancy He understood my Meaning.[15]

The full extent of her disgust and disillusionment, and the shift in her outlook from mild contempt and derision to bitter acrimony, not just against the doctor but against his supporters, is clearest in her description of reading the account of the trial three months afterward:

> I have Skim'd over the Tryal of Sacheverel but dare not Read it thro', Such Horrour and Detestation Rises in me att those Miscreants who Cou'd Rake up Such Blasphemy to be Read in Publick Court and after that print it, which else had never been Seen or Known to Ten Thousand Such as I, who will know no more of it than what I catch'd by Casting my One Eie on the beginning Swiftly run Over the Margin till I saw the

End. Detestable Villains do all his Abettors Seem to mee, Nor Can I bear the Company of my Own Sex who take Part with them. Do not I hate them O Lord that Hate Thee; I hate them with perfect Hatred, I Count them mine Enemies.[16]

Furthermore, as with her judgments of people's writing on the basis of their moral character, Sarah thought the sins and vices of Sacheverell and his supporters infected the body politic as a whole. They reflected the corruption of the nation and the decline of religion; trends which (as her readings in history showed) invited God's judgment to fall upon England and destroy it.

The Tryal of this Man has given Occasion to lay Open the prodigious Wickedness of Mankind. How is this famous Protestant Church of ours Sunk and Declin'd in Her glory, and reduc'd into a very Narrow Compass? as a Beseig'd Citty hemm'd in on all Parts by the Impudence of Atheism, the Insolencies of Popery and the Turbulency of Faction; all Which do every Day Visibly and apace gain ground upon Her. There is almost an Universal Degeneracy and Impentence among Us. The Sinners of this Age are grown Impudent and appear with a Whores forehead forsaken of all Modesty; turning the Word of God it Self, and the most Serious Manners of Religion into Raillery. Such Clamorous Sins are almost Come to be the Garb and Fashion, and to be accounted the Witt and Gallantry of these Times!

And Shall not God Visit for those Things and be Aveng'd on Such a Nation as This? . . . [17]

Sarah recognized in herself increasingly fervent enmity and misanthropy and her unwilling gravitation toward the Whigs, reflecting on the situation in tones that emphasize her age and experience in political observation:

I have Liv'd to See Changes of Faction and Partys, yet never felt so Bitter Zeal against any, as These 'Cheverel Miscreants; who make me that was a Staunch Church:Woma^n become one of the Staggering Party; and to me it seems that our first Motion Shou'd now be to Distrust the World in general, and even to have a Bad Opinion of it.[18]

Furthermore, the trial and the increasingly high-flying tone of the Tories in general drove her away from her natural affinity for the party. Sarah's distancing from the Tories provides a lay, female, nonparticipant parallel to the phenomenon historians have noted occurring among some of her friends in the episcopacy. Some of the bishops who under different circumstances would have been able to adhere to a nonpartisan middle ground, or who were actually "natural" Tories, were driven by the extremes of high church sentiment into association with the Whigs.[19]

An important cause of Sarah's move away from a natural affinity with and defense of the established church and the party most associated with that stance was her deepening anticlericalism. This increasingly prevalent sentiment occasioned some intensely virulent attacks on the profession as a whole, the majority of whom were high church. In preaching the Gospel but not living according to it, or worse yet, not even preaching the Gospel but turning their calling to political ends, churchmen were the worst possible example of the disparity between words and deeds on which Sarah based her opinions of men and books:

> All our Dissentions are owing to the Vileness of persons in the Sacred Ministry' none of the present Schisms Cou'd have Crept in but by their Negligence. The Pretences made by the preisthood from Time to Time that the Church was in Danger, is only a Trick to make the Laiety passionate for that of which they themselves have been Negligent. The practise of piety is the only Method to Support the highest of all Honours; that of A Preist who Lives and Acts according to His Charecter.[20]

In this context, Doctor Sacheverell personified the worst traits of the clergy: their arrogance, search for power, hypocrisy in not living or even preaching according to Christian tenets, instead employing a political, zealous, intolerant, violent, seditious rhetoric that ruined rather than improved their parishioners.[21] Furthermore, Sarah made a direct connection between the clergy's hypocritical, manipulative preaching of nonresistance and the church in danger, and what she decided was their treasonable Jacobite agenda:

> Sacheverel's High: Church:, has brought me from Low: Church, to be of No Church; Except the Christian. I ha' been amaz'd to think what people are Doing; and to sattisfy my Wonder was Inquisitive about it, untill I mett with this Clear Account. Tho' Loyalty and Church is the pretence, Inherent Birth:Right is the Secret Sense. And Restauration is the Consequence.[22]

Because of their particularly egregious sins, the clergy bore the largest part of the blame in Sarah's mind for the judgement that was likely to fall upon the English:

> When They who are the Guides of Souls have by their Ill:Conduct brought Matters to that pass that people are become almost Indifferent

whither they have any Religion or Not, What Can the End of these Things be; But that The Kingdom of God will be taken from Us, and given to a Nation that Will Bring forth the Fruits of It.[23]

Clerics were responsible as well as for the form the punishment was likely to take, which was the subjection of England to the government of (and consequently persecution by) papists—James the Pretender specifically—and through them to be dominated by France.

This distaste for members of the priesthood is a remarkable alteration of opinion for Sarah, who after all had based her domestic and social identity on the character of a pious churchwoman. It is ironic that a woman who had recurring arguments with her husband in which she defended the clergy of the Church of England against his attacks should end up (like many of her contemporaries)[24] holding them as a group in such disesteem. It is just as well Sir William died before the Sacheverell affair began, as Sarah would have been placed in the intolerable position of either having to agree with her husband or defend what she considered by and large a reprehensible company of men.

There is probably a generational and perhaps a social element to her feelings about the clergy. Many of her favorite churchmen had been pillars of the establishment in earlier decades. Isaac Barrow and John Wilkins had died in the 1670s, John Tillotson and Edward Stillingfleet in the 1690s, and Simon Patrick in 1707. Of those churchmen who were still living with whom she most often associated, John Sharp had voted in favor of Sacheverell, Thomas Manningham and John Hough had avoided voting at all, and though Gilbert Burnet was a staunch defender of many of her political principles, and of course had voted against Sacheverell, Sarah did not think much of his preaching or his demeanor in general. So many of the members of the profession whom she most admired and from whose work she had adopted both theological and political prescription were no longer present to counterbalance high church excesses. Nor could they provide leadership to obstruct high churchmen, which is the second point: Aside from Isaac Barrow, these men, though in the minority in their low church or moderate views, were all bishops. If largely a matter of principle and temperament, Sarah's gravitation toward them may also have had to do with their high status in the ecclesiastical and social hierarchy. At any rate, they certainly contrasted with the humble standing and high church allegiance of most of the priesthood.

The Sacheverell trial and its repercussions touched on the contentious questions of the validity of the Revolution settlement, the place and responsibilities of rulers and ruled, the proper relationship of church and state (specifically the role of the clergy and the purpose of their pulpit), and the nature of the popish threat. These were the political issues upon which Sarah continued to focus in the remainder of her diary, throughout the fall of the Whigs, the Tory administration, and the accession of George I (1714) and Whig ascendancy thereafter. Accordingly, her observations in this period ran to attacks on hereditary right and passive obedience, fears for the Protestant succession, and corresponding alarms about the revivification of popery. They were not, however, reflections that ran very far into the realm of theory. Rather, they were personal and practical, based on assumed connections between political doctrine and their implications for real events, drawn from previous experience. As did many other English citizens who had lived through the reign of James II (1685–1688), Sarah thought about hereditary right, nonresistance, and Catholicism in terms of what had already happened, which gave real impetus, urgency, and application to prognostications about the potential implementation of these ideas.

Moreover, in the figure of Robert Harley, the lord treasurer, Sarah had a focal point for expressing her distaste of the Tory government. If in Sacheverell she saw the embodiment of the excesses of the high-flying Tory clergy, Harley was his counterpart in secular government, a minister who epitomized her favorite themes of hypocritical, place-seeking, deceitful political rulers. She collected whatever unflattering descriptions she could find of Harley and applied appropriate discussions of his vices, as in this commentary early in his ministry:

> Heaps upon Heaps of Honor and profit is Laid on This Meritorious Favorite. The Q: has made Him Lord Treasurer. Never did Man Bear a more general Charecter for Hypocrisy and Artifice than He—All Insincerity is mean in it Self having Falshood at the Bottom. Dissimulation Consists in a Vain Shew of What wee are Not; and Infinite litle Crafts, and Acts of Deceit, which Men practise upon one another in their Ordinary Conversation and Intercourse, which Is Gross Iniquity.[25]

The immediate linkage of the succession and its effect on individuals is evident in Sarah's ruminations on which was worse, living amidst atheism or popery. In one case she decided the present state of affairs was worse:

I Cannot Think Him [the Pretender] to have a Divine Right to bring Popery and Slavery hither; yet if it must be So, as Things go now it will Seem
to me No great Matter; ffor, the first is preferable to Atheism and Infidelity which Spreads here apac[e] and the later is good enough for People
who pull it on Themselves.[26]

Two years later, she was more worried about the presumed inevitability
of persecution of Protestants under a Catholic monarch:

Others say In Favor of the Pretender, that wee had better have a papist
than an Atheist (meaning Hanover) to Rule over us. But I say No. ffor an
Atheist may Do me no hurt; but a papist may Think Himself Bound to
Conscience to Cutt my Throat if I will not Conform to His Opinion.[27]

The same fear of aggressive Catholicism informed her observations when
the Tories introduced the Schism Act in 1714, a bill designed to elimi-
nate Dissenting academies by requiring schoolmasters to declare conformity and obtain a license from the bishop of the diocese in order to
teach. She raised arguments against the bill that exemplify the low
church position and conflicting fears of Dissent on the one hand and
popery on the other, concerns that forced Anglicans to make decisions
based on which was perceived to be the lesser of the two evils. At this
time, in the last days of Queen Anne and the Tory government, Sarah
echoed Whig sentiments that popery was the far greater threat, and this
bill, as well as being extraordinarily mean-spirited, was evidence of suspiciously tolerant regard to the papists and failed to recognize the common interest of all Protestants in England.

Our Senators are Now very Busy to Prevent The Growth of Schism. The
Design is to Suppress all Schools and Academies kept (popish Seminaries
Excepted) by Protestant Dissenters: which will be a litle too Severe; Because 'tis a Breaking in upon the Toleration, which Her Majesty has Assured Shall be Inviolably maintain'd as A Principle of Natural Justice. Besides, This Suppression of Their Schools is a degree of Persecution; and is
Contrary to the Common Rules of Charity.

   Is This a Time to weaken The Protestant Interest in England and
make The Dissenters Uneasy? Are wee Sure that This Establishment will
last alwaies, and that The Church will never want the Assistance of the
Dissenters again as She did att The Revolution? Is not the Malice of our
Common Enemies The Papists as great as ever? Do not the French Insult
us with their pompous Accounts of the good Qualitys of The Chevalier
and of the Respect that is paid Him Abroad and Shall wee Strengthen

him at Home? For if Protestants are Set against Protestants; His Cause is Strengthned by It.[28]

Clearly, the Hanoverian succession was of serious concern to Sarah and the continued threats to it alarmed her. But even after George's accession in August 1714 and the reappointment of her son William as lord chancellor in October, Sarah was still worried about political stability, an alarm exacerbated by the election riots and then the rebellion in 1715. After the nationwide Jacobite riots from May to July, and the news arriving in London of the Pretender's plan to land in England, Sarah concluded future likelihoods under Jacobite rule from immediate events:

> Any Body may See what the Nation is to Expect in case the pretender Should be Enabled to go on with his invasion now. The barbarous practises of those English Mobs who have appeared in so many parts of the nation for him are enough to give us a Speciment of what wee are to expect from them when joined by French and Irish papists whose principles it is to destroy all Protestants as well as to demolish all places of worship.[29]

There is evidence of her continuing disenchantment with and dislike of the clergy as a group in her charging them specifically with the blame for the popular disturbances:

> It is deplorable to see human kind so infatuated, but we may impute it to be infused by those profligate high priests whose doctrines have corrupted the people and made them mad.[30]

Associating the high-flying clergy with the Jesuits in terms of their fanaticism and sedition, Sarah explicitly reflected on her changed view of churchmen:

> When a Jesuit was preaching his seditious sermon at Rouen against the Duke Regent, a gentlewoman rose up and told him Father, I came hither to hear the word of God and not your Fooleries. And then she went out. I have been ready to do the same when I could hear our high church preists prate on what they had nothing to do with. Time was, none paid more reverence to the clergy than myself, but now have the generality in huge contempt, as perceiving they have done much mischeif in this nation.[31]

Sarah kept close track of the progress of the 1715 rebellion and the trials, sentences, and executions of its leaders. On her scale of moral offenses, in this rebellion the Jacobite Tories actually outdid the Catholics, since in the latter case attempting to bring James the Pretender to the throne was entirely consistent with their principled exercise of their religion (however bigoted that might be); while in the former, Protestants were betraying their religion as well as the monarch to whom they had sworn allegiance.

> I have compassion for the popish rebels, I think their conspiracys and treasons to be more excusable than those of the members of our own communion who have joined with them. For not only their ignorance, and their erroneous consciences but their apparent interests in this world, as well as their hopes of merit and salvation, call them to the setting up their own creature to bring in their own church; while their aiders and abettors call'd Protestants are in a more deplorable condition of guilt and shame; and labour under the wickedness and madness of common parricide and self-destruction.[32]

Nonetheless, Sarah had doubts about the sufficiency of the government's punishment of the rebels. In the course of advocating severe treatment of the "perjurers" (breakers of their oaths of allegiance to the king), remarkably enough, she echoed the preference she had declared fifteen years previously for the order associated with the Tory party over the "licentious liberty" of the Whigs:

> To me it seems the Whig party manage their affairs so ill that little good is to be expected from such conduct. I have long thought the tories more fit to govern, such is the steadiness to their friends and cause.[33]

It is likely that in this instance, as perhaps previously, she was thinking of the moderate, rather than the extreme wing of the Tory party. Not all Tories were Jacobites, of course, though they were often painted as such by the Whigs. If she had lived longer, Sarah might very well have ended up most sympathetic to the Hanoverian Tories, though as ever, not labeling herself with a party name.

The turbulent politics of this period had repercussions for Sarah's practice of piety as well. Especially on government-appointed holy days, such as November 5 (celebrating the discovery of the Gunpowder Plot), January 31 (Charles I's "martyrdom"), and May 29 (the restoration of Charles II), the visible act of going to church signified the acceptance and countenancing of state ideology—a form of political participation in the shaping of the nation's history and its meaning and perhaps even a civic duty. Although she explicitly distinguished between state and church-appointed holy days, and expressed some doubts even early on in the diary about the validity of such feasts and fasts,[34] Sarah also noted that she formally observed those appointed days, expressing allegiance to the state "with loyal zeal."[35] From 1710, however, she became increasingly reluctant to attend services, not least because of her mounting physical infirmities, but also because of the Sacheverell trial. Sarah was disgusted by the clerical use of the pulpit to preach Tory doctrine. By politicizing their sermons, Sarah felt the clergy were impeding her efforts at personal salvation, behaving improperly before God, and, moreover, twisting the statement of political affiliation and loyalty to the state that she made in attending church into ideological directions she was unwilling to countenance. In turning the church into a Tory political space, high-flying churchmen were affecting Sarah's reputation when she appeared there, especially since she saw in their sermons a direct line to Jacobitism, a treasonous and personally dangerous political stance with which she entirely refused to be affiliated. It was thus this new climate that Sarah blamed for her distancing herself from the Church of England. This distancing included the general practice of going to church, which she confessed to having thought to abandon, but met with biblical prescription otherwise:

> I have been under a Temptation to Neglect going to Church Especially att this Time when too many preachers meddle with Matters beside their Function, and Omit Teaching the Doctrines of Faith and Holy Life. Besides my Hearing fails me so as I cannot give due attention if the Sermon be good and profitable. Wherfore methought it might be more Usefull to Read the Words of Such Men as we have all Reason to think Sincere Beleivers and Practisers of what they Taught. Dean Tillotson, D[r] Barrow and Such like. But 'tis Observable the very Day I did so It was my Chance to meet with this Scripture. Not forsakeing the Assembling of our Selves togather as the Manner of Some is. Also Davids Zeal to Serve God in the in the Temple.[36]

But being reproved, as she thought, by scriptural prescription from neglecting churchgoing altogether, she began to note starting in November 1710 on the occasion of Gunpowder Plot day, "I leave off to Observe State Fasts and Festivals—While I thought the Directors were in Earnest I did Use to Attend Them. But now the Preachers So Rant; And their Collects So Cant, as Damps my Devotion att Such Assemblies, so much do they Seem to be in Jest."[37] She echoed this sentiment on many of the succeeding state holy days, repeating her condemnation of them as insincere, hypocritical, or perilously jesting with what should be holy purposes.[38] So that while she still attended church on regular holy days, she boycotted days associated with the government and its policies, protesting the politicization of the pulpit and refusing to countenance the preaching of Tory ideology by her public appearance at such events.

Moreover, she cited the behavior of the congregation as another reason for disaffection with church attendance on national feast days. Perhaps these are the same women who were so in evidence as Sacheverell supporters during the trial:

> On the 29:[th] of May the Happy Restauration, I went to the Queens Chappel; having not been there Since Ash Wednesday was two year; I had a Mind to See if at Court they behav'd themselves better on Festival than Fasts. But I find it much What on both Occasions. The Men Ogle and Cring to the Ladys. ffor which they return Smiles and Drop Curtesies the whole Time of Divine Worship. Indeed so unsuitable is Such Behavior to the Dread Majesty before whom wee are, that I purpose never to Appear there more.[39]

Even her attendance at regular Sunday services became problematic in 1713 when ironically, Henry Sacheverell, whom she held personally responsible for the high Tory flavor of the church and the incitement of popular disturbances, eventually was rewarded with the rectory of Saint Andrew's, Holborn, Sarah's home parish. It is unclear how she dealt with this intrusion into her home territory by a man she had vowed never to hear, since she had declared:

> But unless He wou'd hold forth att a Bear:Garden, or Punch's Theatre I shou'd not give way to Curiosity So much as to hear him; which no Doubt but many will in the place Appointed for Worship of The Great God. Such preists and their Doctrins may make us Cry out Either this is not the Gospel which wee Read, and that Christian Religion which wee profess, Or wee are No Christians.[40]

By 1714 Sarah still regularly attended monthly Communion and resolved to do so while she was still physically able, but she lamented that her deafness prevented her from going every Sunday, since she could not hear the sermon.[41] Instead, on Sundays, she often copied into her diary selections from published sermons. By this time, she was physically quite debilitated, and making the effort to receive the Sacrament may have been the most she could manage.[42] The question remains, however, whether she received the Sacrament at Saint Andrew's or went elsewhere. References to what was preached at her home parish specify that she obtained her information indirectly. For example, when (as usual by then) in 1715 she boycotted the service celebrating the Restoration (although it was on a Sunday), she said:

> It is Said that 'Cheverel being out of Town his Curate preach'd on this Text. And King David sent to Zadock and to Abiather the preists saying; Speak unto the Elders of Judah why are ye the last to Bring the King Back to His House? No doubt The Parson meant to apply it to King James The Third. I was told 'tis a Threadbare Text among the High:Church priests.[43]

Suggestively, she commented on one Sunday in 1715,

> The Preaching as it is Call'd of our populer Men is now Come to that Degree of Offence that in many Places, persons of Sense and Seriousness Stay att Home out of Piety and Absent themselves for Fear of Hearing Men Preach their own Passions and Indignation and Resentment under their Disappointed Expectations; which is Call'd by too many preaching the Gospel and Delivering Messages from Heaven. Yet wee have Some Still among Us of whom the World is not Worthy. But Alas! I am Deaf and Cannot Hear Them.[44]

It may be, then, that Sarah sought out a church presided over by one of the more moderate clergymen for her monthly duty of attending the Eucharist.

Sarah's inclination to benevolent giving suffered as well in these years. In 1711, assessing her total charitable activity since her widowhood, she concluded that she had spent over £150 in "mistaken bounty and charity" and in the severe words of sermons on the subject, justified decreasing her donations and judging potential recipients harshly:

> But I now purpose to Slacken my Hand with Discretion; Gather up the Fragments that Nothing be Lost. A Direction how to Mannage our Substance to the Best Advantage; and So to Approve our Selves Charitable and Kind as att the Same time not to be profuse and Indiscreet. All Reserving for the Future is not unlawfull; Charity is very Consistent with Frugality. God will make a Difference between the Vertue, and the Specious Extream beyond it: between the Liberal and the Lavish Man—
>
> Wee Shou'd generally bestow our Charity on Such as are least in a Condition of Sustaining Themselves; as Old Age, Maim'd Limbs, the Blind, Long Sickness, and the Calamitys which Visibly Come from the Hand of God. But as for them, who pride or profusion, Sloth or Vice, have reduced; They who Continue poor, only because they will not take any Truble to be Otherwise; The Laws of God have Not Commanded the Same Compassion for Such, who Choose the Shame, but Ease, of That,

before an Honest and Laborious Livelyhood. To Such, the best and truest Charity is, What Solomon has Prescrib'd; A Scourg for the Sluggard, and a Rod for the Fools Back.[45]

In one subsequent case at least, her resolve seems to have translated into action, even toward kin, as it seems she refused to help two of Sir William's cousins on the grounds that their poverty was self-inflicted:

Two yong Women, whose Mother left them fourteen Pound a year for Life, and 200.[l] a Peice in Mony Beside She brought them Up to make Monto's [manteaus]; yet now are become Poor thro' their own Folly; and Ask Mee to Releive their Wants. But I am taught Due Care Shou'd be taken to Enquire out the proper Objects of our Alms. Be they Good or Bad, Friends or Foes; If their Needs be Urgent wee must treat 'em Kindly. Yet we must Distinguish in the Dispensation of our Charity. To all near Relations, Where Nothing of Barr is put in against it: and the Better and More Vertuous they are, the more Free we Shou'd be to 'em But all that are unavoidably poor not self procured must Share in our Alms: if Otherwise wee are not Bound to give them Bread.[46]

Moreover, at the end of that year, Sarah stopped recording her quarterly donations, though she hastened to add that she was not ceasing to be charitable: "The Quarter past, I leave off to Set down here, what I Give in Charity. But forget not what Solomon Saith He that giveth to the Poor, lendeth to The Lord."[47]

After her discouraging experience with donating to the SPG in 1708, she ceased contributions to missionary societies as well. When the next obvious opportunity arose, she put off the solicitor, probably indefinitely:

In the Hands of a Bishop I did formerly Deposit a 100.[l] for propagation of the Gospel. . . Now Comes the Reverend Mr Shute to Solicite mee for Contribution to Carry on the Work of Conversion att Malabar in the East:Indies. He left two Books to Inform mee of the Undertaking; But they rather make it Hopeless, by Setting forth the Strife and Tricks of the Popish Missionaries, and Vicious Living of those Christians already among Them. And 'tis to be fear'd the Example of Protestant Christians in Our Days will give as litle success to the Attempt. So I Desir'd Time to Consider His proposal.[48]

Here, her lack of interest may have something to do with social considerations as well as with worries about the mission's efficacy. Previously her donations had been large enough to garner the attention of and favors from the top of the clerical hierarchy. This solicitation was from Mr. Shute, an active but not high-ranking member of the SPG, which Sarah may have viewed as a social slight, not at all in keeping with the returns due her for her previous scale of benevolence.

In contrast, while it is unclear whether she actually gave any more money, Sarah seems to have been satisfied with the purposes and efficacy of the charity schools, since she mentioned a sermon she heard Bishop Dawes preach on behalf of Saint Giles's school and despite casting aspersions on his sincerity, cited his advice to be prudent and regular in giving, presumably to institutions and not random individuals.[49] More important, in early 1712 she heard through her son of a plan to found a charity school in Hertford and, noting the need for such places to train faithful, deferential servants, announced her intention to subscribe.[50] In any case, Sarah does not seem to have made any other large gifts to charity, though in announcing her intention to do so at Hertford, there is at least the indication that in the proper circumstances, where she could expect the money to be well spent, she might have continued to donate to schools. The following year, though, she commented on her increasing reluctance to give to institutions: "The Air is Cold as Charity; which I must own as to The Publick grows Chill in mee; tho' I Hope 'twill not Decay as to Private Objects who are worthy of It."[51]

In 1712 Sarah contemplated her birthday from the perspective of having achieved full rationality. She may have been echoing Cicero's *On Old Age*, a work reprinted during this period, which lauded "the tranquil and serene old age of a life spent quietly amid pure and refining pursuits,"[52] though in her observation there is an ironic tone not present in Cicero's essay: "My Birth:Day. 68. I am arriv'd at a state of tranquility which few people envy. I mean that of an old woman. . . . There are few who can grow old with a good grace, and enjoy a pleasing indolent old age, in which passion is subdu'd, and reason exalted."[53]

But by that time, Sarah was also apparently beginning to experience a degree of isolation that she had worried about in her fifties and that seemed to be coming true in her seventies. She became more and more a living stereotype, and one that presumed an inability to interact well in society. Concrete evidence of the social isolation of very old ladies, and Sarah's keen sense of injury on this count, can be seen in her experience of rejection, even from her own family:

> This day Lord C[owper] and Lady dine with D[uke] Roxborough. The Dutchess courteously invited mee, but I forbear to go, saying I am too old

to appear in such company from home; which was readily assented to. Love to be conceal'd and litle esteem'd be content to want praise, and never troubl'd when slighted ffor thou canst not undervalue thy self, and if thou thinks't so meanly as there is reason, no contempt will seem unreasonable and therfore it will be very tollerable. Be ever unconcern'd, and secure a good name by living vertuously and humbly.[54]

In this case, Sarah recognized and acceded in her social disability, but was nonetheless hurt when her relatives accepted her offer of self-isolation. She immediately equated this assent with contempt, even though she had initiated the suggestion herself. She recognized some of the reasons why her company might not be welcome, due to her age, but found it painful nonetheless to experience rejection because of membership in a social category that she even acknowledged as legitimate.

By this time too, she was quite straightforward about her less laudable reading:

We are now over:Stock'd with Books Concerning the Managment of State Affairs. But I Eschew to Read long Laborious Nothings, with which Some get rid of a Tedious Quantity of their Time. The pamphlets, Libels, and Ballads are Diverting enough.[55]

The Cheif Amusment of Life to mee is to go Abroad in my Chariot and take the Air, and Read printed papers att Home; ffor in Company the Subject Matter which these Times Afford is often Tiresome to mee.[56]

Perhaps the "subject matter" was particularly distasteful now that her son was out of power, but in the single passage where she described her typical schedule, as in earlier years both reading current events and visiting take up significant portions of her day:

My Journal. At Six, Up I Rose, put on my Cloaths, and then Drink a Dish of Bohe:[mian] Tea. My Employment till Eight is what it Ought to be. Then I Eat a Crust of Bread and Butter. Then I Comb my Head, Wash my Face and Hands, without Attendance to do any thing for me which I Can Do my Self. Then Read the Spectator and Scribble till Twelve. Then ffinish to Dress, and Dine at One, upon Two Dish's. If Alone I take a Nap after it. Then Reckon with the Cook and pay Her Bill, She is in Love and grown Careless. From four to Seven, jogg Abroad in the Coach, for Air, and Excercise; Or to Enter Some House where I find the Door Open to Let Me In. At Eight I Eat my Scrap, Drink half a Pint of Wine, Then Do my Duty. And So to Bed at Nine.[57]

The theme of immortality of the soul resurfaced frequently in these years, perhaps because of increasing age, but also because occasions arose for considering the question from her devotional life and from what appeared in the literary periodicals she was reading. Some of the material she marshaled in defense of her position she would have run across in the course of her devotions, as they followed the church calendar. For instance, the issue was taken up in commentary on the appointed Scripture for Sundays, saints' days and other holy days, as in George Stanhope's explanation of the chapters of Acts of the Apostles relevant to Saint Stephen's day:

> Lord Jesus Receive my Spirit [Acts 7:59]. An Act of Faith, which dos Evidently Imply a firm Belief; That his Soul was a Substance Distinct from his Body. That it Shou'd not Die with, but Continue to Exist when Separated from the Body. That the Same Jesus whom he had acknowledged to be very Man, is likewise very God: One able to Hear and Grant this prayer, and to preserve the Souls Commended to His protection and Care; And That the Spirits Received by Him, are in a State of Safety and Happiness.[58]

Her lengthiest assertion of immortality filled the entries for three successive days in her diary, and was drawn from an essay in *The Spectator* that had appeared ten days previously:

> The proofs for [the immortality of the soul] are Drawn from its passions and Sentiments; Its Love of Existence, its Horrour of Annihilation, and its Hopes of Immortality; with that Secret Satisfaction which it finds in the practice of Virtue, and that Uneasiness which falls upon it upon the Commission of Vice; From the Nature of The Supreme Being; whose Justice, Goodness, and Wisdom, and Veracity, are all Concerned in this Great Point.
>
> But among those and other excellent Arguments for the Immortality of the Soul, there is One Drawn from the Perpetual Progress of the Soul to its perfection without a possibility of ever Arriving at it. How Can it Enter into the Thoughts of Man, that the Soul which is Capable of Such Immense Perfections, and of Receiving New Improvements to all Eternity, Shall fall away into Nothing, almost as Soon as it is Created? . . . Would an Infinite Wise Being make of Such a glorious production of Such Abortive Intelligences, Such Short:Liv'd Reasonable Beings?[59]

While a good deal of *The Spectator* had a distinctly secular tone in its observation of society and its foibles, the Saturday editions (most often written by Joseph Addison) regularly treated a moral subject. The concern of this periodical with theology, and Sarah's use of it as a source for articulating her own position, indicate the level to which religion and this sort of lay piety infused polite society. Sarah even found useful material in contemporary drama. Despite claiming not to read plays, on one occasion she asserted the immortality of the soul by using a speech from Addison's tragedy *Cato*:

> It must be So—Plato Thou Reasonest Well! Else whence this pleasing Hope, This fond Desire, this longing after Immortality. Or Whence this Secret Dread and inward Horrour of ffalling into Naught? Why Shrinks the Soul Back on Her Self and Startles at Destruction? 'Tis the Divinity that stirs within Us, 'Tis Heaven it Self that points out an Hereafter and Intimates Eternity to Man.[60]

This passage also illustrates the popularity of the classical world in early modern literature; contemporary authors both lay and clerical frequently drew on the pagan philosophers to prove the point that the existence of a soul and an afterlife was a given not just in revelation but in "natural religion." It was the logical conclusion of rational thought even outside the Christian framework.

Another diary entry on the topic displays again the widespread reliance on classical models but is especially interesting in that it comes not from moral essays or explicitly theological works but from a highly partisan Whig broadsheet, *The Medley*, much of which is a vitriolic attack on the Tories and in particular on their mouthpiece, *The Examiner*. The original context of this passage was to assert Cicero's moral uprightness and thus his entitlement to demand of the Roman priesthood whether they were going to allow sedition to be cloaked with a pose of religious zeal—the current charge against the Tories. *The Medley* used the speech, then, to contrast the virtue and orthodoxy of even pagans with the low standards of the Tories as well as to accuse them of sedition under hypocritical religious cover. The original diatribe begins:

> I will not have any little ignorant hot headed clergymen . . . imagine that the Roman Orator was a Deist, or a Latitudinarian, or a Socinian; his character is sufficiently established as to his religion: and everybody knows his opinion of the immortality of the soul which is denied.

But Sarah refocused the passage, not eliminating entirely the swipe at the high church, but emphasizing the exemplary reply Cicero furnished to the challenge of Henry Dodwell and others of his ilk:

> The Opinion of the Immortality of the Soul which is Denied by the Pillar
> of the High Church Mr. Dodwell is profess'd by Cicero who Says; If in
> this I Err; That I Think the Souls of Men Immortal I Err with pleasure
> Nor will ever whilst I Live be forced out of an Opinion with which I am
> So much Delighted. So that it may be Said of Him he was a better Chris-
> tian, than Some of our High Churchmen who Broach Such Doctrine as
> the Mortality of the Soul.[61]

This particular case of borrowing shows not just the variety of sources
from which Sarah set out her position, but again, the extent to which
belief in the soul's immortality was used a measure of basic moral character and religious feeling.

By 1713 her complaints not only of physical discomfort, but mental
stultification increased in their frequency and vehemence. As she had
feared and predicted, extreme old age rendered her unfit for the medita-
tive life that was supposed to dignify her later years:

> The same insipid life. To mee the days are come, when I may say I have
> no pleasure in them. My facultys are broken by the infirmitys of age,
> fflatt and dull, irksome and tedious, apt to nothing but complaint under
> the weight of one evil or another that befalls mee. The powers of soul and
> body are in a languishing condition unfit for the offices of piety, or the
> acknowledgment of God's benefits which are so slipt out of mind as to
> have but a dull perception of them.[62]

The only redeeming feature of her own increasing infirmity was that it
helped to reinforce her increasingly appreciative view of her eldest son.
Those few complaints she did make were primarily directed at Spencer,
mostly on the old theme of infrequent visits.[63] She stopped her regular
summer visits to Hertford in 1713, ostensibly (as she told her friends)
because she disliked Hertford during an election, because she was
ashamed to bring her misbehaving servants into another household, and
because her advancing blindness and deafness kept her from being entertained. That she was not entirely pleased with her family, perhaps especially Spencer, can be seen by her closing statement in that entry: "But
the most ponderous reasons prudence bids me keep to myself."[64]

In contrast, for emotional and financial reasons, she was alarmed by
William's bouts of illness, as they could leave her bereft in her old age:

> Some While ago, when my Son was Seiz'd with a Fitt of the Strangury;
> 'tis not to be imagin'd what a Dread it Cast mee in, least He Shou'd Dy
> before me. . . . The Parting with a Beloved Son is at any Time an Afflic-

tion; But when they have attain'd prosperity, then it adds weight, by the Loss of Comfort and Assistance to a Solitary Mother. Such are as the Arrows in the Hand of the Giant; they Defend an Aged parent, and Enable 'em to Bear up against Adversity, by becoming the Stay and Support of Her Age and Infirmitys.[65]

The theme begun here, of William as a comforter and an assist as she becomes more and more infirm, recurs occasionally in the last two volumes.[66] It may be too that William actually became more solicitous, perhaps moved by the visible decline of Sarah's health and abilities. Certainly soon after he resigned as lord chancellor, he sent Sarah a letter indirectly assuring her of her continued financial stability, urging her not to hesitate to send for her annuity payment, if she needed it sooner than he delivered it. Then in 1712 William increased her annuity by £30 per year.[67] An entry in her last volume epitomizes Sarah's habits of placing individual examples of conduct into the context of generalizing, moralizing rhetorical structures. In this case, she made her standard distinction between the good behavior of her elder son and the bad behavior of her younger son in the context of a discourse on the pain sons can bring to their mothers and the obligations of children in their parents' old age:

> A Foolish, that is a Vicious Son, is a Heavyness to his Mother; The Miscarriages of a Child being apt most Tenderly to Affect the Mother. Good Children are the Best Comforts at Such a Time as we most Stand in need of Comfort, the Time of Sickness and Old Age; Then there is no such External Comfort as Good and Dutyfull Children. They will be the Light of our Eies, and the Cordial of our fainting Spirits; and will Recompense all our former Care of Them, by their present Care of Us. And when wee are Decaying and Withering away, we Shall have the pleasure to See our Selves fflourishing again in our Children. This, I have Reason to Hope for from my Eldest Son, who now is very Good to me.[68]

In the last year that Sarah kept a diary (1715–1716), her handwriting visibly degenerated, and her entries grew shorter and shorter. Taking stock on her birthday in 1716, she wrote:

> I am now 72 years of Age, very Crazie and Infirm, Lame with Rhumatick Pains in my Thighs. . . . Also my Hands Shake with the Palsey, I am Dull of Hearing, Dim of Sight, and What Is Worse a Cough Disturbs me Night and Day; So as Life it Self No Relish dos Afford.[69]

Her health became progressively worse, and in August of 1716, Mary and William both pressed her to come to Cole Green to try to improve.

By this time, she frequently referred to William as "my dear son," and in general was pleased and grateful for his attention. Even more interestingly, in noting that Mary had written to invite her to Cole Green, she said:

> the kindness of my Dear Son and His Lady does Cheer my Spirits. I so little Expected it from Her who in sixteen Months made me but One Visit, that I Thought She had laid by all Regard for mee. It may be my not Complaining of it to any One, has Oblidg'd Her to Shew me more Respect and Kindness in Word and Deed.[70]

What is remarkable in this passage is not that Mary had stopped visiting her (which was hardly surprising, since Mary was at this time lady-in-waiting to Princess Caroline while William lived in Hertford, so she was either in attendance on the princess or in the country seeing her children and husband), but that Sarah's response is so comparatively mild: this is the first mention of such a lack of visits. It may be that Mary was writing fairly regularly; but in any case, this is a far cry from her attitude toward such lack of visits either early in the diary, or from her second son.

After much encouragement, she went to Cole Green in August 1716. Unable to move around much, with a persistent cough, breathlessness, and rheumatism, she wrote less and less, primarily briefly mentioning the comings and goings of William and Mary to Hampton Court. It is clear she expected to die momentarily: First, she proposed to William and Mary that she live the rest of her (presumably short) life at Cole Green, giving up her house in London, on which the lease was due to run out, and thus avoiding the need to supervise servants. The suggestion indicates the extent of her infirmity and emotional and physical dependence by this time. "To which she [Mary] gently Reply'd, She Desired a Day or two to Consider of It."[71] This is a recounting of the episode altogether unlike her depiction of her family when she was in her fifties and sixties; and an acceptance of Mary's hesitation, which would earlier have displeased her—though earlier, she would not have been so ill and dependent, either. The next day, William dissuaded her from the idea by pointing out how much less pleasant, and how lonely, Cole Green would be in the winter. The same episode is documented in a letter from William to Mary, in which it is possible to see the pity that by now William felt for his mother in her advanced age and infirmity, and also a closer approximation of the reaction to Sarah's proposal and a reaffirmation that Sarah by this time no longer was so quick to take offense, either in her diary or outwardly:

> I was this afternoon to take the air with my poor Mother, who I think visibly declines. . . . She expresses herself of you with great respect and kindness, so that nothing has been taken ill; and the affair you apprehend not touch'd on. All is well.[72]

Sarah's last memorandum regarding Spencer, however, indicates both her expectation of imminent death and her continuing estrangement from that branch of the family. She recounted the difficulty with which she was transported to Hertford Castle to "take Farewel For Ever," and that "My Dear Son was so kind as to Bear me Company Thither, But I Receiv'd no Sattisfaction There."[73]

The difference between the will Sarah wrote in 1702, after the severe illness in which she lost sight in one eye, and the will she wrote in 1716, thinking she would die soon, is a final encapsulation of the change in her outlook toward her elder son. While the text of the 1702 will does not survive, Sarah described its contents in her diary, noting it "Consists mostly of restoring gifts I formerly receiv'd from my ffriends. ffor that reason my two Sons are not Named because they never gave me any thing."[74] The brief will of 1716 left everything to "my Loving Son William Lord Cowper whom I do make Sole Executor" and asked him to give each member of Spencer's family ten pounds to buy mourning.[75]

For Sarah, the role of mother had allowed her to expect authority as a parent while simultaneously claiming sympathy as a martyr. Nonetheless, in role of mother, as well as of wife, the reality of her family situation clashed with the ideal of the conduct books. Both husband and sons refused to accord her what she felt was her due in the domestic sphere, so that while the ideal of motherhood assisted Sarah in justifying and valuing herself, the rewards came not so much from her relationship with her children, as from the comfort of having performed her duty as a mother, and the righteousness of knowing her expectations of deference in that role were justified. That the emotional rewards of motherhood increased late in Sarah's life was not due to any shift in ideological outlook, but to the altered circumstances of William's family life and to Sarah's increasing physical frailty. When Sarah became more pitiable than formidable, and less demanding of respect as she defined it, William seems to have become more attentive, but from a position of strength—being kind to an infirm elderly woman rather than deferring to the advice and disapproval of an instructing parent.

The conflict with servants did not improve as Sarah aged, though less space in her diary was devoted to describing it and citing authorities about it. It may be that an additional element of alarm and distrust crept in as Sarah grew older; certainly the episodes that merited most detailed complaint were those that put her at risk physically, such as when a servant left a candle on an oil-varnished board and it caught fire, or when a maid left the doors to the house unlocked at night so that the servants could come and go.[76]

Two additional themes surfaced in the entries on servants in her last volume's entries. First, the responsibility servants bore for her fault of contempt for mankind (knowing as she did, that all humans had souls, and so "the meanest" should be pitied, not despised),[77] and second, that together with her increasing mental and physical frailty, they were the burden that made her life uncomfortable:

> Tho' of late I have made no Mention of my Stupid Lying Servants, yet I suffer never the Less by Their Doings. That Added to the Infirmitys of Old Age is almost Insupportable to my Solitary Life.[78]

That she found herself increasingly unable to cope with managing five servants is also suggested in her proposal at the end of her diary to William and Mary to live with them, giving up her house and her staff in London. Even before Sir William's death, she was glad to live with only the minimum number necessary, thinking in terms not of the prestige but of the problems of running an even larger household.[79]

But by the summer of 1716, politics were no longer diverting, and as her physical health deteriorated, so did her mental health. For the first time since 1700, her diary seems to have lost its power to comfort and occupy her mind:

> I was wont to supply my diary with what I read, which now is but litle thro' defect of sight. Or with what I heard from others, which now is less than formerly for want of hearing, or by setting down my own thoughts and meditations, which alas now are so very dull and insipid as to afford me no pleasure nor benefit.[80]

The deterioration in Sarah's health was constant, but became an insurmountable impediment only in the last two months before she stopped keeping her diary. She complained occasionally about her impaired hearing and vision and rheumatism, and six months before the end of the diary her health was at its worst yet,[81] but for another four months she mentioned it only infrequently. It was only in August 1716 that it became an all-consuming concern. Entries began to be consistently shorter as well:

> August 3. My Mind is so intent upon my Pain, that I cannot turn it to Enquire after Publick Affairs; nor Can I Divert my Thoughts to mor Usefull Meditations. . . .

> August 4. The Excessive Heat of Weather takes away my Stomach, makes mee Faint, sinks my Spirits, so that I feel my self Decay apace. O Lord! give Mee Grace to Wait Patiently till my Change Come.[82]

Her heath continued to worsen throughout August and September. She had managed to write for years despite her shaking hands and near-blindness, but her rheumatism was increasingly excruciating; she was constantly short of breath, and she developed a persistent cough. She wrote ever more briefly each day; in late September she skipped five days entirely. Expecting to die soon, she resumed writing for the last three days of the month to record her farewell visit to Spencer and his family and to say goodbye to her diary. On September 29 she wrote: "The palsey encreases on my Hand so that I am forced to leave off my Diary, writing is so troublesome to me." Then on the last day of the month:

> This is the seventh volume. 'Tis to be hoped there are some collections in them, may be useful to posterity. My phrase now is farewell For Ever.

Sarah was seventy-two at this point; she continued in this unhappy state another three and a half years. In 1719 William mentioned to Mary that Sarah was giving up her coach, and said since arriving in town he had "yet seen nobody but my poor mother, more disconsolate than ever."[83] Sarah's actual death on February 3, 1720, passed unremarked in what family correspondence survives, other than a brief note from Spencer to William twelve days after the fact: "I shall be entirely satisfied with whatever your Lordship shall doe with respect to Rings or Monuments, and submit everything to your disposall as you shall think proper."[84] On the public front, *The Weekly Journal* ran a notice: "On Wednesday last the corpse of the Lady Cowper, mother to the late Lord Chancellor, was carried from her house in Bedford row, in Great State, to be interred in Hertfordshire."[85]

William seems to have fulfilled his obligation as a dutiful son to the last. In the churchyard of Saint Mary's, Hertingfordbury, near the east wall of the church, stands Sarah's very large and impressive funeral monument, inscribed:

> Here lyes enterred, by her own appointment, the body of SARAH LADY COWPER widdow of SIR WILLIAM COWPER of Hertford Castle in this County Baronet of England and Scotland. She was a great Example of Industry Virtue Wisdom and Piety. Her two surviving Sonns, WILLIAM EARLE COWPER and SPENCER COWPER ESQ: CHEIF JUSTICE OF CHESTER, caused this monument to be erected. She dyed the 3rd day of February 1719 [1720] Aged 76 years.

Sarah Cowper's epitaph is a final testimony to the mentality of the world in which she lived and to her working out of a place in that world. As is typical of the thinking of this period, Sarah is primarily identified by her relationship with her male relatives, particularly her husband. Also epitomizing the period's overwhelming concern with rank and hierarchy are the specifications of the station and titles of those male relatives and the grandeur of the monument itself. There are, however, intimations of Sarah's own individual imprint on society—her interpretation of and reaction to the way of dealing with her cultural context. In her choice of burial place, Sarah allied herself emotionally with her son and with his image as a nobleman with a country estate rather than with her husband, his status, and London. Moreover, regardless of how intentionally they were chosen, the words used on her tomb to praise Sarah—to make her an "exemplar"—are in and of themselves an epitome of the ideologies, selections, omissions, and interpretations at work in Sarah's life and approach to her environment. "Industry, virtue, wisdom, and piety" were all valued attributes in early modern society, but were not the same attributes insisted upon time and time again in conduct books and "characters" of women—chastity, silence, obedience, modesty, meekness, patience. Nor were they attributes that specifically applied to the domestic roles that identified and categorized women as a sex: She was not described as a devoted wife, a loving mother, a prudent mistress. Instead she was characterized by religious and intellectual characteristics not specifically directed at women—achievements not of resignation and submission, but of accomplishment, action, and understanding.

Sarah Cowper fashioned for herself multiple identities that she chose and reinterpreted from the prevailing ideological conceptions of gender, status, and age, with mixed success in acting as she would wish within those roles, depending on the extent to which those to whom she presented herself in reality would accept her conceptions of her identity and rights. Nonetheless, this final description of Sarah by her sons after her death suggests that many of the images that she strove to enact in herself were effectively represented. In her diary—the testing ground of her efforts at self-realization—Sarah left her own textual monument that asserts those identities and inscribes those images of herself for posterity. Her epitaph shows her part and parcel of her culture, constructing an identity that affirmed her individuality in ways that were valued and respected, within the boundaries, conceptions, and language of the society she inhabited.

APPENDIX

Herts. PRO D/EP F36
"Catalogue of Books att Lon: in the year 1701"

Sarah's Catalogue Entry	Full Citation (from the English Short Title Catalogue)
1. Dr Hammond on the New Testamt	Henry Hammond, *A Paraphrase and annotation upon all the books of the New Testament.* 2nd ed. 1653.
*2. Hookers Ecclesiastical Polity	Richard Hooker, *Of the laws of ecclesiastical polity.* 1611.
*3. Dr Taylor. Life of Christ	Jeremy Taylor, *The Great Exemplar of sanctity and holy life according to the Christian institution. Described in the history of the life and death of the ever blessed Jesus Christ the Saviour of the world.* 1649. Or perhaps *Antiquitates Christianae: or, The history of the life and death of the Holy Jesus: as also the lives, acts and martyrdoms of his apostles.* 1678.

*4. Cudworths System of the Universe

Ralph Cudworth, *The true intellectual system of the universe*, 1678.

*5. Browns Works

Thomas Browne, *The works of the learned Sir Thomas Brown.* . . . 1686.

6. Barrow[?]s Works folio

Isaac Barrow, *The works of the learned Isaac Barrow.* 1683.

7. Paraphrase on Job Manuscript

Sir Richard Blackmore, *A paraphrase on the book of Job.* 1700.

*8. Dr Pearson on the Creed

John Pearson, *An exposition of the Creed.* 1659.

*9. Dr Goodman Penitent Pardon'd

John Goodman, *The penitent pardoned or A discourse on the nature of sin and the efficacy of repentance.* 1679.

10. Origines Sacra

Edward Stillingfleet, *Origines sacrae: Or a rational account of the grounds of Christian faith, as to the truth and divine authority of Scriptures.* 1662.

*11. Charron of Wisdome

Pierre Charron, *Of wisdom. Three books. Written originally in French.* Transl. George Stanhope, 1697.

*16. B^p Pattrick on the five Books of Moses

Simon Patrick, *Commentary upon the First [through Fifth] book of Moses* . . . . 1695–1700.

*17. Kettlewel of Obedience

John Kettlewell, *The measures of Christian obedience: Or, a discourse shewing what obedience is indispensably necessary to a regenerate state* . . . . 1681.

*18. L'Strang's Seneca

Seneca's Morals abstracted . . . by Roger L'estrange. 1679.

21. Montaigns Essays in three parts	Michel de Montaigne, *Essays of Michael, seigneur de Montaigne. In three books* . . . transl. Charles Cotton, 1685.
22. Memoirs of China	Louis Le Comte, *Memoirs and observations topographical, physical, mathematical, mechanical, natural, civil, and ecclesiastical. Made in a late journey through the empire of China.* 1697.
27. Plutarchs Lives in five parts	Plutarch, *Plutarch's Lives. Translated from the Greek by several hands. In five volumes.* 1683–1686.
32. Plutarchs Morals in five parts	Plutarch, *Plutarch's Morals. In five volumes. Translated from the Greek, by several hands.* 1684–1694.
33. Philip D'Comines	Philippe de Commynes, *The History of Philip de Commines, Knight, Lord of Argenton.* 3rd ed. 1665.
*34. Kempis Christian Pattern	Thomas à Kempis, *Christian pattern or a treatise of the imitation of Jesus Christ* . . . Transl. George Stanhope, 2nd ed. 1664.
*35. Parsons Resolution	Robert Parsons, *A booke of Christian exercise appertaining to resolution.* 1586. [reissued as: *A Christian Directory, Guiding men to eternal salvation, Commonly Called the Resolution.* . . . 1687.]
*36. Blackhalls Sermon	Offspring Blackall, *The sufficiency of a standing revelation. A sermon preached at the Cathedral-Church of St.Paul, January the 1st. 1699/1700. Being the first* . . . *of the lecture founded by the Honourable Robert Boyle.* . . . 1700.

*37. Bradford

Samuel Bradford, *The credibility of the Christian revelation . . . in eight sermons, preached in the Cathedral Church of St. Paul, being the lecture for the year 1699. Founded by the Honourable Robert Boyle.* . . . 1700.

*38. Harris

John Harris, *The atheistical objections against the being of a God, and his attributes, fairly considered and fully refuted. In eight sermons, preached in the Cathedral-Church of St. Paul, London, 1698. Being . . . the lecture founded by the Honourable Robert Boyle.* . . . 1698.

*39. Gastrel

Francis Gastrell, *The certainty and necessity of religion in general: or, The first grounds and principles of humane duty establish'd; in eight sermons preached at St. Martins in the Fields at the lecture for the year 1697, founded by the honourable Robert Boyle.* . . . 1697.

*40. Dr Williams

John Williams, *Twelve sermons preach'd at the lecture founded by Robert Boyle, esq. Concerning the possibility, necessity, and certainty of divine revelation.* 1695.

*?41. Dr Bentley

Richard Bentley, *The folly and unreasonableness of atheism demonstrated . . . in eight sermons, preached at the lecture founded by the Honourable Robert Boyle.* . . . 1693.

*42. Wilson of the Resurrection

William Wilson, *A discourse of the Resurrection shewing the import and certainty of it.* 1694.

*44. Colliers Essays. Review of Jeremy Collier, *Essays upon several*
    yᵉ Stage   *moral subjects.* 2nd ed. 1697.
                             [Originally published as *Miscellanies.*
                             1694.] *A short view of the immoral-*
                             ity and profaneness of the English
                             stage. 1698.

46. Witness to Christianity 2 Sir David Hamilton, *The private Chris-*
    parts   *tian's witness for Christianity to the*
                             notional and erroneous apprehen-
                             sions of the Arminian, Socinian, and
                             Deist of the age. . . . . 1697.

47. The Glorious Epiphany   Simon Patrick, *The glorious Epiphany,*
                             with the devout Christians love to it.
                             1678.

48. Pattrick on the Sacremᵗ   Simon Patrick, *Mensa Mystica; or A*
                             discourse concerning the sacrament
                             of the Lords Supper. 1660.

50. On Ecclesias: Proverbs   Simon Patrick, *A paraphrase upon*
                             the books of Ecclesiastes and the
                             Song of Solomon. . . . 1685. and
                             The Proverbs of Solomon para-
                             phrased. . . . 1683.

51. On the Psalms 2 parts   Henry Hammond, *A paraphrase and*
                             annotations upon the books of the
                             Psalms, briefly explaining the diffi-
                             culties thereof. 1659.

54. On Job. The Pilgrim Par- Simon Patrick, *The book of Job*
    able   *paraphras'd.* 1679. *The parable of*
                             the pilgrim: written to a friend.
                             1665.

55. Devout Christian

Simon Patrick, *The devout Christian instructed how to pray and give thanks to God: or A book of devotions for families and for particular persons in most of the concerns of human life.* 1673.

*56. Wolsely Scripture Beleif

Charles Wolseley, *The reasonableness of Scripture-belief.* 1672.

57. A Dictionary

Thomas Wilson, *A complete Christian dictionary wherein the significance and several acceptations of all the words mentioned in the Holy Scriptures are fully opened.* . . . 1661. Or perhaps Thomas Blount, *Glossographia: or A dictionary, interpreting all such hard words of whatsoever language, now used in our refined English tongue.* . . . 1661.

*73. B^p Tillotsons Works 16 parts.

John Tillotson, *The works of the Most Reverend Dr John Tillotson* . . . . 1696.

*74. Wakes Sermons

William Wake, *Sermons and discourses on several occasions.* 1690.

*76. Whichcotts Serm: 2 parts

Benjamin Whichcote, *Select sermons of Dr Whichcot.* 1698.

*79. Barrows Serm: 3 parts

Isaac Barrow, *Sermons preached upon several occasions.* 1678.

*80. Wilkins Natural Religion

John Wilkins, *Of the principles and duties of natural religion.* 1675.

82. His Sermons in 2 parts

John Wilkins, *Sermons preached on several occasions.* 1682.

83. Dr Goodmans Sermons

John Goodman, *Seven sermons preached upon several occasions. To which is added, the golden rule.* 1697.

84. His Evening Conference

John Goodman, *Winter-evening conference between neighbors.* 1684.

85. The Old Religion

[n.a.], *A brief survey of the old religion. . . .* 1672.

*86. Mons: Allix on ye Script:

Pierre Allix, *Reflections upon the books of the Holy Scripture to establish the truth of the Christian religion.* 1688.

*87. Fran: Sales Devotion

Francis de Sales, *Introduction to a devout life.* 1613.

88. Pattricks Psalms

Simon Patrick, *The book of Psalms paraphras'd: with arguments to each Psalm.* 1691.

*89. Bright Of Prayer

George Bright, *A treatise of prayer* 1678

90. Taylor on ye Sacrem^t

Jeremy Taylor, *The real presence and spirituall of Christ in the blessed sacrament proved against the doctrine of transubstantiation.* 1653.

*91. Bacons Essays

Francis Bacon, *Essays.* 1597.

?92. Erasmus in English   Desiderius Erasmus, *The Colloquies, or familiar discourses of Desiderius Erasmus of Roterdam, rendered into English.* 1671, or perhaps *Twenty Select colloquies out of Erasmus Roterodamus; pleasantly representing several superstitious levities that were crept into the Church of Rome in his days.* Transl. Roger L'Estrange, 1680.

93. Epictetus   *Epictetus, his Morals, with Simplicius his Comment.* Transl. George Stanhope, 1694.

94. Miltons Poem   John Milton, *Paradise lost. A poem written in ten books.* 1667.

95. Sandys Survey   Edwin Sandys, *Europae Speculum, or, A view or survey of the state of religion in the western parts of the world. . . .* 1629.

96. Moor of Vertue   Henry More, *An account of virtue, or, Dr Henry More's abridgment of morals.* 1690.

97. Puffendorf   Samuel Pufendorf, *The whole duty of man according to the law of nature.* 1691.

98. Osborns Works   Francis Osborne, *The works of Francis Osborne, Esq; Divine. Moral. Historical. Political. In four several tracts. . . .* 7th ed. 1673.

*99. Boyls Theology   Robert Boyle, *The excellency of theology compar'd with natural philosophy. . . .* 1674.

100. Hearts Ease

Simon Patrick, *The hearts ease.* 1659.

101. Advice to a ffriend

Simon Patrick, *Advice to a friend.* 1673.

102. Search Scrip: Dr Patt:

Simon Patrick, *Search the Scriptures. A treatise shewing that all Christians ought to read the Holy Books; with directions to them therein.* 1685.

103. Treatise of Fasting

Simon Patrick, *A treatise of repentance and of fasting, especially of the Lent-fast.* 1686.

104. Dr Patt: on Comunion

Simon Patrick, *The Christian sacrifice. A treatise shewing the necessity end and manner of receiving the Holy Communion. . . .* 1670.

*112. Turkish Spy 8 parts

Giovanni Paolo Marana, *The eight volumes of letters writ by a Turkish spy who lived five and forty years undiscover'd at Paris. . . .* 1694.

116. Moral Essays 4 parts

Pierre Nicole, *Moral essays.* Vols. 1–4, 1677–1682.

117. Cicero of ye Gods

Marcus Tullius Cicero, *Cicero's three books touching the nature of the gods done into English. . . .* 1683.

118. Blounts Essays

Sir Thomas Pope Blount, *Essays on several subjects.* 1691.

119. Reflec: on Philosophy — Margaret Cavendish, Duchess of Newcastle, *Philosophical letters, or Modest reflections upon some opinions in Natural philosophy.* . . . 1664.

*120. Tully's Offices — Marcus Tullius Cicero, *Tully's Offices.* transl. Roger L'Estrange, 1680.

121. Grotius of Religion — Hugo Grotius, *On the truth of Christian religion.* 1669.

122. Lipsius of Constancy — Justus Lipsius, *A discourse of constancy in two books.* 1654.

123. Gent: Religion — Edward Synge, *A gentleman's religion: with the grounds and reasons of it.* 1693.

124. Rational Catechism — William Popple, *A rational catechism, or, an instructive conference between a father and son.* 1687.

125. Letter to a Deist Stilling: — Edward Stillingfleet, *A letter to a deist, in answer to several objections against the truth and authority of the scriptures.* 1677.

126. Erasmus Praise of Folly — Desiderius Erasmus, *Moriae encomium, or the praise of folly.* Transl. John Wilson, 1668.

*127. Advice to a Daughter — George Savile, Marquess of Halifax, *The lady's new year's gift, or advice to a daughter.* 1688.

128. Rules of Health — Santorio, Santorio, *Medicina statica, or Rules of health, in eight sections of aphorisms.* 1676.

129. Humane Reason Clifford   Martin Clifford, *A treatise of humane reason*. 1674.

130. Dʳ Taylor of ffriendship   Jeremy Taylor, *A discourse on the nature, offices and measures of friendship, with rules of conducting it. Written in answer to a letter from the most ingenious and vertuous M[rs] K[atherine] P[hillips].* 1657.

131. Indifference in Religion   Benedict Pictet, *An antidote against a careless indifferency in matters of religion.* . . . 1694.

132. The Countess of Warwick   Anthony Walker, *Eureka, Eureka. The virtuous woman found her loss bewailed, an character exemplified . . . At the funeral of that most excellent lady the right honorable, and eminently religious and charitable Mary, Countess Dowager of Warwick.* . . . 1678.

133. Erasmus Christian Souldier   Desiderius Erasmus, *A manual for a Christian soldier, written by Erasmus, and translated into English.* 1687.

*This title is also located in D/EP F43, Lady Sarah Cowper's Index to Thoughts and Meditations.

Reference Matter

Notes

Chapter 1

1. For the bare facts of Sarah and William's union, see Hertfordshire Public Record Office (hereafter Herts. PRO) D/EP F30 Diary of Sarah, Lady Cowper, vol. 2 (1703–4), pp. 20, 106, 174; and *Victoria History of the County of Hertfordshire* supp. vol. *Hertfordshire Families*, p. 138.

2. Herts. PRO D/EP F23 Correspondence of Sarah, Lady Cowper and Sir William Cowper, February 14, 1662. Sarah's birthday was February 14 as well.

3. Herts. PRO D/EP F31, Diary of Sarah, Lady Cowper, vol. 3 (1705), p. 162.

4. London Public Record Office, Prob. 11: Will of Samuel Holled, reel 305, no. 125; Will of Anne Holled, reel 314, no. 68.

5. Herts. PRO D/EP F25 Memorandum Book of Sir William Cowper contains notes on the births of William (June 24, 1665), Samuel (August 17, 1666), John (December 5, 1667), and Spencer (February 23, 1669), and the deaths of Samuel (October 8, 1666) and John (April 27, 1686).

6. For the discussion that follows on the careers of Sir William, William and Spencer, see: *Dictionary of National Biography*; *Victoria History of the County of Hertfordshire*, pp. 137–38; Foss, *Biographia Juridica*, pp. 199–200.

7. Herts. PRO D/EP F29–F35 Diary of Sarah, Lady Cowper: F29 Volume 1, July 25, 1700, to December 31, 1702; F30 Volume 2, January 1, 1703, to December 31, 1704; F31 Volume 3, January 1, 1705, to November

21, 1706; F32 Volume 4, December 1, 1706, to June 30, 1709; F33 Volume 5, July 1, 1709, to June 30, 1711; F34 Volume 6, July 1, 1711, to September 30, 1713; F35 Volume 7, October 1, 1713, to September 30, 1716. References are abbreviated hereafter to volume, year, and page. The vast majority of entries were daily, but occasionally Sarah made one entry stretch to fill more than one date. Once, at an especially low point in her life, she took this practice to extremes, stretching one entry across five dates, with breaks in the middle of sentences and sometimes even in the middle of a word. Vol. 2 (1703), pp. 125–26.

8. Vol. 2 (1704), penultimate page; vol. 4 (1708), p. 148.

9. Bell and Yalom, eds., introduction to *Revealing Lives: Autobiography, Biography, and Gender*; Atwood, p. 8.

10. As Patricia Spacks puts it, "reading autobiography, we expect truth, yet always suspect the reliability of self-interpretation." *Imagining a Self*, pp. 41–42.

11. In contrast to earlier ideas of autobiographical writing as coherent, consistent, and unified (see Mandel, "The Autobiographer's Art," or Pascal, *Design and Truth in Autobiography*), more recent literary scholarship characterizes autobiography as an evolving and dynamic process of self-invention that produces multiple, changing, inconsistent identities. Nussbaum, pp. 18–19, 223–32. See also Olney, *Autobiography: Essays Theoretical and Critical*; Spengemann, *The Forms of Autobiography: Episodes in the History of a Literary Genre*. Social context is also crucial in that writers are governed by socially defined standards of plausibility and by a vocabulary of shared meanings. Sinfield, pp. 24–25.

12. Mandel, p. 222. See also Bell and Yalom, p. 4; Graham et al., p. 22. For diaries as lacking retrospection, see Blodgett, p. 21; Mendelson, "Stuart Women's Diaries," pp. 182–183. Some go even further and characterize diaries as uniquely feminine products on two levels: first, "the idea that oneself, one's feelings, one's spouse and domestic relations were properly and innately worth writing about was essentially a female idea" (Pomerleau, p. 19); and second, that women's gendered experience of domestic life ("daily," "discontinuous," and "formless") was mirrored in their writing style. Jelinek, *Tradition of Women's Autobiography*, p. 4. See too Lensink, p. 40. Stanton (pp. 11–13) has criticized this association of femininity and formlessness on the grounds of overgeneralizing a single pattern for women's writing.

13. Culley says "all diarists are in a process, even if largely unconscious, of selecting details to create a persona" (p. 12); while Nussbaum (p. 26) warns that diarists purport to be transcribing their experiences, their 'truth', but are necessarily selecting topics and details.

14. Fothergill, pp. 40, 42, 48. Another possible regulator of the form of diaries comes from devotional books and sermons that advocated keeping a formal record of self-examination—channeling, perhaps restrictively, the diarist's introspection. Sara Mendelson notes that some of the diaries she studied went so far as to respond directly to specific catechism questions about daily duties, in a sort of "spiritual ledger in diary form" ("Stuart Women's Diaries," p. 186). Nonetheless, as the editors of *Her Own Life* assert, the "relationship between doctrinally-required interpretation and experience is dialectical" (Graham et al., p. 4).

15. Vol. 2 (1704), p. 209. She again paraphrased this passage five years later. Vol. 5 (1709), p. 67.

16. Barash, p. 60. The original reads "Ladies . . . [will] find a Picture of my Mind, my Sentiments, all laid open to their view; . . . they'll see me struggling with my Passions, blaming my self, endeavoring to pay a homage to my Reason, and . . . with a decent calmness, an unshaken Constancy, and a resigning Temper, to support all the Troubles, all the uneasinesses of Life, and then by unexpected Emergencies, unforseen Disappointments, sudden and surprizing Turns of Fortune, discompos'd, and shock'd, till I have rallied my scattered Forces, got new Strength, and by making an unweary'd Resistance, gain'd the better of my Afflictions, and restor'd my Mind to its former Tranquility."

17. Nussbaum notes the long tradition, beginning in the seventeenth century, that the private self of the diary is more authentic than the public self (p. 25), a view Blodgett reiterated when she made the absence of an intent to publish the criterion for inclusion in her study of women's diaries, arguing that if a diarist wrote with an immediate audience in mind, it would "adulterate her self-expression" (pp. 13–14).

18. Crawford, "Women's Published Writings," p. 216.

19. There were some ways around this prohibition, such as writing about religious or maternal topics, which might act as a sanction for female public expression, but this was not a foolproof strategy. Paul's admonition 'Let your women keep silence in the churches' (1 Corinthians 14:34–35) was frequently cited as a general prohibition, and women were attacked for disregarding it. Despite the pressure, some did publish, though the frequent appearance of apologies and disclaimers in prefaces reveal anxiety about public exposure and a "consciousness of the need to justify their activity." Hobby, "'Discourse so Unsavory'," pp. 16–17, 22. See also Crawford, "Women's Published Writings," pp. 217–22.

20. See Ezell, pp. 64–73 on the possibilities for manuscript circulation among friends and acquaintances as an informal, but still significant means of dissemination of writing for both men and women.

21. Samuel Pepys, for example, probably kept his diary for his eyes only during his lifetime, but the fact that he cataloged it and bequeathed it along with his library to Magdalene College indicates a different intention for the work after his death. *The Diary of Samuel Pepys,* vol. 1, introduction. Nussbaum even suggests that although they might claim they wrote in secret, women often assumed posthumous publication, so that complete privacy was an "affectation" (pp. 26, 136, 161).

22. Herts. PRO D/EP F43 "Thoughts and Meditations" (1690). There is a similar dedication to Judith in Herts. PRO D/EP F41 "History of the World" and Life of Mohammed (1686), preface.

23. Vol. 1 (1702), p. 176.

24. Vol. 3 (1706), p. 304.

25. Fothergill, pp. 66, 73; Mendelson, "Stuart Women's Diaries," pp. 181–85; *Diary of Samuel Pepys,* pp. cvi–cvii.

26. Blodgett (pp. 69–76, 206), especially, is correspondingly doubtful of their validity; she suspects they often disguised less socially acceptable motives, including the indulgence of self-interest and nostalgia.

27. Spacks considers it a universal "human need to declare not only the identity but the larger-than-life significance of the self." *Imagining a Self,* pp. 14–18.

28. Vol. 4 (1706), preface.

29. Vol. 4 (1708), pp. 247–48.

30. Vol. 1 (1701), p. 67.

31. Vol. 2 (1704), p. 250.

32. Vol. 4 (1706), preface.

33. Vol. 1 (1700), first page.

34. Vol. 1 (1702), p. 176.

35. Vol. 4 (1708), p. 260.

36. Examples of this kind of writing include William Gouge, *Domesticall Duties* (3d ed. 1634), William Nichols, *The Duty of Inferiors Towards their Superiours in five Practical Discourses* (1701), Samuel Pufendorf, *The Whole Duty of Man and Citizen According to the Law of Nature* (1691). On prescriptive literature about (and for) women, see Hull, *Chaste, Silent and Obedient: English Books for Women 1475–1640.*

37. Mendelson and Crawford, pp. 31–34; Amussen, "Gender, Family and the Social Order," pp. 196–98.

38. For addressing this problem by studies such as this one, see Anthony Fletcher, *Gender, Sex and Subordination,* pp. 409–10. See also Ezell, pp. 2, 6, 37–38; Mendelson, "Stuart Women's Diaries," p. 181.

39. Even taking into account Margaret Spufford's caution that reading was taught before writing ("First Steps in Literacy," pp. 407–35), only about 30% of men and 45% of women in the early eighteenth century were

literate, with higher rates in London. Cressy, *Literacy and the Social Order*, pp. 176, 147.

40. For a brief discussion of the source problems, see Mendelson and Crawford, pp. 8–10.

41. See, for example, defenses of women by William Austin, *Haec Homo* (1639); Charles Gerbier, *Elogium Heroinium* (1651); Thomas Heywood, *The General History of Women* (1657); François Poulain de la Barre, *The Woman as Good as the Man Author Is* (1677). On the 'woman question' in general, see Rogers, *The Troublesome Helpmate: A History of Misogyny in Literature*, and Henderson and McManus, *Half Humankind: Contexts of the Controversy About Women in England 1540–1640*. For women's written contribution to the formal debate, see Joan Kelly, "Early Feminist Theory and The Querelle des Femmes," pp. 4–28.

42. Feminist historians began the exploration of female consciousness by documenting oppression and individual women's heroic attempts to name and resist it. By the later 1970s, responding to criticisms that this approach tended to imply a single, homogeneous history of women, an anachronistic feminist consciousness, and a corresponding ahistorical roll call of achievements of personal transcendence, scholars began reading the documents for signs of women dealing with their contradictory, repressive social position with a more subtle conception of what constitutes awareness and resistance, both in nature and degree (see Davis, "Women's History in Transition: The European Case," Kelly, "Early Feminist Theory and The Querelle des Femmes," p. 7). Despite these warnings, see M. Ferguson, ed., *First Feminists: British Women Writers 1578–1799*, as an example of the continuing search for individual "feminist" resisters.

43. Blodgett, pp. 4–5, 145, 194–95. See also Hull, p. 140.

44. Spacks, p. 73; Nussbaum, p. 203. See also Rogers, *Feminism in Eighteenth-Century England*, pp. 4, 231; Graham et al., p.10.

45. See Copelman's critique of the disproportionate attention paid to these unrepresentative women, pp. 315–45; but note, too, Mendelson and Crawford's conscientious effort to address this problem in their recent survey (p. 10).

46. Newton, et al., pp. 2–5; and Kelly, "The Doubled Vision of Feminist Theory," pp. 260–68. Other discussions of the relative weight to be given to the categories of gender and rank include: Scott, pp. 1054–65; and Rhode, ed., *Theoretical Perspectives on Sexual Difference*.

47. Astell, p. 71.

48. Pomerleau, pp. 22–24; Jelinek, *Tradition*, p. 25.

49. Lilley suggests that some women utilized a strategy of valorizing stoicism and duty in the face of affliction, able to do so because "a conservative women's heroism—and this seems especially true for aristocratic women—is

located in (and can afford to be located in) embracing submission . . . "p. 91. See Hobby "'Discourse so Unsavory'," p. 21, where she describes Margaret Cavendish's conservative attitude toward class.

50. Foucault (p. 98) contests the notion of comprehensive hegemony, offering instead the idea of dispersed social power "which circulates or functions in the form of a chain." His view has been widely influential; see for instance Scott, p. 1067, where she advocates the adoption of his conception of power and its implications for limited human agency; and Judith Newton et al. (p. 7), who note the agreement of many feminist historians with this view.

51. Ezell (pp. 4, 9, 35) doubts that even the literary presentation of patriarchalism per se was as repressive, or as hegemonic, as it appears to historians and literary critics. See also Hobby's argument that women "turned constraints into permissions, into little pockets of liberty or autonomy." *Virtue of Necessity*, pp. 7–8.

52. Women in particular focused on the implications of a genderless Christ and genderless souls in their defenses of the worth of their sex and, in the case of sectarian women in the period of the Civil War and Commonwealth, of the validity of their prophecies and admonitions. Crawford, "Women's Published Writings," pp. 224–25; 229–30.

53. Kelly, "Early Feminist Theory," p. 8.

54. Mendelson, "Stuart Women's Diaries," p. 194; Hobby, "'Discourse so Unsavoury'," p. 30; Pomerleau, p. 28.

55. Barash, p. 61.

56. Stone, *The Family, Sex and Marriage in England 1500–1800*.

57. Although Stone admitted that his evidence most properly applied only to the upper layers of society, in his recent series of case studies he has firmly reiterated this position. *Road to Divorce*, pp. 6–12; and *Broken Lives*, pp. 14–15.

58. See Wrightson, pp. 66–88 and Houlbrooke, *The English Family*, pp. 63–95.

59. Hunt, *The Middling Sort*, pp. 152–54, 82; Vickery, *The Gentleman's Daughter*, pp. 40–45, 60. See, too, Ezell (pp. 160–63) who argues for a loose, contested system: she describes the active involvement of women in arranging marriages for their children and relations, and the opportunities for intellectual discourse in correspondence networks and circulation of manuscripts.

60. This line of thought was instigated long ago by Powell in *English Domestic Relations 1487–1653*. It was taken up by: Haller and Haller, pp. 235–72; Johnson, pp. 429–36; Douglass, p. 303. Patrick Collinson reiterated the theme in *The Birthpangs of Protestant England: Religious and Cultural Change in the Sixteenth and Seventeenth Centuries*, p. 93.

61. Davies, "Continuity and Change in Literary Advice on Marriage," pp. 60–64. Her views on the continuity of the ideal of mutuality are accepted by Macfarlane, *Marriage and Love in England*, pp. 175–208, and Houlbrooke, *The English Family*, pp. 30–35.

62. Collinson, pp. 70, 93; Amussen, *An Ordered Society*, pp. 41–47. Vickery also takes up this point, asserting that obedience remained in the eighteenth century the "indispensable virtue of a good wife" (*Gentleman's Daughter*, p. 59). More optimistically, Anthony Fletcher sees a new, radical, and potentially egalitarian shift in these Puritan authors, not in their continued unquestioned assumption of female inferiority, but in their approval of frequent, mutually satisfying sex as a support to loving, companionate marriage. ("The Protestant Idea of Marriage," pp. 168, 175, 177.)

63. Allestree organized his discussion this way in *The Ladies Calling* (1673), p. 180; more generally, Kelso noted this characteristic, p. 2.

64. Allestree explained the relationship of allegiance and support a wife owed her husband in terms of duties owed to his person, his reputation, and his fortune. *Ladies Calling*, p. 191. See also Gouge, pp. 24–25. The same message is in sermons; for example, Barrow, vol. 1, Sermon 2, "The Profitableness of Godliness," p. 16.

65. Allestree, *Ladies' Calling*, pp. 210–12; 222–23.

66. Allestree, *Ladies Calling*, pp. 223–26.

67. Vol. 1 (1700), pp. 7, 19.

68. Vol. 6 (1711), pp. 28–29; from *The Spectator* no. 153, August 25, 1711.

Chapter 2

1. Vol. 1 (1702), p. 185. See also vol. 2 (1704), p. 200: "My Wedding day full 40 year Since, all which time I have lived with a greivous generation."

2. Clay (p. 174) surmises John Cowper was a moneylender from the large number of small sums, totaling 7450 pounds, that were owing at his death. See Heal and Jones (pp. 97–135) regarding moneylending as one of an increasing number of ways to enter into the ranks of the gentry and maintain oneself there.

3. Clay, p. 174.

4. See *Victoria History of the County of Hertfordshire*, p. 137, and Herts. PRO D/EP F 25 Sir William Cowper's Commonplace Book. Clay suggests the first baronet's wife was also from a mercantile background (p. 177).

5. *Victoria History of the County of Hertfordshire*, p. 136.

6. Clay, p. 175; Herts. PRO D/EP T1138 Will of Sir William Cowper, first baronet (August 14, 1663), and D/EP F20, Marriage Settlement of John Cowper and Joyce Hukely (1638).

7. See Gregory King's estimates in Holmes, *The Making of a Great Power*, Table B.5, p. 410; and Holmes, "Gregory King," p. 55. See also Speck, p. 44 and Sharpe, p. 179 for the general estimate that about four-fifths of the merchant rank were making roughly 200 pounds per annum and the remaining fifth more like 400 pounds.

8. Clay, p. 175.

9. Henning, p. 165; *Victoria History of the County of Hertfordshire*, p. 138.

10. Sir William notes in his Commonplace Book (Herts. PRO D/EP F25) the Fire of London "in which calamity I lost all my houses in Cornhill besides a great sum of money".

11. Clay, pp. 175–77. Mingay suggests that in the later seventeenth and early eighteenth centuries the wealthy gentry (about 1,000 families) had a minimum annual income of above 1,000 pounds, lesser gentry (about 2,000 families) an income of between 250 and 1,000 pounds, and 'county gentlemen' (about 10,000 families) under 250 pounds. (*The Gentry*, pp. 13–14.) Wrightson (p. 25) uses the same income groupings to describe the regional example of the Yorkshire gentry in the mid-seventeenth century. He also gives an overall range for gentry incomes in Kent of between 200 and 10,000 pounds. To assess average income of the gentry in the early years of the eighteenth century, historians most often use as a starting point the ranking scheme and population and income estimates Gregory King made in 1696, combined with the checks provided by the estimates of Edward Chamberlayne in 1669 and Joseph Massie in 1760. It is clear from the general assumptions and principles upon which King was basing his table of "The Income and Expenses of the Several Families of England" and from comparison with Chamberlayne's higher income calculations for an earlier year, that Gregory King seriously underestimated the incomes of the four ranks of the gentry in 1688. Holmes points out that King was projecting backward to 1688 in an intensely conservative attempt to argue for reestablishing the social order as it stood before that time." Gregory King," pp. 54–55. A comparison of King and Massie's estimates is in Holmes's *The Making of a Great Power*, Table B.5. Looking at baronets (of whom there were 935 in 1700), King suggested that their average income would have been approximately 880 pounds. Beckett, p. 491 Table A5; p. 288.

12. Herts. PRO D/EP F24 Correspondence of Sarah, Lady Cowper and Sir William Cowper, fol. 7, Anthony Ashley Cooper to Sir William Cowper, September 8, 1678. The letter is addressed to "much honored Kinsman" and begins "dear cousin"; no further information is available on the nature

of their blood ties, which presumably were distant. The tone of the letter is very cordial; as well as discussing political news, and in reference to the Cowper's visit, says "I really estem you the worthyest gentleman I know and the best friend I have."

13. This was the third wife of Lord Shaftesbury, Margaret Spencer, sister of the First Earl Sunderland and niece of the Earl of Southampton. Haley (pp. 90–91) describes her as pious, intelligent, and devoted to her husband, living with him in the Tower of London during his imprisonments, and mourning his death in 1683 for years afterward.

14. For instance in a speech declaring that "whoever was against exclusion was against their religion and their liberty." Henning, p. 166.

15. Henning, p. 166 and Haley, p. 633.

16. Vol. 1 (1700), p. 16.

17. Henning, p. 166 and Haley, p. 645.

18. Haley, p. 677.

19. Henning, p. 166.

20. Lords Russell and Montagu, Sir John Sydenham, and Francis Charlton also assisted with bail. Haley, p. 682.

21. Haley, p. 727.

22. For a discussion of the plausibility of insurrection plans in late 1682, their connection to the Rye House Plot, and Shaftesbury's involvement, see Haley, pp. 709 and 723, and from the perspective of Lord Russell's involvement, see Schwoerer, pp. 101–24.

23. Henning, p. 166.

24. For Sir William's political career, see Henning, pp. 165–66. I am also grateful to Mark Knights of the History of Parliament Trust for allowing me to see his draft biographical entry for Sir William.

25. Herts. PRO D/EP F23 Correspondence of Sarah, Lady Cowper and Sir William Cowper. The first dated letter from William at St Albans to Sarah is October 1672. On the occasion of being in St Albans in 1707, Sarah remembered, "Thirty five years ago my Son W[illiam] was Carried to the Free School there." Vol. 4 (1707), p. 101.

26. *Register of Admissions to the Honorable Society of the Middle Temple*, vol. 1, pp. 206, 220.

27. Vol. 3 (1706), p. 205.

28. Vol. 3 (1705), p. 116.

29. Vol. 7 (1714), p. 143. Marriage date and names, Herts. PRO D/EP F25 Sir William's Memorandum book.

30. Herts. PRO D/EP F81 Cowper Family Correspondence, fol. 5, William to Judith, June 1, 1686.

31. Clay, p. 177; Herts. PRO D/EP T1217 Marriage Settlement of William Cowper and Judith Booth, July 7, 1686.

32. Herts. PRO D/EP T4445 Letter Robert Booth to Judith Booth, April 15, 1685.

33. Herts. PRO D/EP F58 Cowper Family Correspondence, fol. 2, Sir William to William, July 14, 1698, mentions the recent separation.

34. Stone, *Family, Sex and Marriage*, p. 84.

35. Herts. PRO D/EP F81 Cowper Family Correspondence, fol. 64, William to Judith, May 4, 1695; fol. 97, William to Judith, September 18, 1701; D/EP F58 fol. 8, Sarah to William, September 24, 1692[?].

36. Herts. PRO D/EP F81 fol. 14, William to Judith, June 14, 1687.

37. Herts. PRO D/EP F58 fol. 32, Judith to William, April 29, n.y.

38. Herts. PRO D/EP F58 fol. 5, Sarah to William, n.d.

39. *Victoria History of the County of Hertfordshire*, p. 284.

40. Herts. PRO D/EP F58 fol. 1, Sir William to William, March 17, 1690.

41. Herts. PRO D/EP F58 fol. 4, William to Sarah, 1692[?].

42. Herts. PRO D/EP F58 fol. 2, Sarah to William, n.d.

43. Herts. PRO D/EP F58 fol. 31, Judith to William, April 29, n.y.

44. Herts. PRO D/EP F81 fol. 62, William to Judith, April 30, 1695.

45. Herts. PRO Penshanger MSS Catalogue regarding D/EP F84–F86, Will of Elizabeth Culling, Correspondence, Culling children to William. See also Campbell, vol. 4, p. 260; and *Dictionary of National Biography*.

46. In his memorandum book (Herts. PRO D/EP F25) Sir William noted the birth of his grandson William on September 10, 1687. The last mention of this child is in letter from Judith to William, June 14, 1691 (D/EP F58 fol. 33). By the time of Sir William's Will in 1700 (D/EP T1141) there are provisions for there being no male heir from Judith and William's marriage.

47. Herts. PRO D/EP F58 fol. 4, Draft letter, William to Sarah.

48. Vol. 1 (1701), p. 43.

49. Herts. PRO D/EP F58 fol. 3, Sarah to William, October 4, 1692: "Without further argument I desire to have my money for so I may justly call it. I have ask'd nothing more because I too well know 'twas in vain and if he will not send 20l let it be 19 and ten shillings for that is my due. My Michalmas quarter and four pound ten of the last. . . . "

50. Herts. PRO D/EP F58 fol. 5, Draft, William to Sarah, September[?] 1692[?].

51. Herts. PRO D/EP F58 fol. 8, Sarah to William, September 24, 1692[?].

52. The allegation for the marriage license is dated February 4, 1688, when Spencer would have been not quite nineteen. *Victoria History of the County of Hertfordshire*, p. 145.

53. Herts. PRO D/EP F81 fol. 116, Pennington to Judith, April 2, 1688[?].

54. Herts. PRO D/EP F81 fol. 117, Pennington to Judith, October 3, 1696.

55. The Commonplace Books of arah, Lady Cowper: Herts. PRO D/EP F36 Poems and Sayings (1670); F37 "The Medley" (1673); F38 Moral and Scriptural Collections (1675); F39 Bible Commentary and Notes on Heresies (1680); F40 Prayers (1680); Uncatalogued Collection from Plutarch's Morals, Lives of Bishops, and Precepts (1683); F41 "History of the World" and Life of Mohammed (1686); F42 Topical Index to Sermons (1686); F43 "Thoughts and Meditations" (1690); F44 "Collections from the Bible" and Sarah Cowper's own Biblical Commentary (1700); F45 Scrapbook (1700). References to these commonplace books are abbreviated hereafter to number, title, and year.

56. Clifford wrote *A Treatise of Humane Reason* (1674) and was thought to have helped Buckingham compose *The Rehearsal*. He lived in the Master's Lodge of the Charterhouse from 1672–1677 during which years Sarah lived in Charterhouse Yard. Pritchard, p. 255.

57. It is also likely to be because of her friendship with Clifford that six of Cowley's letters ended up in the Cowper family papers. (Pritchard, pp. 253–57) surmises that three of these letters were addressed to Martin Clifford and one to the Duke of Buckingham.

58. Herts. PRO D/EP F36 Poems and Sayings (1670); F37 "The Medley" (1673).

59. Herts. PRO D/EP F37 "The Medley" (1673), preface.

60. Herts. PRO D/EP F38 Moral and Scriptural Collections.

61. Herts. PRO D/EP F41 "History of the World" and Life of Mohammed (1686); F45 Scrapbook (1700).

62. Herts. PRO D/EP F39 Bible Commentary and Notes on Heresies (1680); F40 Prayers (1680); Uncatalogued Collection from Plutarch's Morals, Lives of Bishops, and Precepts (1683); F42 Topical Index to Sermons (1686); F43 "Thoughts and Meditations" (1690); F44 "Collections from the Bible" and Sarah Cowper's own Biblical Commentary (1700).

63. Campbell, vol. 4, p. 258.

64. Letter from William to Judith, December 15, 1688, reprinted in Campbell, vol. 4, pp. 258–59.

65. "Patronage structured early modern society" says Linda Levy Peck in her study of the Jacobean court, "at once symbiotic and symbolic, those private, dependent, deferential alliances were designed to bring reward to the client and continuing proof of power and standing to the patron." Moreover, Peck demonstrates how in the neo-stoic rhetoric of Senecan language found in courtier's conduct books patronage was explicitly validated and disguised as disinterest and generosity—part of the mutually beneficial exchange of gifts and favors that reinforced reciprocal bonds and thus

helped to cement society and the social order, in which the virtue of liberality displayed by the bestowing of favors by the magnanimous patron would be repaid by "duty and deference" from "grateful recipients" (pp. 3, 13–15).

66. Much of the scholarship on patronage in this period has come in the form of studies of the history of the House of Commons and the role of alliances on the basis of party, patronage, and principle in the passing of legislation, the rise and fall of ministries, and the relationship with the Crown. The leading authority in this debate has been Holmes (*British Politics in the Age of Anne*, and *Politics, Religion and Society in England*). The scholarly work that has followed, such as Roberts, in "Party and Patronage in Later Stuart England," and Hayton, "Moral Reform and Country Politics in the late Seventeenth Century House of Commons," pp. 48–91, responds to his characterization of the relative importance of party, crown, and patronage in managing parliamentary business successfully.

However, the Jacobean court has received attention that specifically considers the patronage activities of notable women courtiers. Studies by Peck (pp. 70–74) and Lewalski, (pp. 95–99, 115–23) both recognize Queen Anne of Denmark's household as an important locus of political, artistic, and literary networks, where women acted as patrons themselves, or brokered influence through their kin and connections, and established future networks through arranging marriages and designating godparents. They were involved in a whole range of interactions, from clerical appointments, through business and legal favors, to defending or advancing court factions While the same sort of study of elite women as patrons later in the century is only beginning, the biographies of the Duchess of Marlborough (Harris, *A Passion for Government: The Life of Sarah, Duchess of Marlborough*), and Lady Rachel Russell (Schwoerer, *Lady Rachel Russell: "One of the Best of Women"*), demonstrate their continuing importance.

67. The Cowpers declared early for the Prince of Orange; both of Sir William's sons went to meet the prince at Wallingford after his landing in England. Herts. PRO D/EP F68 is part of an account William wrote of the flight of James II, the landing of the Prince of Orange, and William and Spencer's journey to meet him.

68. Margaret Spencer was the sister of the first earl of Sunderland and niece of Thomas Wriothesley, fourth earl of Southampton and Lord Treasurer under King Charles II, who was Rachel Wriothesley's father. Rachel's father-in-law was William Russell, first duke of Bedford. Rachel inherited a vast estate from her father including very profitable property in the growing Bloomsbury area of London. See Haley, p. 91; Schwoerer, pp. 27–31.

69. See Schwoerer, pp. 76–77, regarding Lady Russell's friendship with Lady Shaftesbury; and see pp. 28–30, 150–54, 194–95 regarding her relig-

ious outlook, connections to the highest clergy, and patronage for the lesser clergy.

70. Herts. PRO D/EP F24 Correspondence of Sarah, Lady Cowper and Sir William Cowper, fols. 1, 3, Lord Halifax to Lady Russell, March 28, 1689; fols. 2, 4, Sarah to Lord Halifax, March 20, 28, 1689; fol. 5, Lord Halifax to Lady Russell, n. d.; *Letters of Rachel, Lady Russell*, vol. 1, pp. 272–74, Lady Russell to Lord Halifax; pp. 275–76, Lady Russell to Sir Henry Pollexfen, 1689.

71. Schwoerer, pp. 192–93.

72. In a further demonstration of the pervasiveness of kin connections in the elite patronage workings of Stuart England, George Savile, the Marquis of Halifax, was Lady Shaftesbury's nephew by marriage and cousin-in-law, and Lady Russell's cousin by marriage. In additoin, Savile's daughter was married to Rachel's first husband's brother. (Haley, pp. 91, 347; Schwoerer, p. 25.)

73. It should be noted, however, that Sarah's son William in a letter to the Duke of Marlborough several years later gave credit to Sir Robert Howard for obtaining the appointment (Herts. PRO D/EP F 63 Cowper Correspondence with the Churchill Family, October 16, 1705). There does exist a letter from Sir Robert Howard to the Earl of Shrewsbury in his capacity as Secretary of State: "Sir William Cowper presents this to your Lordship and I humbly desire . . . that you will be pleased to certify his majesty's commands that his sonne should be of his council Learned in the Law." (D/EP F 94 Letters Patent for William Cowper as King's Counsel). Certainly, then, at the formal stage of drawing up the legal documents for the appointment William's father and his connections appear to the fore.

74. Campbell, vol. 4, p. 262; Henning, pp. 12–22.

75. Foss, *Biographica Juridica*, p. 199.

76. The sources for this discussion of Spencer's trial are the trial transcript and five polemic pamphlets reprinted in T. Howell, vol. 13, pp. 1105–1250; *The Tryal of Spencer Cowper, esq.*; Herts. PRO D/EP F96 William, Earl Cowper's copies of the trial transcript and notes entitled "Argument for my brother Spencer, at Lord Keeper Wright's Chamber in the Inner Temple, May 27, 1700"; Foss, *Judges of England*, vol. 8, pp. 115–19; and his *Biographica Juridica*, pp. 199–200; Campbell, pp. 269–75; *Dictionary of National Biography*.

77. T. Howell, p. 1217.

78. T. Howell, pp. 1116–24.

79. T. Howell, pp. 1124, 1158.

80. And pointing out that four of the prosecution's physicians, the three doctors Dimsdale, and Dr. Nailor were deadly political enemies of the Cowper family. T. Howell, p. 1132.

81. For instance, Stout's allusive comment in a letter dated March 5, "I am sure the winter has been too unpleasant for me to desire the continuance of it; and I wish you were to endure the sharpness of it but for one hour, as I have done for many long nights and days; and then I beleive it would move that rocky heart of yours, that can be so thoughtless of me as you are: . . . When you come to H– –d . . . do not do as you did the last time; and be sure order your affairs to be here as soon as you can, which cannot be sooner than you will be heartily welcome. . . . " T. Howell, pp. 1172–73.

82. T. Howell, pp. 1157–64.

83. T. Howell, pp. 1181–82.

84. T. Howell, p. 1151.

85. T. Howell, p. 1190.

86. Foss, *Biographia Juridica*, p. 199.

87. See Luttrell, p. 539: "We have a particular account by several gentlemen of good reputation, who were yesterday present at the tryal of Mr. Spencer Cowper, and the three others at Hartford, that there was no room to think that either of them were concerned in the murther of Mrs Stout the quaker . . . it appearing . . . in all probability she had drowned her self. . . . " Campbell (pp. 275–76) notes too that by 1710, even Mrs. Manley, a virulent Tory who included in her *Memoirs from the New Atalantis* a scandalous account of the Cowper family, depicted Sarah Stout's death as suicide. In a melodramatic scene at the riverside, Spencer rejects Sarah and leaves; then Sarah "flounced with all her strength into the river." *New Atalantis*, p. 129.

88. Initiated under Henry VII, it was not repealed until the early nineteenth century, in the reign of George IV. Campbell, vol. 4, p. 275.

89. T. Howell, p. 1198.

90. Campbell, vol. 4, p. 275.

91. T. Howell, p. 1201.

92. T. Howell, p. 1201.

93. "The Case of Spencer Cowper," in T. Howell, pp. 1194–96. And see Campbell, p. 275.

94. Diary, vol. 1 (1701), p. 104, the entry for June 25: "The parlement is now prorogu'd without so much as having read M Stouts petition against Spencer."

95. T. Howell, p. 1149.

96. "The Case of Spencer Cowper, esq., Ellis Stephens, William Rogers, and John Marson . . . " in T. Howell, p. 1194.

97. "A Reply to the Hertford Letter," in T. Howell, p. 1237.

98. Sarah mentions such conversations in her diary, vol. 1 (1700–1701), pp. 18, 35, 79, and 133.

99. Vol. 4 (1707), p. 33.

100. Vol. 1 (1701), p. 71.

101. Vol. 1 (1700), p. 23. Vol. 1 (1701), p. 54: That afternoon Came Pen: to visit me. Some discourse with her about the unkind manners of my Sons gave me a litle disturbance that Night. . . . I told her, that I meant not to enter in any talk about it, nor wou'd I have admitted any but for this reason, that if herafter She did see Some suitable neglects, to so much ingratitude, She might not apply it to any remaining prejudice toward her Self whom I had forgiven. This sure must be allow'd Charitable, but for her sattisfaction to tell her so, must needs be thought kind.

102. Vol. 1 (1700), pp. 1, 3–4.

103. Vol. 1 (1700), p. 33.

Chapter 3

1. Vol. 1 (1701), p. 156.

2. Vol. 1 (1701), p. 130 and vol. 2 (1703), p. 88; vol. 2 (1703), p. 136; vol. 1 (1701), p. 100 and vol. 2 (1704), pp. 194, 282; vol. 2 (1703), p. 154.

3. Vol. 1 (1702), p. 207.

4. Vol. 1 (1700), p. 7.

5. Vol. 1 (1700–1702), pp. 4, 203, 179.

6. Vol. 1 (1701), p. 162.

7. Vol. 1 (1701), p. 161: "ffor a litle Ugly variety, a Visiting go I, where they tell of Ladies that mannage their Domestick affairs in Such manner as argues they have much power. then home I Come an humble Mouse gnawing on the thought that in 40 year I have not gaind the priviledg to Chang a Cook Maid upon any account whatsoever."

8. Gouge, p. 152.

9. Vol. 2 (1704), pp. 316–17.

10. Vol. 1 (1701), p. 55.

11. Allestree, *Ladies' Calling*, p. 201; Diary, vol. 1 (1702), p. 194.

12. Vol. 2 (1704), p. 190; and copied out in her collection of Thoughts and Meditations, D/EP F43 pp. 544–45; the original is: Mary Astell, "Reflections upon Marriage," 1706 ed. reprinted in Hill, *First English Feminist*, pp. 90–91.

13. Halifax (see under Savile), *The Lady's New Year's Gift*, pp. 46–48, 57–60.

14. Halifax, pp. 52–56.

15. Vol. 3 (1705), p. 82; Halifax, p. 51.

16. Halifax, p. 30.

17. Halifax, p. 32.

18. Vol. 1 (1701), p. 168.

19. Vol. 1 (1702), p. 288. There is even an indication he fulfilled his promise for some time, as six months later Sarah wrote, "If the Next half year Concludes so Well as this, twill be the best as to Domestick Affairs that in almost 40 years I have known. Sir Wm having left off to Meddle with the Maids I dispose of them as is fitt." Vol. 2, p. 53.

20. Vol. 1 (1702), p. 200.

21. Vol. 1 (1702), p. 230.

22. Vol. 1 (1702), p. 230.

23. Herts. PRO D/EP F23 Correspondence of Sarah, Lady Cowper and Sir William Cowper, fols. 2, 3, Sir William to Sarah, July 26 and 31, 1702.

24. Vol. 1 (1702), p. 249.

25. Vol. 1 (1702), p. 252.

26. Herts. PRO D/EP F44, p. 88.

27. Herts. PRO D/EP F 44, p. 94.

28. Herts. PRO D/EP F 44, p. 96.

29. Patrick, *A Commentary on the First Book of Moses.*

30. Herts. PRO D/EP 44, p. 91.

31. Patrick, *A Critical Commentary Upon the Old and New Testament.*

32. Herts. PRO D/EP F 44, pp. 116–17.

33. Vol. 1 (1701), p. 61.

34. Hammond, *Paraphrase and Annotation upon all the Books of the New Testament.* Hammond was a leading defender of Anglicanism during the interregnum. He juxtaposed chastity and purity again regarding 1 Corinthians 6:13 ("Now the body is not for fornication, but for the Lord . . . "), where he commented: "Your bodies are to be consecrated to God in chastity whether in marriage or single life, and being kept pure here, must be made capable of rising to everlasting life. . . . " Sarah also copied out this passage in her collected Bible Commentary and Notes on Heresies (D/EP F39 [1680]).

35. Margaret Thickstun uses these verses in Timothy to help build her case that there was a literary effort to denigrate women through identifying their sex with the flesh, in which writers indirectly asserted that for women, childbirth was what saved, not faith through God's Grace. *Fictions of the Feminine,* p. 25. Hammond's commentary did not present it that way at all; he took childbearing in this passage to refer specifically to Mary bearing the Messiah, humankind's promise of redemption, not to all women being required to bear children for their salvation. Moreover, Sarah interpreted it in precisely the opposite direction, connecting abstinence, not childbearing, with virtue, and therefore redemption. Whatever may have been happening in some sections of the literary world of this period, Henry Hammond and Sarah certainly did not see the passage that way.

36. In *Domesticall Duties*, p. 130, for example, Gouge specifically declared that it was undutiful for either partner to deny sex to the other; Jeremy Taylor said the same thing in *The Marriage Ring* in *The Whole Works of Jeremy Taylor*, v. 4, p. 211. Patricia Crawford notes that clergy and medical advisors in general condemned abstinence. "The Construction and Experience of Maternity," p. 20.

37. Vol. 1 (1702), p. 305.

38. For example, Gouge, p. 130.

39. Crawford notes the expectation that gentlewomen would continue to have children until they had produced at least one son ("Construction and Experience of Maternity," p. 20).

40. There is disagreement among historians as to who made this decision. Crawford ("Construction and Experience of Maternity," p. 20) asserts that "little contraception was under exclusive female control." On the other hand, Angus McLaren (*History of Contraception*, pp. 153–56), Randolph Trumbach (*Rise of the Egalitarian Family*, pp. 170–79), and J. L. Flandrin (*Familles*, pp. 217–22), all suggest (but only in passing) that high-ranking women fairly frequently refused to continue sexual relations after they had produced sufficient male heirs.

41. See chapter 4 for discussion of the Cowpers' financial situation.

42. Vol. 1 (1700), p. 13.

43. Vol. 1 (1700), pp. 20–21.

44. Allestree, *Ladies' Calling*, p. 201; Gouge, p. 275; and see Crawford, "Construction and Experience of Maternity," pp. 11, 27.

45. Taylor, *Ductor Dubitantium*, pp. 693–718; Pufendorf, p. 230.

46. Gouge (p. 274) explicitly argued that children should continue to obey their parents when they were adults; Allestree (*Whole Duty of Man*, p. 279) indirectly suggests a similar view by lamenting the lack of obedience of adult children; Pufendorf (*Whole Duty of Man*, p. 234) stopped short of insisting on obedience, but argued that adults still owed their parents "piety and observance." Other writers who mentioned children's inability to repay their parents include Richard Baxter, *Christian Directory*, pp. 550–51; and Isaac Barrow, "Exposition of the Decalogue," in *The Works of the Learned Isaac Barrow*, p. 531.

47. Generally, see Amussen, *An Ordered Society*, p. 100; Schlatter, *Social Ideas of Religious Leaders*, p. 33. Specifically, see Allestree, *Whole Duty of Man*, p. 280; Barrow, pp. 530–33; and Patrick, "A Book for Beginners," in *Works*, vol. 1, p. 618.

48. Gouge, pp. 274, 307; Allestree, *Whole Duty of Man*, p. 286.

49. Allestree, *Whole Duty of Man*, pp. 288–91.

50. See, for instance, vol. 1 (1702), p. 233; vol. 3 (1705), p. 126.

51. Vol. 1 (1700), p. 42.

52. Gouge, pp. 274–75.

53. Vol. 1 (1701), p. 92.

54. Allestree, *Ladies' Calling*, p. 221; copied out in Herts. PRO D/EP F 43, p. 152.

55. Vol. 1 (1700), p. 11.

56. Vol. 1, p. 125 (1701); vol. 2 (1703), p. 93, 143.

57. Vol. 1 (1701), p. 45: "Came my Son W: to learn I suppose the Circumstances of his Fathers ill success. About half an hour past before he so much as askt how I did; to which I reply'd wel: enough. After that he address'd no perticuler discourse to me, tho' his stay was about two hours, I was much out of Countenance, but Since he Said nothing to excuse himself; disdain wou'd not let me shew Concern enough to accuse, so let it pass off in Silence and Wise:dumb. The ill usage from S^r W had almost made me Callous, but adding the trouble my Sons have Caus'd, hath petrify'd me; and (like the Fable of Niobe) much weeping hath turned me into Stone." And p. 58: "After 5 weeks absence, in Came my Son Spenc: just as we were going to dinner. He Said nothing to me, so I behaved my self in the Same fashion, as to any indifferent person, only much out of Countenance which I Endeavor'd to hide."

58. Vol. 2 (1703), p. 34.

59. Patrick, in *Works*, vol. 3, p. 522.

60. Patrick, in *Works*, vol. 3, p. 521.

61. Vol. 2 (1703), p. 29.

62. *Diaries of William Nicolson*, p. 200. This relationship was a political vulnerability for William again in early 1707 when Francis Atterbury included William's "bigamy" in the catalog of "abominable impurities" of the Whigs and the Junto in particular. Kenyon, *Revolution Principles*, pp. 116, 228 n. 45.

63. The small social world of Hertfordshire is apparent in her hearsay knowledge of her son's mistress: "I was told by one who did averr it to be true that Bet: Cul: shou'd say, every one had some Fault and she had but one, and that otherwaies she led a better Life than Ever. but by her favour robbing another woman of her Hus: is a Swinger, and pulls after it a long train of vices. . . . She hath been heard to say she Cou'd never live Easie till she gott rid of her Vertue the most troublesome thing in ye whole World." Vol. 1 (1700), p. 26.

64. Vol. 2 (1703), p. 93.

65. Vol. 2 (1703), p. 98.

66. Vol. 2 (1704), p. 261.

67. Vol. 1 (1702), p. 189.

68. Vol. 1 (1701), p. 133, "Upon some talk about that Rampant Shaker who Drown'd herself, I had this Reflection. That immodesty of behavior

makes way to lust, and gives life to wicked hopes. Schechem Sinn'd, but Dinah tempted him. She that was so light as to wander abroad alone I fear was not over difficult to yeild. Lust given way to is a pleasant madness, but is a desperate Madness when it is opposed. This hated Truth (so strongly proved) the Quakers Cannot bear to hear"; and p. 141, "Comes goodwive Burr and tells us . . . she heard it said Mad:[am] Coop:[er] [Pennington] did drown Sa: Stout. I reply'd 'twas well it Cou'd be proved She was all the while at London. Ay. quoth the Gammer, but she hired and Sent down the 3 men that did it. Said I, indeed there was most Cause why she shou'd dispatch her. They have been often urg'd to render a Reason why Sp:[encer] Shou'd, and Cou'd never give any likely account, which perhaps hath put 'em upon this Device."

69. Vol. 1 (1701), pp. 67, 80.

70. It is also worth noting here that there are no letters at all from Spencer to anyone except his brother William, and those are dated 1717. This may be partially an effect of the circumstances of preservation, but it may well reflect distance and divisions among the family, especially during the period after Spencer's marriage.

71. Throughout the period of the diary, the Cowpers kept five servants. While Sir William was alive, they comprised a footman, coachman, cook, and two maids (Vol. 1 [1702], p. 247). Hecht, *Domestic Servant in Eighteenth-Century England*, p. 7, puts the average number of staff at seven for the "moderately well-to-do" gentry, and five for the lesser gentry.

72. Hecht initially put forward this idea; recently it has been wholeheartedly endorsed by Bridget Hill, *Servants*, pp. 5, 89.

73. Hecht, pp. 71–76. For specific contemporary prescription, see for example Patrick, *A Book for Beginners* . . . in *Works*, pp. 619–20; Allestree, *Whole Duty of Man*, pp. 311–13.

74. Hill (*Servants*, p. 2) notes the wave of complaints seen in letters to newspapers, and authors such as Daniel Defoe and Bernard de Mandeville; see also Hecht, pp. 80–82.

75. Hecht, p. 77.

76. Vol. 2 (1703–1704)), pp. 88, 260.

77. Vol. 2 (1704), p. 173.

78. On the problem of servility in master-servant relations and the question of whether domestic service was an attractive career option as opposed to a job necessitated by lack of alternative employment, see Hill, *Servants*, pp. 93–103; Kent, "Ubiquitous but Invisible," pp. 111–28. Specifically with regard to servants in London, see Meldrum, "Domestic Service," pp. 27–39.

79. For instance, vol. 2 (1704), pp. 173, 233, 260. See Hill, *Servants*, p. 185, for evidence of these problems in even the relatively harmonious households of three clergymen.

80. Vol. 1 (1700), pp. 16–17. Hill suggests that ordinarily, a maid's pregnancy was cause for immediate dismissal by the mistress of the house who would fear that her husband or son was the father. Hill also suggests that the ever-present possibility of this kind of sexual relationship involving the men of the family contributed to tension between women and their maids. *Servants*, p. 51.

81. Vol. 1 (1700), pp. 19–20.

82. In *An Ordered Society*, Susan Amussen notes that husband and wife were legally bound to bring servants to church, to observe the Sabbath, and to catechize them. Hecht mentions these obligations more generally (p. 99); a contemporary description of these duties is in Allestree, *Whole Duty of Man*, p. 314.

83. Herts. PRO D/EP F44, p. 117.

84. An instance of Sir William's prolonged bad temper when Sarah pressured him to dismiss a servant is registered in the following entry: "Ever Since the Cook had order to be gone S^r W hath been very Shaggrin and often Vents his Spite and impatience att having his humour Controul'd but this Evening burst forth an expression so Diabolical that for pitty and Shame I forbear to Register but sure from my Memory it can never depart an must require a Consummate Charity to forgive." The dismissal had occurred ten days earlier. Vol. 1 (1701), p. 150.

Chapter 4

1. Wrightson, p. 17.

2. Wrightson, pp. 22–24; Sharpe, p. 153; Mingay, *The Gentry*, p. 2.

3. Stone, *An Open Elite?*, p. 290; Speck, p. 38. See also Heal and Holmes, pp. 276–318.

4. Wrightson, p. 24.

5. Mingay, *The Gentry*, p. 14.

6. Wrightson, p. 26.

7. Beckett, *The Aristocracy in England 1660–1914*, pp. 40–42; 92–93.

8. Beckett, pp. 23–24.

9. Stone, *An Open Elite?*, p. 284. See also Cannon's figures on peer creations, pp. 26, 33.

10. See especially Prest, "Lawyers," pp. 64–86; Holmes, *Augustan England*, pp. 120–24.

11. Prest, p. 86.

12. Speck, p. 45.

13. Moreover, there was a significant expansion in the number of lawyers from the mid-sixteenth to the mid-seventeenth century, partially just in line with population trends, but also because of a large increase in litigation,

as business shifted from church and manor courts to London and grew because of a busy land market. The increasing costs of becoming a barrister and separation of their activities from those of attorneys contributed to an increase in social exclusivity, and high status was reinforced by sharply increased legal fees: Barristers raised their fees fivefold between 1590 and 1660, and they doubled them again between the 1680s and 1720s. If the law in general was a particularly effective stepping-stone to higher social status, its highest echelons were simultaneously reducing mobility into their own rank, while enhancing their own prospects for movement even further up the social scale. Prest, pp. 74–84.

14. Clay, p. 178.

15. D/EP T1218, Settlement of Hertford Castle on Sarah Cowper for her life, July 13, 1686; and see at Hatfield House the Leasebook for the Earls of Salisbury, 1688. Many thanks to Mr. R. Harcourt-Williams, Hatfield House archivist, for this information.

16. Leasebook, and see H. Andrews, pp. 75–82.

17. See the addresses in D/EP F23 Correspondence of Sarah, Lady Cowper and Sir William Cowper (1662–1719). Earliest is the Charterhouse Yard address in the 1670s; in the 1690s it was the upper end of Hatton Garden; then Bedford Street in Holborn. Finally Sir William and Sarah moved to Bedford Row in March, 1706 (Diary, vol. 3, p. 214).

18. Beckett, p. 268.

19. Vol. 3 (1706), p. 206.

20. *The Making of the English Middle Class*, p. 206.

21. Vol. 1 (1700–1702), pp. 38, 149, 162, 303; vol. 2 (1703), p. 54.

22. See vol. 1 (1702), p. 179; vol. 3 (1706), p. 303.

23. Vol. 1 (1701), p. 120.

24. D/EP T1141 Will of Sir William Cowper (1700) and D/EP F50 Account of Sir William Cowper's Estate by Spencer Cowper (1706). Narcissus Luttrell's report has been taken up by Henning and by *Victoria History of the County of Hertfordshire*.

25. Vol. 4 (1708), p. 175.

26. Bourdieu, *Outline of a Theory of Practice*, pp. 179–83, offers this term to describe the intangible assets that make up a family's honor and reputation—their manner of living, direct or indirect display of wealth, and their connections to others within and without the family.

27. Vol. 1 (1700), p. 15.

28. Vol. 1 (1701), p. 67. There is a similar assertion of lack of complacency in vol. 2, p. 69.

29. *Women and Religion*, p. 91.

30. Mendelson, "Stuart Women's Diaries," p. 190; Beckett, p. 341.

31. Beckett, p. 350.

32. Sharpe, *Early Modern England*, p. 196. Regarding the efforts of the monarchy to assert control (initially over the aristocracy) through imposition of a code of behavior at court, see especially Elias. Regarding subsequent developments and the effect on distinctions between public and private, see vol. 3 of *A History of Private Life*, general eds. Philippe Ariès and Georges Duby, pp. 163–87.

33. See originally Alice Clark, *Working Life of Women in the Seventeenth Century*. Later historians such as Susan Cahn, in *Industry of Devotion: The Transformation of Women's Work in England 1500–1660*, or Lindsey Charles and Lorna Duffin, eds., *Women and Work in Pre-Industrial England*, have altered the timing and the definition of capitalism somewhat, arguing for an earlier retreat into the private sphere than the industrial revolution, but have accepted the fundamental thesis. See for example Elaine Hobby, *Virtue of Necessity: English Women's Writing 1649–1688*, where women's writing is taken as a means of resistance to an assumed trend of confinement in the domestic sphere.

34. "Golden Age to Separate Spheres?" pp. 383–414.

35. As Vickery (*The Gentleman's Daughter*, p. 10) does in her recent comprehensive treatment of her earlier argument.

36. Vickery, *Gentleman's Daughter*, p. 196, emphasizes the power of women as hostesses and that "social exchanges in homes have a 'public function'" as part of her overall rejection of the notion of the eighteenth century as a period when a woman's world constricted, confining her to a "private" domestic arena. Work on sociability and gender relations and the fluidity of public-private boundaries on both sides of the Atlantic is growing daily; see for instance Westhauser, "Friendship and Family in Early Modern England"; Whyman, *Sociability and Power in Late-Stuart England*; Hanson, *A Very Social Time*; and C. Dallett Hemphill, *Bowing to Necessities: A History of Manners in America 1620–1860*, especially pp. 105–22.

37. Mendelson, "Stuart Women's Diaries," p. 190.

38. For the surge in interest in the issue of structured social interaction by contemporary writers and the agenda of the most famous author on manners, see Lawrence Klein, "Liberty, Manners, and Politeness in Early Eighteenth-Century England," and further expansion in his book *Shaftesbury and the Culture of Politeness: Moral Discourse and Cultural Politics in Early Eighteenth-Century England*. On the development of the concept of "civility" in social interaction in the seventeenth century, see Anna Bryson, *From Courtesy to Civility: Changing Codes of Conduct in Early Modern England*.

39. Allestree, *The Ladies' Calling*, pp. 9–19; Halifax, pp. 95–108.

40. Halifax, pp. 95–96.

41. Allestree, *Ladies' Calling*, p. 70; Halifax, p. 116.

42. Jeremy Taylor, *A Discourse on the Nature, Offices, and Measures of Friendship*, pp. 25, 29, 101.

43. Halifax, pp. 118–19.

44. Halifax, pp. 126, 154.

45. Vol. 3 (1705), pp. 76–77, citing Halifax, p. 118.

46. Vol. 2 (1703), pp. 30–31.

47. Vol. 1 (1702), p. 253.

48. From sermons she heard, as well as texts she read, for instance: "A good Day I hope to my Soul, if I improve by a most Excellent Sermon I heard from Doctor Man:[ningham] teaching us how to order Conversation aright. that our Discourse in Company be such as may Edify our Selves and others" (Vol. 1 [1700], p. 22).

49. Vol. 1 (1700), p. 13.

50. Vol. 1 (1701), p. 140, citing 1 Timothy 4:7 and John 16:33.

51. Vol. 2 (1703), p. 11, citing Psalm 119:46.

52. Arditi, *Genealogy of Manners*, sees, beginning with Locke's *Some Thoughts Concerning Education*, "the separation of manners and morals in the English concept of civility" (p. 184).

53. "If I outlive this Winter I intend to lay aside formal Visiting daies, being no longer able to bear the impertinence that attends them. It dissipates all Usefull thoughts, and sets me in a ferment to hear the Vile talk of most people. If my acquaintance do not mend, I'le break off whatever it Costs mee He who walketh with Wise men Shall be Wise, but a Companion of Fools Shall be the Worse for it. He that Converses with the Just pertakes of their good Manners and Carries away a Sweet remembrance of their Words." Vol. 2 (1703), p. 31, citing Proverbs 13:20.

54. The first eighteen pages of the diary, covering the end of July to mid-October 1700, for much of which she was in Hertford and often alone, illustrate her ambivalence at its height. She alternated between claiming that she preferred the entertainment of reading and meditation to the idleness and distraction of conversation with those acquaintances she did see and observing frequently that she was "alone all day" or "living solitary."

55. Vol. 2 (1704), p. 219.

56. Vol. 1 (1701), pp. 50–51: "Two La: who I think bear me no ill will, yet abruptly fell into an Extravagant praise of S^r J: Holt [Chief Justice Holt who had refused to grant Spencer bail] whom they must needs know I have no reason to Commend. . . . To these La: I made no manner of reply, ffor of whom I cannot Speak well I choose to say Nothing. besides in this case I have been most Especially Circumspect, being very Secure that no Indiscretion of mine hath in the least added to the danger or suffering of my ffamily, which assurance gives me no small Sattisfaction."

57. In a particularly benevolent moment, having just received a supportive letter and perhaps practical assistance from Lady Rachel Russell regarding Spencer's troubles she commented, "Among my Acquaintance and Common ffriendships I meet with very good reception and Esteem far beyond what in Reason I coud expect. A letter I received from a friend full of kind and Compassionate expressions of a tender sense of what she beleives me to Suffer, is the occasion of this saying. I do ingeniously Confess to have found the world very Charitable to me, and that I never mett with any Censure, but what upon due reflection I was Conscious that something had been done by me which gave the occasion. tho' Some mistake might Carry it further than it was deserv'd." Vol. 1 (1701), p. 67.

58. In descending order of frequency, the "top ten" names are: Colonel Plummer (her neighbor from 1706 and known before then); John Hough, bishop of Litchfield and Coventry; Lady Holt (the wife of Chief Justice Holt, who had presided at Spencer's trial—not to Sarah's satisfaction, as she called him "Cheif Injustice Holt"—but having broken their social connection during and after the trial, the relationship was reestablished in 1703, on Lady Holt's initiative, according to Sarah); Doctor Manningham (rector of her parish, Saint Andrew's, Holborn, and then bishop of Chichester); Gilbert Burnet (bishop of Salisbury); Lady Rachel Russell (a clearly unequal relationship, with Sarah as a deferential inferior and sometimes client); Lady Calverly (a connection of Mary Cowper); Simon Patrick (bishop of Ely); John Williams (bishop of Chichester); and Lady Nevil (perhaps a connection of Judith Cowper). John Sharp, archbishop of York, is mentioned four times as well.

59. Vol. 1 (1702), p. 220.

60. In a very rough and unscientific count, there are twenty-nine people mentioned as Mr. or Mrs, twelve referred to as sir, thirty-eight referred to as lady, and five referred to as lord. Lady and lord, however, are very misleading as indicators of rank without more specific information; for example, the hated Chief Justice Holt and his wife are termed lord and lady because of his office, obviously, rather than his birth.

61. See vol. 2 (1703), pp. 54–55: "In my travels I mett with a Stupify'd dull Atheist the most Nauseous of all Creatures. Some of 'em have Witt which renders them more tollerable tho' more dangerous, what they wou'd infuse is Subtile and apt to infect, but this wretched Old fellow So Sensless and inconsistent in his babling, Stirrs nothing but loathing of his folly, so I quickly left him. In the next place I mett a Whig:woman who Consumes herself with fiery Zeal for the party. . . . Methinks these people with divers Such like one may reckon Stark Mad before they Come to dy."

62. Vol. 1 (1701), p. 111: "To our Hartford Enemies, and false ungratefull friends when they Come in my way, this is my fashion. I cast 'em the

best looks with the finest Speech I can frame, but withdraw so soon as may be, and by all means possible avoid having any thing to do with 'em." And the next day, "My Solitary Circumstances in this place force me to read; more than enough, for the litle Company I am Condemn'd to is Such, that I must not only bear with their impertinence but keep Strict watch that I say nothing w^c they may pervert to mischeif. While among 'em, I take Special Care to appear alwaies in good humour, but get away when I can."

63. Vol. 1 (1701), p. 136; and see also vol. 1 (1700), pp. 13, 14, 18.

64. Vol. 1 (1700–1701), p. 26: "A Dissenter . . . told me that he refused to pay his Builders . . . pleading priviledg of parliment to avoid his Creditors. . . . Let him that thinks he standeth take heed lest he fall. how Empty and vain is a formal profession, and loud praying without Sincerity."; p. 111: "This Day Dined with me a preaching Anabaptist who piously denounceth ruin on the now prevailing party whom he Stiles his Enemies. upon my seeming to dislike his presuming, he put to me this question. how he Cou'd fulfill that precept. If thine Enemy hunger give him meat, if he thirst give him Drink, unless poverty reduced them to want it? Did ever any one so hear an Infidel Burlesque Christianity more than this precious Saint."

65. Such as her conflation of both in an early complaint: "The litle Company this place affords me, is mostly dissenters, who seem to me very ignorant of what they profess. So that by their Conversation I daily find Reason to Bless God that hath kept me in the Communion of the Establish'd Church." Vol. 1 (1700), p. 12.

66. Vol. 1 (1701), p. 108.

67. Holmes, *British Politics*, p. 315.

68. Vol. 1 (1700), pp. 53–54.

69. Vol. 1 (1701), p. 89.

70. Sara Mendelson in fact contrasts Sarah's mobility with the earlier experience of Lady Anne Clifford, who was marooned in the countryside, and did not expect (as Sarah did) to accompany her husband to London in the season. "Stuart Women's Diaries," p. 200.

71. For instance, she visited Flamsteed, the Royal Astronomer, in Greenwich. Vol. 1 (1702), p. 250.

72. See Pritchard, pp. 255–56.

73. Vol. 2 (1703), p. 131.

74. See for example Sarah's account of Lady Rachel's assistance, probably in helping to prevent Spencer's retrial: "The Excellent La: Russel, to whom (the day before) I address'd my Self for some help against the proceedings of that Melencholly Matter, most readily undertook, and did Effectually perform it, which in a most Compassionate Endearing manner She Let me know by her letter. . . . Being laid up I cou'd not wait upon this Great La: I return'd humble thanks in paper." Vol. 1 (1701), p. 68.

75. See Hirschberg, "Episcopal Incomes and Expenses," pp. 213–16; there is not complete information for every bishopric, and figuring in commendams presents an additional complication, but Canterbury, York, London, Durham, and Winchester all probably had annual incomes of over £2,500 during the period of the diary—some well over. Salisbury and Ely may not have been much below this figure; Lichfield and Chichester were in the £1,000 to £1,500 category—a distinct rung up from the roughly £500 annual income of a see like Bristol, Exeter, or Oxford.

76. Aside from the obvious allegiance of someone like Gilbert Burnet, and characterizations in brief biographical sketches for some of the lesser-known figures, concrete evidence at least on one issue comes from Norman Sykes's reprint of the division lists for the bill against occasional conformity in 1703 and the bill for the repeal of the act against occasional conformity in 1718. Burnet, Patrick, Hough, and Williams all voted against the bill in 1703 (and all had been appointed by William III); Hough voted for the repeal in 1718 and Manningham (appointed by Anne) voted against. *Church and State in England in the Eighteenth Century*, p. 35.

77. She had some reluctant contact with Parson Hodgkin, since he was rector of her son's parish church, which was also where she wished to be buried, but she despised him: "there's a Tory Jacobite Parson of the Parish where my Son has Built his Seat; Who 'tis said for years past has made it his Business to Libel the Family in Prose an Rhimes but now this Hypocrite Comes and makes Court to him and the Week he was made Lord Keeper; this Wretch took his Text. Let your Moderation be known unto all Men; The Lord is att Hand." Vol. 3 (1705), p. 159.

78. Vol. 1 (1701), p. 162.

79. Sykes (*Church and State*, pp. 239, 254–56) cites contemporary commentary by Steele, Fielding, and Wesley, condemning the destruction of a devotional atmosphere, as some churchgoers came late, looked around to see who else was there, bowed to each other, and carried on conversations during the service. Earle (*The Making of the English Middle Class*, p. 247) sees this attitude in the middle classes and even among Dissenters.

80. Sykes, *Church and State*, pp. 237, 258.

81. G. R. Cragg, "The Churchman," p. 55; O'Day, *English Clergy*, p. 103.

82. O'Day, "Anatomy," p. 53. While it is a matter of debate just how extensive the poorest ranks of the clergy were, and how grim their prospects of advancement, it does seem that there was a slow, erratic improvement in both the incomes and status of the clergy over the course of the early modern period. Sykes calls the system of preferment for the mass of the clergy a "lottery" with very low chances of drawing a prosperous ticket and is doubtful about the overall effect of Queen Anne's Bounty (*Church and*

State, p. 227); Holmes is more positive about the prospects for the lower clergy and the effect of the Bounty (*Augustan England,* pp. 86, 95, 100); and O'Day notes studies by Pruett and Virgin showing a significant, if uneven, improvement in clerical salaries and a rise in social origin and standing for the clergy (O'Day "Anatomy," pp. 54–55).

83. This frequency would not make her entirely unusual according to W. Jacob (*Lay People and Religion,* pp. 60–62), who notes that often people with leisure might well go to Sunday services twice and perhaps morning prayers two or three times a week as well, belying the often-articulated notion that the early eighteenth century marked a period of rampant nonattendance at church.

84. Vol. 1 (1700), p. 20.

85. Vol. 1 (1701), p. 54.

86. Sarah most often cited prescriptive sources when reminding herself of her duty to attend services; for example, vol. 3 (1705), p. 123 and on the more specific duty not to neglect receiving the Sacrament, see vol. 3 (1706), pp. 278–79.

87. Vol. 1 (1702), p. 196. See also her criticisms of the way the bishop of Salisbury preached: If Modesty be the Science of Decent Motion (as Some have defin'd it) to my thinking I never saw less. they who made him a priest Spoil'd a good player, the Same manners without Lawn Sleeves wou'd incurr the Title of Tub:preacher. tho' he talks very Earnest, yet for my life I know not how to Think[?] is more than in jest. . . . Most Certain a Comely Deportment is an Essential qualification for a good preacher. Vol. 1 (1702), p. 299.

88. See vol. 1 (1702), p. 222, where she commends the bishop of Gloucester for "abundance of honest meaning, but not much judgment" in his sermon; vol. 2 (1703), p. 11: "There are some preachers I take great delight to hear, because they Seem in good Earnest to Beleive what they Teach."

89. Vol. 1 (1701), pp. 156–57.

90. Vol. 1(1701–1702), pp. 67, 174; vol. 3 (1705–1706), pp. 27, 206.

91. In vol. 1 (1702), p. 298, she said explicitly: "On holidays appointed by the State, I choose to hear what men Say at Court."

92. During Lent 1702 she heard Dr. Smalridge and mentioned going to the Boyle Lecture, and in Lent 1704 she heard and commended Dr. Pratt. Vol. 1 (1702), pp. 192, 212; vol. 2 (1704), p. 186.

93. Vol. 1 (1701–1702), pp. 76, 283.

94. Sykes in particular describes the London fashionable preaching scene and notes that in 1714 there were 72 churches with twice daily services (*Church and State,* pp. 254–55).

95. As when complaining of how bereft of good company she is in London in the summer: "Here I can come at no Company, either from home or gone out of Town, sure 'twas never more Empty. The good preachers are likewise absent, which abates the Solace even of going to Church." Vol. 1 (1702), p. 266. Or on the subject of good preaching in general: "Tho' I am very much indisposed, yet having been accustom'd to follow the Lent Lectures, I go on in that way. ffor were it not a Religious matter, I know no greater pleasure, than to hear learn'd and 'tis to be hoped good men discourse their best for an hour." Vol. 1 (1702), p. 195.

96. Owen, *English Philanthropy*, p. 20.

97. Jones, *Charity School Movement*, pp. 7, 10. See also W. Jacob, pp. 155–56.

98. Gray, *History of English Philanthropy*, pp. 267–70; Beckett, p. 356.

99. Vince, "Man's Economic Status," p. 33, where he points to Thomas Tenison's 1681 Sermon, "Concerning Discretion in Giving Alms," as the beginning of a long line of sermons advocating "prudent restraint" in giving.

100. Vince, p. 33; Owen, p. 27.

101. Speck, p. 79. A number of concurrent trends may have been responsible for this shift in attitude; in *Order and Disorder in Early Modern England*, pp. 13–15, Anthony Fletcher and John Stevenson suggest that the institutionalization of poor relief so that almsgiving could be viewed as a responsibility of the state, not the individual, reduced both the personal feeling of obligation to the poor and personal contact with them. See also Baugh, "Poverty, Protestantism and Political Economy: English Attitudes Toward the Poor," pp. 86–91, where he argues for a slightly later trend (from the mid-eighteenth century rather than the late seventeenth) toward a severe and fatalistic attitude toward the poor based on economic prosperity and progress followed by a period of pauperization brought on by harvest crises, declining wages, and rising prices.

102. Vol. 1 (1702), p. 175: "This Chris:mas [1701] I have given in Charity and Bounty Seven pounds."

103. Vol. 1 (1701), p. 78.

104. Beckett also points out that land gifts, setting up schools, and other forms of benevolence are difficult to quantify, and thus not really taken into account (pp. 355–56).

105. Lummis and Marsh, *Woman's Domain*, p. 35.

106. Vol. 1 (1700), p. 25. It should also be noted that despite her poor opinion of his generosity and piety, Sir William apparently was in the habit of disbursing £12 pounds each year at Christmas himself. He left £12 pounds to the poor in his will, explicitly as a final gesture in accordance

with his practice while alive. D/EP T1141 Will of Sir William Cowper (1700).

107. Vol. 1 (1701), p. 120.

108. Vol. 1 (1700), p. 25. The society had been founded just a year earlier with two concurrent goals of spreading the gospel to the English plantations abroad and encouraging the establishment of charity schools at home. The SPCK was run by an association of philanthropic individuals and supported by what was essentially joint stock financing, where numerous people subscribed small sums to the endeavor. Jones, p. 3. For a recent discussion of the organization's political, social, and ideological context, see Craig Rose, "The Origins and Ideals of the SPCK 1699–1716," pp. 172–90. On the founding of schools, often charitable, in the sixteenth and seventeenth centuries, see Charlton, *Women, Religion and Education*, pp. 142–52.

109. Jones, pp. 4–8, 35; Rose, pp. 180–85; and Owen, pp. 13 and 24, where he notes that the two earliest Anglican charity schools were set up in 1685 by Simon Patrick at Saint Margaret's Westminster and by Thomas Tenison at Saint James Westminster, specifically to counter Jesuit schools. See also Unwin, *Charity Schools*, p. 2.

110. Rose, p. 173, calls the early members "politically a motley crew"; the five founders were of all stripes—Tory, Whig, and self-consciously undefined. Jones (pp. 6–8, 41) categorizes the members as "active Christians."

111. To be a member, as opposed to subscriber, one had to be proposed twice and then approved at an SPCK meeting. While women were subscribers, there were no women members. See *A Chapter in English Church History: SPCK Minutes 1698–1704*. The bishops of Worcester, Chichester, Bath and Wells, and Chester are listed, as is Sarah's pastor, Dr. Manningham. *SPCK Minutes*, pp. 4–6. See also Allen and MacClure, *Two Hundred Years of the SPCK 1698–1898*, p. 21, who note that both archbishops and the bishop of London countenanced the society, and at least ten bishops eventually became members.

112. *SPCK Minutes* pp. 25, 41–42. The number of girls was doubled to eighty in 1701 (p. 135). Aside from Saint George's, Southwark, where fundraising began a week earlier, Saint Andrew's was the first parish to begin the charity school movement from 1699. Jones, p. 56.

113. *SPCK Minutes*, pp. 91, 100.

114. The survival rate for these schools is varied and seems to have depended on whether and how soon they were endowed rather than having to rely entirely on subscriptions, which could fluctuate from year to year and were hard to sustain. Owen, pp. 25, 30; Jones, pp. 52, 57. The data on charity school income from the *Account of Charity Schools Lately Erected in Great Britain and Ireland* (beginning in 1704 and published annually with updates and the text of each year's sermon) is self-reported, incom-

plete, not always consistent in categories, and suspiciously unchanging in some amounts and schools, but broadly speaking, taking into account the number of pupils in each parish, the estimated costs, and the reported income from various sources (the 1707 edition figured that ordinarily it would cost £75 per year to educate fifty boys, including their clothes, schoolmaster salaries, and building and materials costs, and £60 per year to educate fifty girls), Saint Andrew's subscription income alone in 1706 exceeded its costs, not to mention its gift and sermon collection income, both of which were well above the typical amount reported. The 1709 Account for 1708 shows a similarly comfortable income, with an increase in the number of pupils and a concurrent increase in subscriptions.

115. Jones, p. 39.

116. Vol. 3 (1705), p. 57.

117. Vol. 3 (1706), p. 229; vol. 4 (1707–1708), pp. 50, 176.

118. See *An Account of the Society for Propagating the Gospel in Foreign Parts . . . With their proceedings and success . . .* (1706) pp. 15, 34. Thomas Tenison, the archbishop of Canterbury, was very much at the forefront of this endeavor—named as the first president, he donated 20 guineas for the initial expenses, and offered his library at Saint Martin-in- the-Fields as a meeting place. *Account*, p. 17; and C. Pascoe, *Two Hundred Years of the SPG*, pp. 5–7.

119. The 1706 *Account* (pp. 40–53) describes the difficulty the society had in convincing anyone to go and try to counter the influence of French missionaries among the Iroquois; after the salary was doubled a Mr. Moor went but despite assuring the Society of his continuing efforts, he reported no success at Albany. By 1707, over £500 promised in subscriptions remained unpaid—roughly half of that year's expenditures. Pascoe, pp. 823, 830.

120. Pascoe, p. 822.

121. *Account*, pp. 85–87.

122. Mrs. Stephens of Epsom and Mrs. Littleton of Windsor, p. 87.

123. *Account*, p. 85. Certainly Patricia Crawford (in *Women and Religion*, p. 207) suggests that women were active supporters of these charity endeavors.

124. *Account*, p. 86.

125. John Tillotson, *The Works of the Most Reverend Dr John Tillotson*, sermon 24, p. 278, at the funeral of Dr. Benjamin Whichcote (1683).

126. Vol. 4 (1707), p. 50.

127. See Isaac Barrow, sermon 21, "Of Quietness and Doing our own Business"; and sermon 31, "The Duty and Reward of Bounty to the Poor," in *Works*, vol. 1, pp. 288–93; 423–30.

128. Borsay, *English Urban Renaissance*, p. 251.

129. Borsay, p. 252.

Chapter 5

1. Vol. 1 (1701), p.67.
2. Vol. 1 (1701), p.95.
3. Vol. 1 (March 1702), pp.196–202.
4. Vol. 1 (1702), p.229. While not in direct quotation, this passage in the diary strongly echoes Charron, *Of Wisdom* (1697), p.308; Parsons, *Christian Directory* (1660), pp. 184–89; and Ranew, *Practical Discourses Concerning Death and Heaven* (1694), pp.43–44. Warnings about the dangers of waiting to prepare for death were standard in many devotional works of the period.
5. Vol. 3 (1705), p. 99.
6. At the back of D/EP F36 Poems and Sayings (1670) and published here in the Appendix. There is some, but not a lot, of overlap with Sommerville's discussion of forty-nine of the most popular works of this period: Thomas à Kempis, Jeremy Taylor, and Simon Patrick are on both lists. C. John Sommerville, *Popular Religion in Restoration England*, pp. 33–56. Sarah's book titles in general were quite highbrow.
7. Vol. 1 (1702), p. 312.
8. For a thoughtful treatment of the development of Anglican thought in the Restoration period, see John Spurr, *The Restoration Church of England*, pp. 234–353. See also Cragg, *From Puritanism to the Age of Reason*.
9. Rivers, *Reason, Grace and Sentiment*, pp. 5–25.
10. There is still no consensus on exactly what "latitudinarian" means and where its conceptual and temporal boundaries are to be located, but it is at least safe to say that in the latter half of the seventeenth century, the term refers to the principles and program of a group of English churchmen, most notably John Tillotson, archbishop of Canterbury, Simon Patrick, bishop of Ely, and Edward Stillingfleet, bishop of Worcester, who in their sermons and treatises elevated morality at the expense of spirituality or doctrine, and argued for "the reasonableness of Christianity." These three men were particularly influential advocates because they wrote extensively, were famous preachers, and as bishops under William III had a chance to implement their vision on a wide scale. Griffin, *Latitudinarianism*, pp. 3–17, 26. See also Spurr, "'Latitudinarianism' and the Restoration Church"; Kroll et al., eds., *Philosophy, Science, and Religion in Restoration England 1640–1700*; Cragg, *Puritanism*, pp. 61–84; Rupp, *Religion in England*, pp. 29–38; and John Walsh's introduction to *The Church of England c. 1689–c. 1833*, pp. 29–51.
11. Herts. PRO D/EP F 44, preface.

12. Vol. 2 (1703), p. 132; vol. 4 (1709), p. 355.

13. Vol. 1 (1701), p. 132. Thomas Manton was a moderate Presbyterian and Joseph Hall, bishop of Norwich, was deprived in the Interregnum and ordained Simon Patrick and others covertly.

14. Vol. 2 (1703), p. 53.

15. Vol. 1 (1701), pp. 112, 152.

16. Sommerville, p. 38.

17. Spurr, *Restoration*, pp. 308–11; Allison, *Rise of Moralism*, pp. 94, 206–7.

18. Vol. 2 (1703), pp. 157–58.

19. Vol. 2 (1704), p. 197.

20. "But if wee wou'd Spend that time in recounting God's Mercies to us, and giving him our Solemn Thanks for them; which wee Spend in Complaining, in finding fault with one another, and aggravating every thing which displeases us; Wee Shou'd be perfectly Cured of these Distempers, and ashamed to make such a bustle and stir as we about Such Small things as now disquiet us. Wee Shall soon suppress Anger and Rage at those that offend us when wee remember with due thankfulness as wee ought to do perpetually how oft we have provoked God and have been mercifully forborne and forgiven by his patient Goodness toward us." Vol. 2 (1703), pp. 97–98.

21. Vol. 1 (1701), p. 147, and vol. 2 (1703), p. 91: "Of K: Charles 1st it is said he was kind to his Servants, yet they felt Sometimes the hasty Sallies of his Anger, Which Shews the Greatest of Men may be left without a Guard against passion."

22. Vol. 2 (1703), p. 78.

23. Vol. 1 (1701), p. 164.

24. Vol. 1 (1702), p. 224.

25. Vol. 2 (1704), p. 285.

26. Vol. 1 (1701), p. 82.

27. Vol. 1 (1701), p. 106. This annual preoccupation continued through the rest of the diary; see vol. 6 (1713), p. 259: "Tho' I have not been quite rid of my Usual Whimsy on This Day; yet thro' Mercy no Accident happening to increase my Imaginations, I past it without Terror, Blessed be God."

28. See Spurr, "'Rational Religion' in Restoration England," pp. 563–85, on the rhetoric of "reasonable" religion and the challenge by defenders of revelation in a struggle between laity and clergy for supremacy in the intellectual world.

29. For a full statement of this view, see Sommerville, *The Secularization of Early Modern England*; the archetypical opposing view is Clark (*English*

Society: 1688–1832), who argues for the omnipresence of Anglicanism in society as a whole for the entire eighteenth century.

30. Vol. 1 (1701), pp. 55–56.

31. Vol. 1 (1701), p. 84.

32. On saints' days see for example vol. 2 (1703–1704), pp. 129 and 319, where it is explained that saints are to emulate, not to worship or to ask to intercede.

33. Champion, *Pillars of Priestcraft Shaken*, pp. 24, 107–18. See also Sullivan, *John Toland and the Deist Controversy*, and M. Jacob, *The Radical Enlightenment: Pantheists, Freemasons and Republicans*.

34. "I Receiv'd the Blessed Sacrament. Doth there Remain No more Sacrifice for Sin? then it Stands us in great Stead to take heed to the utmost of Sining beyond what this Sacrifice will Atone for; that is indeed to take heed of Sining at all. For Since the Merits of this Sacrifice will be available to None but Such as Repent of their Sins, become Obedient, and are Sanctify'd in this Life." Vol. 4 (1709), p. 358.

35. As in her extract on the Thursday before Easter from George Stanhope's *Paraphrase and Comment* (vol. 2, p. 539) on Luke 23:34 for that day: "Father forgive them—praying God to forgive them implies, that He himself forgave them. 'Tis true that Christ as God, Cou'd Bestow the Blessing he here intercedes for. But in all those Actions w^c Speak Submission (and Such to be Sure Prayer is) he is to be Consider'd as a mere Man And the Powers of the Divine Nature, tho' actually in Seperable from his Humane, yet are at such times to be look'd upon as under a Voluntary Suspension. And therfore neither dos the humble Manner of this Intercession prove any thing against his Divinity. . . . " And see defenses of the entirety of Christ's propitiation for sin in entries just after she has been to Holy Communion, as in "Shall not then his Blood Whose Person is Divine and so his Blood the Blood of God by the Unity of the Same Eternal Spirit be Effectual to Cleanse mens Souls from the guilt of those Sins that make liable to Death." Vol. 3 (1705), p. 47.

36. Vol. 7 (1714), p. 105. The reference is from one of a collection of Tillotson's sermons on these issues called "Concerning the Divinity and Incarnation of our Blessed Savior," preached at Saint Lawrence Jewry in the 1670s and 1680s. Sermon XLVIII, "Concerning the Unity of the Divine Nature and the Blessed Trinity," in Tillotson, *Works*, vol. 1, p. 460.

37. Spurr, *Restoration*, pp. 268–73; Griffin, pp. 150–51.

38. Walsh and Taylor, p. 16.

39. Ashcraft, "Latitudinarianism and Toleration," pp. 151–60.

40. Griffin (pp. 105–17; 132–34) develops this idea for the latitudinarian case, arguing that the insistence on using reason as a yardstick for doctrine opened the way for heterodoxy and also meant that eventually in the eight-

eenth century latitudinarianism would shelter Deist and Socinian thinkers. For a rejection of the idea that the rational rhetoric was "paving the way for Deism by its concessions to reason" see Spurr, "'Rational Religion'," p. 584.

41. Vol. 2 (1704), p. 231; Sermon XLVIII, "Concerning the Unity of the Divine Nature and the Blessed Trinity," in Tillotson, *Works*, vol. 1, p. 462.

42. See Hunter, "Science and Heterodoxy," pp. 438–55, for a discussion of the meaning and importance of the term "atheism" in Restoration England, in opposition to the disparagement of the significance of fears of atheism in M. Jacob's analysis, *The Newtonians and the English Revolution 1689–1720*.

43. Vol. 4 (1709), p. 301.

44. Vol. 2 (1704), p. 186.

45. Spurr (*Restoration*, pp. 218–27) notes the growing lay discussion and publication of divinity.

46. Vol. 1 (1701), p. 152.

47. Vol. 2 (1704), p. 310.

48. Vol. 3 (1705), p. 63.

49. D/EP F41 "History of the World" (1686), from William Howell, *An Institution of General History: or, The History of the World* (1680).

50. Vol. 1 (1701), p. 110.

51. Vol. 3 (1705), p. 28.

52. As noted in Chapter 2 above, Sarah explicitly recognized her dilemma, remarking: "It greives me I no offner Can Comply with his [Sir William's] Sentiments about Government, being enclin'd to Love Order and Obedience, I think him too much a favorer of licentious Liberty, so that these debates make me somewhat uneasie, since the interest of my family bends me to wish well to the party he is engag'd with, and my opinion leads me to think the Contrary best for the good of the Community." Vol. 1 (1700), p. 16.

53. Vol. 2 (1703), p. 36. See also vol. 2 (1704), p. 210.

54. Vol. 1 (1701), p. 124.

55. On two occasions she mentioned reading plays (*Tamerlane* and *The Tender Husband*) and once attempted *Don Quixote*, all on recommendation either of the work or that she approved of the author in a different context. *Tamerlane* she found unrealistic, *The Tender Husband* sentimental, and *Don Quixote* incomprehensible. Vol. 1 (1701–1702), pp. 189, 97; vol. 3 (1705), p. 74.

56. Walsh and Taylor, p. 22; Champion, p. 6.

57. Vol. 2 (1703), p. 152. This passage may be a paraphrase from Edward Stillingfleet's *Irenicum* (1661), a conciliatory work written when comprehension of the Presbyterians looked its most feasible. Stillingfleet later

repudiated parts of it as too accommodating. And see her specific citation of Stillingfleet on this issue in vol. 7 (1714), p. 96: "Bishop Stillingfleet Says, God will one Day Convince Men That the Unity of The Church Ly's more in the Unity of Faith and Affections, than in Uniformity of Doubtfull Rites and Ceremonies. It is a Certain Maxim That no mans Religion is rightly Founded which is Built only upon Custom and Education, and not upon His own Conviction and Choice."

58. Holmes, *Making of a Great Power*, pp. 457–58.

59. Vol. 1 (1702), p. 316.

60. Vol. 2 (1703), p. 10. A marginated addendum to the entry notes that "This bill was at last thrown out of both Houses of Parliment or rather lost."

Chapter 6

1. Sarah estimates Spencer's income on others' report, as £3,000 to £4,000 yearly in 1706. Vol. 3 (1706), p. 264.

2. Campbell, pp. 277–80; Herts. PRO D/EP F 54, fol. 57 Sir Francis Drake to William Cowper n.d.

3. Already in 1699 when the matter first arose William had spoken in defense of Somers, who had as far back as 1690 commended William's performance at the bar and suggested he go into politics. Sachse, *Lord Somers*, pp. 164, 179.

4. Oxford Bodleian i, 78, 69, Sir Richard Cocks, Diary. I am grateful to Mark Knights of the History of Parliament Trust for this reference. See also Cocks, *The Parliamentary Diary of Sir Richard Cocks 1698–1702*.

5. Clay, p. 179.

6. Clay, p. 185.

7. Vol. 2 (1704), p. 228.

8. The two biblical quotations to which Sarah alluded were the parable of the rich man warned against being one who "layeth up treasure for himself and is not rich toward God" and this passage in Jeremiah: "Let not the wise man glory in his wisdom, neither let the mighty man glory in his might, let not the rich man glory in his riches: But let him that glorieth, glory in this, that he understandeth and knoweth me, that I am the Lord."

9. Vol. 2 (1704), p. 312. Lord Halifax had employed William's services in a dispute with Lord Carmarthen over a position in the Exchequer.

10. Vol. 2 (1704), p. 312.

11. Vol. 3 (1705), p. 99.

12. Queen Anne had told Wright when she kept him on as lord keeper after the death of William III that she would not have done so had she known of a fitter person. Under attack in the House of Commons as at best

ineffective, at worst corruptly partisan, by the time he was removed "he had totally lost the esteem of all parties." Glassey, *Politics and the Appointments of Justices of the Peace*, pp. 153, 163, 170.

13. This "hard core of Whig politicians" who since the late 1690s had held important offices of state and had been instrumental in managing elections, patronage, and influencing votes in Parliament were Lord Somers, Lord Russell, the earl of Devonshire, Charles Montagu, viscount Halifax, Wharton, and the younger Sunderland. As well as working together politically, these men formed a social network grounded in their membership in the Kit-Cat Club. "The Junto lords were regarded as greedy, overbearing, and unscrupulous" by many, including Queen Anne. They constituted "a coherent, effective, and reasonably united Whig leadership." Sachse, pp. 113–14.

14. Gregg, *Queen Anne*, p. 204; Sachse, p. 230 n. 101, referring to Brown, *Letters and Diplomatic Instructions of Queen Anne* (London, 1935), p. 172, Holmes, *British Politics*, p. 489, referring to BL Add MSS 28070, fol. 12.

15. Holmes, *British Politics*, p. 242.

16. Green, *Queen Anne*, p. 144. On his first-class oratory skills, fine legal mind, and personable demeanor, see *The London Diaries of William Nicolson, Bishop of Carlisle 1702–1718*, pp. 65, 50; Glassey calls him "a man of great personal distinction; he was eloquent, witty, and polished in manner" (p. 171).

17. It is not clear exactly how much influence Sarah, the duchess of Marlborough, wielded on William's behalf. While she claimed credit retrospectively for the appointment, saying "For my Lord Cowper, I continually laboured with the Queen to make him keeper, to save the Duke of Marlborough and Lord Godolphin from an application so disagreeable to her; and at last, by a great deal of drudgery, I succeeded." *Private Correspondence of Sarah, Duchess of Marlborough*, vol. 2, pp. 149–50. Sir David Hamilton, physician to the Queen and friend of William's, noted in 1710 "The Queen told me that the putting out of Wright and putting in Cowper, made no difference between the Duchess and her, for the Duchess had never spoke but once to her of it." *Diary of Sir David Hamilton*, p. 22. Historians consequently disagree as well. Holmes (*British Politics*, p. 211) doubts that her influence was vital in this appointment, both because of her lack of success at prevailing with the queen over other similarly high-level positions, and because by October 1705, her influence with the queen was on the wane as their personal relationship degenerated. Glassey (p. 168), however, credits Sarah's claim. Green's account of Anne's suspicious attitude toward Sarah's praises of William, suggests that Sarah was exercising sufficient pressure

about William to the point that Anne at least felt impelled to respond (p. 144).

18. Sachse (pp. 164, 179) even credits Somers along with the duke of Marlborough and Lord Godolphin with being instrumental in William's appointment, though evidence is clear only for the duke of Marlborough and Lord Godolphin's involvement.

19. Campbell, p. 284. It is also worth noting that Swift was propagandist for the Tory cause, and as such may have been reviving gossip in retrospect that was not at issue at the time.

20. Gregg, p. 205.

21. Gregg, p. 206. In addition, she apparently specified that "the disposal of certain benefices in the universities was to remain in the hands of Harley." Green, p. 145.

22. Vol. 3 (1705), p. 94.

23. Thomas Trevor, attorney general and then chief justice, had refused the job in both 1701 and 1705, specifically on the grounds that it was too great a risk to his law practice for a position so ephemeral. Sachse, pp. 171, 231.

24. Sachse, p. 70.

25. Lord Somers claimed, justifiably, that the conscientious performance of his myriad duties had ruined his health. Sachse, p. 72.

26. Vol. 3 (1705), p. 160. William himself was apparently of a similar mind, as he noted in his own diary on the day he was sworn in as lord chancellor: "During these great honours done me, I often reflected on the uncertainty of them. . . . and I begged of God that he would preserve my mind from relying on the transient Vanity of the World . . . that I might not be lift up with the present success, nor dejected when the reverse should happen." *The Private Diary of William, First Earl Cowper*, p. 6, October 23, 1705.

27. As his daughter Sarah later recalled. She added, "He looked very young and wearing his own hair made him appear yet more so; which the Queen observing, obliged him to cut it off, telling him the world would say she had given the Seals to a boy." Campbell, p. 287.

28. Sachse, pp. 88, 86. The lord keeper or lord chancellor also stood next to the monarch on the steps of the throne when the king or queen attended the House of Lords on formal occasions. *London Diaries of William Nicolson*, p. 92. Sarah, whether from discomfort at such elevated proceedings or in order to prove her indifference to things of this world, twice decided not to go to see her son honored by his bearing the great seal or sitting next to the archbishop of Canterbury in the queen's presence at chapel. Vol. 3 (1705–1706), pp. 143, 205.

29. Speaking of Lord Somers when lord keeper, Sachse says (p. 69), "Custodian of the Great Seal, he supervised all functions connected with its use. He was Speaker of the House of Lords. He presided in the Court of Chancery, and was the chief exponent of English justice." See Clyve Jones, "Debates in the House of Lords on 'The Church in Danger,' 1705, and on Doctor Sacheverell's Impeachment, 1710." *Historical Journal* 19:3 (1976), p. 771, for the influence William as speaker could bring to bear on debate in the House of Lords by guiding the debaters back to the issue at hand and by calling for the question to be put. See Glassey, pp. 5, 7, for the powers of the lord keeper or lord chancellor to appoint and dismiss justices of the peace and the political use they made of this power.

30. Sachse, p. 87.

31. In *London Diaries of William Nicolson*, pp. 63–64, the editors Jones and Holmes argue that the early eighteenth century was the heyday of the House of Lords, in both initiation and consideration of legislation and because the leaders of both parties were primarily peers and thus to be found in the upper house. See, too, Gregg, p. 142, for the corresponding avidity of rising politicians for peerages, for political gain as well as social prestige.

32. *Lord Cowper's Diary*, p. 1, October 11, 1705. For further discussion of the negotiations and ceremonies surrounding the installation of William as lord keeper, see Campbell, pp. 284–87.

33. Among the other Whig winnings in this round of promotions were earldoms for Lord Godolphin and Lord Wharton. Sachse, p. 246; Gregg, p. 230; Green, p. 162.

34. Jones and Holmes assert that "A Strong-minded Lord Chancellor could . . .do a great deal through his force of personality and knowledge of the rules of the House to steer the House in the direction he wanted. A peer probably carried more weight on the woolsack than a commoner, and, if a respected man of the law, he could do a great deal beyond his role as laid down in standing orders." *London Diaries of William Nicolson*, p. 91.

35. Jones and Holmes estimate that the House of Lords spent up to two-thirds of its time hearing appeals cases and those nobles without legal experience were inclined to defer to the expertise of lord chancellors and former lord chancellors on highly technical questions. *London Diaries of William Nicolson*, pp. 94, 100, 104.

36. Vol. 4 (1706), p. 13.

37. Lord Somers actually refused a peerage in 1695, and Sachse speculates "probably because he doubted his ability to support it without substantial grants, which were not assured" (p. 115).

38. The initial agreement was that he would receive £4,000 per annum salary plus £2,000 equipage; most years in office he averaged rather more than that, often something like £8,000 in income from his position. See the

list "Profits of the Seal" at the back of the manuscript copy of his diary, Herts. PRO D/EP F69, and Clay, pp. 180–81. As noted earlier, in consideration of his lost business as lawyer, he also received the promise of a pension at £2,000 per annum. Ten years earlier, Lord Somers had received the same base salary plus perquisites. Sachse, p. 70.

39. Clay, p. 186.

40. Clay, p. 184.

41. Letter from Sir George Oxenden to William, second earl Cowper, November 23, 1753, cited in Clay, p. 185.

42. Clay, p. 185; Herts. PRO D/EP F193 fol. 78, address of letter to Mary, Countess Cowper, 1720. See also Beckett, p. 331, who cites William as an example of the low end of the scale of aristocratic spending on a country house, the high end being in the tens of thousands of pounds at the end of the seventeenth century.

43. Vol. 3 (1705), p. 158.

44. Spencer also moved up politically; in 1705 he replaced his brother as MP for Bere Alston. Foss, *Biographia Juridica*, p. 200.

45. Vol. 3 (1706), p. 189.

46. Vol. 3 (1706), p. 193.

47. Genesis 43:11 and 45:23.

48. Vol. 3 (1706), pp. 217–18.

49. Vol. 3 (1706), p. 218.

50. William Gouge in his allocation of domestic duties specifically said the wife was to be concerned with "adorning her house." *Domesticall Duties*, p. 152.

51. Vol. 3 (1706), p. 215.

52. Vol. 3 (1706), p. 303.

53. Vol. 3 (1706), p. 234.

54. Herts. PRO D/EP F58 Cowper Family Correspondence, fol. 10, Sarah to William, August 19, 1706.

55. Burnet, *Bishop Burnet's History of His Own Time*, vol. 5, p. 872; M. Cowper, *Diary of Mary, Countess Cowper*, p. 63.

56. *Private Diary of William, First Earl Cowper*, p. 32. For laudatory poetry, see *Poems of Ambrose Philips*, ed. M. G. Segar (Oxford, 1937), p. 118, as cited in Sachse, p. 82 n. 60; Campbell, pp. 296–99; And see Glassey for an important caveat: "He immediately won the applause of laymen, if not of lawyers, by his lofty refusal of the 'New Year Gifts'" (p. 171).

57. Sachse, p. 70.

58. Glassey, p. 18, Sachse, p. 100.

59. Herts. PRO D/EP F63 William Cowper to John Churchill, duke of Marlborough, October 16, 1705.

60. Glassey says "After his appointment, Cowper lost some of his Junto connections, and became, to some extent, a Court Whig" (p. 172), although Holmes notes a concerted and generally successful effort by the Junto after 1708 to "assimilate" not only Cowper, but the second duke of Devonshire and Viscount Townshend into closer cooperation, so that through the period 1710–1714 William consistently voted with the Junto on major issues, with the exception of the Hamilton vote in December 1711, "when Cowper's tender political conscience was offended by the unscrupulousness of his colleagues' tactics." *British Politics*, p. 242. Note too by 1711 Cowper's membership in the Kit-Cat club (Holmes, *British Politics*, p. 297).

61. Glassey, p. 172.

62. Glassey, pp. 172–73.

63. Vol. 3 (1705), p. 142.

64. In the sixteenth century, the Crown held the largest total number of advowsons and delegated to the lord keeper the disposal of those livings below £20 per year. O'Day estimates that Elizabethan Lord Keepers had to deal with roughly 100 vacancies per year, roughly one-third of the national total. *The English Clergy*, p. 113. A later figure comes from Holmes, who states that in the late seventeenth and early eighteenth centuries the lord chancellor had control of just over a thousand clerical places in total. *Augustan England*, p. 101.

65. O'Day, "The Anatomy of a Profession," p. 52; Holmes, *Augustan England*, p. 85; Sykes, *Church and State*, p. 172.

66. Clerical livings are actively bound up with parliamentary politics as well as with the question of the Anglican church's vitality and credibility in this period. Because of the fact that a large proportion of advowsons were held by either the Crown or the lay elite rather than the church itself, the right of presentation to a living was thought of as private property, and "as part of the wider web of patronage (or clientage) in society as a whole." O'Day, *The English Clergy*, p. 86. Places were allotted primarily on the basis of kinship, friendship, dependency, solicitation from bishops for their chaplains, and as political rewards. Sykes, *Church and State*, pp. 149–50, 172, 213; Hirschberg, "Episcopal Incomes and Expenses," p. 225.

67. Apparently he felt the effects of this limitation in some uncomfortable ways, as when he had to apologize to the duke of Marlborough for not being able to appoint Marlborough's candidate to a living, saying "Your Grace knows I am particularly obliged to obey the Queen in things of that kind." Blenheim MSS, B I-23 13 Oct. 1709, cited in Glassey, p. 171 n. 4.

68. Vol. 3 (1705), p. 152.

69. Letters to Lord Chancellor Cowper indicate that Dr. Joseph Rawson got the job instead, and it may be that Sir James Oxenden recommended

him. Herts. PRO D/EP F55 no. 83, October 28, 1706; no. 105, October 16, 1710.

70. Vol. 3 (1705), p. 153.

71. *Private Diary of William, First Earl Cowper*, p. 12.

72. Vol. 3 (1705), p. 154.

73. Vol. 3 (1705), p. 144.

74. Vol. 3 (1706), p. 204.

75. Vol. 3 (1705), p. 157.

76. Vol. 3 (1706), p. 233.

Chapter 7

1. Mendelson, "Stuart Women's Diaries," pp. 191–92, 195–98. For a sobering assessment of the risks of childbirth in the seventeenth century, and the extensive physical debilitation and constant preoccupation with rearing numerous children that awaited women who survived giving birth, see Perry, "Mary Astell's Feminism," pp. 25–43.

2. Mendelson, "Stuart Women's Diaries," pp. 198–99, and Todd, "The Remarrying Widow," pp. 55–81. See also J. Smith, "Widowhood and Ageing in Traditional English Society," pp. 429–49. Regarding the possibility that women's autonomy as widows helps explain low remarriage rates, see Thomas, "Age and Authority," p. 236; Laslett, *A Fresh Map of Life*, p.137; though note O'Day's caution (*Family and Family Relationships*, pp. 97–99) that this situation applies only to a small stratum of society.

3. Vol. 4 (1707), pp. 26–27.

4. Luke 2:36–37. The Revised Standard Version makes an even clearer distinction between the period of Anna's married life and the chastity of her widowhood: "She was of a great age, having lived with her husband seven years from her virginity and as a widow until she was eighty-four."

5. Vol. 4 (1707), p. 90.

6. Vol. 4 (1707), p. 133.

7. This was a period of increasing numbers of court cases involving disputes over marriage settlements. See Stone, *Uncertain Unions*, pp. 12–13.

8. D/EP T1217 Marriage Settlement of William Cowper and Judith Booth (1686), copied also in Diary, vol. 4 (1707), pp. 17–18.

9. Vol. 3 (1705), p. 173.

10. See Staves, *Married Women's Separate Property*, pp. 27–37 and 116–18, for an extended discussion of the process of the replacement of dower rights by jointures in this period. Staves points out the risks for widows as smaller settlements, usually in the form of a cash pension, took the place of customary rights to one-third of a husband's land.

11. Vol. 3 (1706), p. 183.

12. Vol. 3 (1706), p. 206.

13. Although Sarah was named as coexecutor with William and Spencer in Sir William's will, D/EP T1141 Will of Sir William Cowper (1700), she seems to have taken no part in settling his estate, other than signing over her right to Hertford Castle to Spencer, as he requested. Vol. 4 (1707), p. 20.

14. Vol. 4 (1707), p. 16.

15. The original document Sarah copied is D/EP T1217 Marriage Settlement of William Cowper and Judith Booth (1686) in which Sarah surrendered her jointure lands to her son William for a cash annuity—a deal typical of the trend Staves observed (p. 115): women, in order to help their sons, accepted financial settlements that were not necessarily in their own economic interest.

16. D/EP T1141 Will of Sir William Cowper (1700); D/EP F50 fol. 4, Account of Sir William's Estate by Spencer[?] Cowper (1706).

17. Vol. 4 (1707), p. 22.

18. Vol. 4 (1707), p. 29.

19. Vol. 3 (1706), p. 301.

20. In Volume 1 of the diary (1700–1702) there are roughly seventeen complaints of either a lack of visits or invitations, or cold, negligent treatment when Sarah did have contact with her sons. There are five complaints each in volume 2 (1703–1704) and volume 3 (1705–1706); three (all in the first forty pages) of volume 4 (1706–1709), two of which are directed at Spencer solely; and one (less complaint than comparison) in volume 5 (1709–1711).

21. Vol. 5 (1709), p. 83.

22. Vol. 5 (1710), p. 201. Quoting *The Tatler*, no. 207, August 5, 1710 (ed. Donald Bond, Oxford: Clarendon Press, 1987, vol. 3, pp. 97–98).

23. Herts. PRO D/EP F194 Cowper Family Correspondence, fol. 28, Sarah to Mary, July 22, 1707.

24. Vol. 4 (1707), p. 90.

25. Herts. PRO D/EP F194 Cowper Family Correspondence, fol. 30, Sarah to Mary, September 16, 1707.

26. Vol. 4 (1707), pp. 140, 146.

27. Herts. PRO D/EP F59 Cowper Family Correspondence, fol. 5, Mary to William, August or September, 1709.

28. Crawford, "The Construction and Experience of Maternity," pp. 26–27.

29. Schwoerer, pp. 226–27.

30. See Herts. PRO D/EP F193, fol. 51, William to Mary August 23, 1717, that Sarah sent her grandson "Billy" £5 and Billy wrote a thank-you letter back. See also in the diary, vol. 5 (1711), pp. 339–41, where Lady

Sarah transcribed her letter of pious advice to Spencer's son John, and his dutiful reply.

31. Vol. 4 (1707), pp. 22–23.

32. Vol. 4 (1707), p. 23.

33. Vol. 4 (1707), p. 40.

34. Vol. 4 (1709), p. 361.

35. Vol. 4 (1708), p. 254.

36. Vol. 4 (1709), p. 299.

37. Gouge, *Domesticall Duties*, Treat. 8, pt. 40.

38. Vol. 4 (1709), p. 356.

39. See Sarah's summary, vol. 5 (1709), p. 21, of Isaac Barrow's sermon on reproof, in his *Works*, vol. 1, pp. 301–2.

40. Simon Patrick, "Advice to a Friend" (1673), in *Works*, vol. 4, p. 470. Actually, Patrick offered this depiction of how to speak to a servant effectively as an example of how one ought to stir one's own soul in trying to meditate with sincere feeling. As was her general pattern, Sarah used the part of this example that applied to others, not to her.

41. Vol. 4 (1708), p. 287.

42. Vol. 5 (1709), p. 71.

43. Vol. 5 (1711), pp. 299–300.

44. Vol. 5 (1711), p. 297.

45. See, for example, William Gouge, who said that if "neither fair nor foule means will reclaim them, they must then be thrust out of doors." Treat. 8, pt. 40.

46. For a contemporary commentary, see *The Spectator* no. 88, June 11, 1711, where English servants are described as the best treated in Europe but the most disrespectful, negligent, untrustworthy, and apt to change jobs.

47. Vol. 4 (1707), p. 20.

48. Vol. 4 (1709), p. 310.

49. Vol. 5 (1709), p. 4.

50. Vol. 4 (1707), p. 112.

51. Vol. 5 (1709), p. 91.

52. Vol. 4 (1708), p. 174.

53. See Barrow, *Works*, sermon 31, "The Duty and Reward of Bounty to the Poor," and the annual *Account of Charity Schools Lately Erected* (1704–1713), which includes an anniversary sermon preached each year by a different clerical dignitary.

54. See *An Account of the Charity Schools lately Established . . .* , 6th ed. (1707), p. 12, for the year ending June 4, 1707.

55. According to the *Account of Charity Schools* for 1707, Saint Andrew's had received £307 in gifts since the establishment of its charity schools.

56. Looking at the 1707 *Account of Charity Schools*, it appears that Saint Botolph Aldgate, needed about the same amount as Saint Andrew's to operate; and Saint Giles-in-the-Fields, Saint James, Westminster, Saint Margaret's, Westminster, Saint Martin-in-the-Fields, and Saint Sepulchre all needed between £10 and £50 more per year. Using the same rough estimate based on enrollment, most of the other parishes needed about £100 or less, sometimes much less. There is clearly not an exact correlation between this very rough gauge of costs and income, but it is interesting that in these six parishes, the proportions of income through subscription, sermons, and gifts varied significantly: Saint Giles and Saint Sepulchre were the only two reporting subscription income sufficient to meet the cost estimation. A few churches could rely on conspicuously huge gifts for income; the beneficiaries of the largest gifts were Saint Margaret's (£1,500), Saint Mary Whitechapel (£1,140) Saint James (£600), but after Saint Andrew's, at fourth on the list with £307, the gift amount drops precipitously. If annual sermon collection income is added, both Saint Botolph and Saint Martin just about break even on expenses.

57. To operate its schools in 1708–1709, Saint Andrew's would have needed an income that year of around £218—an amount quite close to the £226 reported in subscriptions for that same period. See *An Account of Charity Schools*, 8th ed., 1709, p. 10, where Saint Andrew's is listed as having two charity schools educating a total of 81 boys and 80 girls.

58. Vol. 4 (1709), p. 304.

59. Vol. 4 (1709), p. 335.

60. Vol. 4 (1709), p. 361.

61. Pascoe, p. 823.

62. Hayton, pp. 48–91.

63. Hayton, pp. 56–57, and Slack, *From Reformation to Improvement*, pp. 115–17. For additional tensions over the issue of the imposition of moral reform to the extent of excessively intrusive oversight, see Isaacs, "The Anglican Hierarchy," pp. 391–411.

64. Owen, p. 28. Jones, pp. 111–13.

65. Vol. 4 (1709), pp. 337–38.

66. *An Account of the SPGFP*, p. 79.

67. *An Account of the SPGFP* (1706 ed.), p. 79.

68. For instance, "In thy Fear will I worship toward thy holy temple." Vol. 4 (1708), pp. 243, 249.

69. Vol. 4 (1707), p. 51.

70. W. Jacob, p. 65.

71. See vol. 1 (1701), p. 109: "Sunday, at Church we have very Sorry doings with a ffellow that Spoils what he Reads, Sermon and all. I wou'd not Speak so Contemptuously of that order, but that I think a litle due Care

and diligence wou'd qualify men to perform their Duty better." And again: "Wee have indeed Such Sorry Doings att Church I was tempted to Neglect going there, but lighting on this Scripture; I Resolv'd to obey the Heavenly Call, and give my attendance; how weakly soever the Duties are perform'd." Vol. 3 (1706), p. 255.

72. Vol. 4 (1707), p. 95.

73. Vol. 4 (1708), p. 249.

74. Vol. 4 (1708), p. 275.

75. These authors sometimes borrowed extensively from moral works such as Archbishop Tillotson's sermons. See, for example, an essay on friendship and the evils of insincerity in number 103, June 28, 1711. Editor Donald Bond notes that large sections of this essay were lifted from Tillotson's "Of Sincerity toward God and Man," preached July 29, 1694 (in *Works* [1728], vol. 2, p. 6).

76. Vol. 5 (1711), p. 264.

77. Vol. 6 (1711), p. 12, cited from the *Spectator* no. 119, July 17, 1711.

78. Vol. 4 (1709), p. 342; see also vol. 5 (1709), p. 30: "Nothing Procures Love like Humility, Nothing Hate like Pride. To be Humble to our Superiors is Duty. to our Equals Courtesy, to our Inferiors Generosity, which for all her Lowness Carrys Such a Sway that She may Command their Souls."

79. *Spectator* no. 57, August 19, 1709.

80. Vol. 5 (1709), p. 58.

81. Vol. 4 (1709), p. 321.

82. Vol. 4 (1708), p. 220.

83. Vol. 4 (1707), p.110.

84. Vol. 4, (1707), pp.129–30; quoting Montaigne, *Essays*, vol. 2, ch. 10, p. 94. For an extensive treatment of Sarah Cowper's attitude toward death, see Clare Gittings, "The Hell of Living: Reflections on Death in the Diary of Sarah, Lady Cowper," *Mortality* 2:1 (1997): 23–41. I am grateful to Clare Gittings as well for supplying information on a portrait of Sarah Cowper.

85. Minois (*History of Old Age from Antiquity to the Renaissance*) consistently refers to a religious life and practices as "bigotry" (see for example, p. 264); Rosenthal (*Old Age in Late Medieval England*) refers to characterizations of old age as a period when one has time for religious contemplation as "unexceptional pieties" (p. 94).

86. Vol. 4 (1707), p. 138.

87. Vol. 4 (August, 1708), pp. 239–40. And also the following summer: "Sixty five years is a great deal of Sand in ye Hour:Glass. Now I find thro' Age, Greifs, and Infirmitys, my Sense is become Dull, my Memory Decay'd, my Sight failing, my Hearing imperfect, and in all the Powers and Facultys

of my Mind and Body great Debility. My Judgm:ᵗ of Men and Things Seems more Strong, but Whenever that grows Weak 'tis like I Shall not perceive it." Vol. 5 (July 1709), pp. 12–13.

88. Vol. 4. (1708), p. 245.

89. Vol. 4 (1707), p. 138.

90. Vol. 4 (1708), p. 250.

91. Vol. 4 (1708), p. 270.

92. Vol. 4 (1707), p. 106.

93. Vol. 5 (1709), p. 36.

94. Thomas, "The Perception of the Past," pp. 1–3; A. B. Ferguson, *Clio Unbound*, pp. xii, 349–50; Champion, pp. 20–25. Both Thomas and Champion also point out history's function as a means to defend an ideological position (pp. 2 and 20–21, respectively). And note Ferguson's more extended discussions in chapters 10 and 11 of the beginnings of a competing idea of history that traced the slow, painful, but in the main uphill progress of humanity.

95. For a good account of the crises and divisions that faced Queen Anne's government in 1708, see Sundstrom, *Sidney Godolphin*, pp. 214–20.

96. Vol. 4 (1708), p. 160.

97. Vol. 4 (1708), pp. 163–64.

98. Vol. 4 (1708), p. 276.

Chapter 8

1. Holmes, *Sacheverell*, pp. 65–75; 124–26.

2. Holmes, *Sacheverell*, pp. 157–75.

3. Holmes, *Sacheverell*, pp. 228–29, 252–54.

4. Harley apparently assured William that it was "A Whig game intended at bottom," but William said "To keep in when all my friends were out would be infamous." *Private Diary of William, First Earl Cowper*, p. 46. For Harley's strategy and the reasons for William's resignation see, too, Glassey, pp. 192–97, and *Diary of Sir David Hamilton*, pp. 17, 80–81. Even Jonathan Swift said the queen showed Cowper "As great a Personall regard and Esteem as her nature was capable of admitting." *An Enquiry into the Behaviour of the Queen's Last Ministry*, ed. Irvin Ehrenpreis (Indiana University, Humanities Series No. 36, 1956), p. 23, cited in Sachse, p. 292.

5. William wrote in his diary of his resignation that the queen "strongly oppos'd my doing it, and giving it me again at least five times after I had laid it down." *Diary of William, First Earl Cowper*, p. 46. For indications of the pressure of fellow Whigs for his resignation, see Hamilton, *Diary of Sir David Hamilton*, pp. 80–81, and for indications of offers to continue,

and perhaps William's interest in continuing as lord chancellor, see Sachse, p. 291.

6. For accounts of William's discussions with the queen, see *Diary of Sir David Hamilton,* pp. 19, 33, 47, 49, 53. For their continuing relationship even when Anne was convinced that William was biased by partisan loyalty in his opposition to the Peace of Utrecht, see pp. 53, 60, 88, and regarding his role as intermediary in the tricky issue of retaining the duchess of Somerset in her household while dismissing the duke of Somerset, see p. 37. On Anne's tendency in the last years of her reign to maintain connections to ousted Whig ministers, see Gregg, p. 332.

7. Holmes, *Sacheverell,* p. 170.

8. Vol. 5 (1710), p. 129.

9. Vol. 5 (1710), pp. 118–19.

10. Vol. 5 (1710), p. 120.

11. Holmes, *Sacheverell,* p. 170.

12. Vol. 5 (1710), p. 131.

13. Holmes, *Sacheverell,* p. 228.

14. Vol. 5 (1710), p. 136.

15. Vol. 5 (1710), p. 240. In the margin Lady Sarah gave the citation for this motto as 2 Corinthians 11:13.

16. Vol. 5 (1710), pp. 181–82.

17. Vol. 5 (1710), p. 130. These lamentations became a recurring refrain: The same quote, though without specific reference to Sacheverell, is also in vol. 6 (1712), p. 84, and vol. 7 (1714), p. 79.

18. Vol. 5 (1710), p. 190.

19. See Rupp, p. 74, who suggests that Edmund Gibson, eventually bishop of Lincoln, was Tory by inclination but allied to the Whigs because of the Protestant succession; and that Tenison, Sharpe, and Wake all tried to keep to the middle ground but were forced to take sides. See also Holmes, *The Making of a Great Power,* p. 362.

20. Vol. 5 (1710), p. 212.

21. Sarah frequently used the epithet "'Cheverel' preachers" to designate those who emulated Sacheverell's reprehensible character.

22. Vol. 5 (1710), p. 148. The full text of the verse from which the rhyme here is taken is written out at the back of volume 5, p. 14, of the new set of page numbers. Titled "A Letter to Queen Anne by the Duchess of Marlborough," it begins: "Madam look to't your title is arraign'd/- Sacheverel saps the ground whereon you stand."

23. Vol. 6 (1712), p. 107.

24. Spurr, *Restoration Church of England,* pp. 383–84, describes widespread anticlericalism among the laity.

25. Vol. 5 (1711), p. 323.

26. Vol. 5 (1711), p. 284.

27. Vol. 6 (1713), p. 222.

28. Vol. 7 (1714), pp. 90–91.

29. Vol. 7 (1715), pp. 241–42.

30. Vol. 7 (1715), p. 271.

31. Vol. 7 (1715), p. 269.

32. Vol. 7 (1715), p. 273; see also similar sentiments expressed about the sentencing to death of Lord Derwentwater, "who was educated in the popish religion, so perhaps might act out of principle as believing it to be his duty to promote the interest of his church. But for our perjur'd protestants I have no more bowels than a nitt. And do think no severity can be too much for such miscreants." Vol. 7 (1716), p. 290.

33. Vol. 7 (1716), p. 283.

34. Vol. 1 (1701), p. 94: "The Ascension of our Lord. and the Restauration of Char: 2$^{\rm d}$. The first oblidg'd me to attend upon the Offices of the Church. As for the later I do own to have no Manner of Understanding or inclination for politick Devotion." And the next year at the Restoration feast: "To the Court I went to hear what men talk there on this political Holy:day, which I have no zeal to observe; so go where Curiosity leads mee." Vol. 1 (1702), p. 222. The same sentiment applied on the anniversary of the Gunpowder Plot: "On holidays appointed by the State, I choose to hear what men Say at Court." Vol. 1 (1702), p. 298.

35. Vol. 5 (1711), p. 273.

36. Vol. 5 (1710), pp. 130–31.

37. Vol. 5 (1710), p. 240.

38. See vol. 5 (1711), p. 273; vol. 6 (1712–1713), pp. 130, 186, 250; vol. 7 (1713–1714), pp. 13, 90.

39. Vol. 5 (1710), p. 165.

40. Vol. 6 (1712), p. 130.

41. "My Hearing is grown So Dull that now I go not every Lord's Day to the Publick Worship but Resolve, not to Leave the Communion of the Establish'd Church while I am able to go There." Vol. 7 (1714), p. 134; see also p. 174.

42. She continued to receive the Sacrament monthly until she missed it the last week in August 1716 (vol. 7, p. 341), a month before she ended her diary because of ill health.

43. Vol. 7 (1715), pp. 223–34.

44. Vol. 7 (1715), p. 222.

45. Vol. 5 (March 20–21, 1711), pp. 291–92.

46. Vol. 5 (1711), p. 311.

47. Vol. 6 (1711), p. 39.

48. Vol. 5 (1710), p. 236.

49. Vol. 6 (1711), p. 74.

50. Vol. 6 (1712), pp. 94–95. The scheme may actually have been a plan to restart an overflow branch of London's Christ's Hospital, a bluecoat school for boys and girls. It had been built between 1683 and 1695, and, according to Sarah, was not in operation in 1701, when she commented, "A few years since was built in this Town, a larg House and School for the Children of Christs Hospital and stand° now uninhabited. The Reason given is for that the late warrs hath peel'd people so near they Cannot afford to maintain those foundations as formerly. . . . This thought came in my head because about this time of year I used to line the Hedgs with pretty Blue:Coats and fill their Caps with Goosberies." Vol. 1 (1701), pp. 113–14. Something must have been done in the earlier 1700s along the lines of what Sarah describes, since much later in the century it seems that a grammar school was added (*Victoria County History*, p. 97), and a school continued on the site until the mid-1980s.

51. Vol. 6 (1713), p. 247.

52. Cicero, *De Senectute* transl. William Falconer (Cambridge, Mass.: Harvard University Press, repr. 1985), p. 23. Though there is no explicit mention of this work in the diary, Lady Sarah listed Cicero's *Of the Gods* in her "Catalogue of Books at London" at the back of commonplace book D/EP F36 in the Panshanger MSS and in the Appendix here. She may well have read more of Cicero's works; her catalogue is by no means a complete record of her reading but at least indicates her familiarity with this classical author.

53. Vol. 6 (February 14, 1712), p. 93.

54. Vol. 6 (1712), p.158.

55. Vol. 6 (1711), p. 64.

56. Vol. 7 (1713), p. 22.

57. Vol. 6 (1712), p. 102.

58. Vol. 5 (1710), p. 259, and Stanhope (Dean of Canterbury), vol. 1, p. 202.

59. Vol. 6 (1711), p. 8, from *The Spectator* no. 111, July 7, 1711.

60. Vol. 6 (1713), p. 243. In the original, however, this affirmation of an afterlife is part of a speech in which Cato argues the benefit of suicide, secure in the thought that in the next world his soul will "flourish in immortal Youth/Unhurt Amidst the War of elements/The wreck of Matter, and the Crush of Worlds." *Cato*, act 5 scene 1. This scene was reprinted with a Latin translation in *The Spectator* no. 628, December 6, 1714, but Sarah wrote it out in her diary just a few weeks after the play's first performance on April 14, 1713.

61. Vol. 5 (1711), p. 269; *The Medley* no. 14, January 8, 1711. Sarah may have been specifically replying to Mr. Dodwell, in that she apparently

had read his book a few years earlier or at least had read a condemnation of it. Vol. 3 (1706), p. 223.

62. Vol. 6 (1713), p. 274.

63. One in volume 6 (1711–1713); and in volume 7 (1713–1716) four, all directed at Spencer, two of which specifically approve William's behavior in comparison to Spencer's.

64. Vol. 6 (1713), pp. 262–63.

65. Vol. 5 (1710), p. 222.

66. Vol. 6 (1713), p. 257; vol. 7 (1714), p. 164.

67. Vol. 6 (1712), p. 156.

68. Vol. 7 (1713), p. 8.

69. Vol. 7 (1716), p. 293.

70. Vol. 7 (1716), p. 336.

71. Vol. 7 (1716), p. 340.

72. Herts. PRO D/EP F193 Cowper Family Correspondence, fol. 41, William to Mary, September 1, 1716.

73. Vol. 7 (1716), p. 343.

74. Vol. 1 (1702), p. 207.

75. Herts. PRO D/EP F50 fol. 6.

76. Vol. 5 (1709–1711), pp. 9, 319; vol. 7 (1716), p. 287.

77. Vol. 7 (1713–1714), pp. 23, 94, 98.

78. Vol. 7 (1714), p. 88. See also vol. 7 (1715–1716), pp. 271, 274, 307, 326.

79. Vol. 2 (1703), p. 54.

80. Vol. 7 (1716), p. 324.

81. "I never was in so Ill Health all my Life. I think the great Frost Bound Up my Rhumes, and Now the Thaw brings a Defluxion from my Head which Causes me to Cough Night and Day. Besides I lose my Stomach which was good but never great; so that I grow Weak not Eating enough to Sustain Life. But I meet with many in a more painfull condition than my self, so as I ought to be contented and Thankfull it is no worse. An Exact Diary is a Window to the heart that makes it." Vol. 7 (1716), p. 296.

82. Vol. 7 (1716), pp. 335–36.

83. Herts. PRO D/EP F193 Cowper Family Correspondence. Letter from William to Mary, September 2, 1719.

84. Herts. PRO D/EP F 58 Cowper Family Correspondence, Spencer to William, February 15, 1720.

85. *The Weekly Journal or Saturday's Post* no. 63 (February 13, 1720).

Bibliography

Primary Sources: Manuscripts

Hertfordshire Public Record Office, Panshanger MSS:

D/EP F23–F24 Correspondence of Sarah, Lady Cowper and Sir William Cowper. 1662–1719.

D/EP F25 Commonplace Book of Sir William Cowper. 1658–1690.

D/EP F29–F35 Diary of Sarah, Lady Cowper. 1700–1716.

D/EP F36–F45 Commonplace Books of Sarah, Lady Cowper:

F36 Poems and Sayings. 1670.

F37 "The Medley." 1673.

F38 Moral and Scriptural Collections. 1675.

F39 Bible Commentary and Notes on Heresies. 1680.

F40 Prayers. 1680.

F41 "History of the World" and Life of Mohammed. 1686.

F42 Topical Index to Sermons. 1686.

F43 "Thoughts and Meditations." 1690.

F44 "Collections from the Bible" and Sarah, Lady Cowper's own Biblical Commentary. 1700.

F45 Scrapbook. 1700.

Uncatalogued Collection from Plutarch's Morals, Lives of Bishops, and Precepts. 1683.

D/EP F50 Will of Sarah, Lady Cowper. 1716. Account of Sir William Cowper's Estate. 1706.

D/EP F58, F59, F81, F193, F194 Cowper Family Correspondence. 1682–1722.

D/EP F84 Will of Elizabeth Culling. 1702.

D/EP F85–F86 Correspondence of Culling children to William Cowper. 1716–1720.

D/EP F96 Documents pertaining to the trial of Spencer Cowper. 1699–1700.

D/EP T1138 Will of Sir William Cowper, first baronet. 1663.

D/EP T1141 Will of Sir William Cowper, second baronet. 1700.

D/EP 1217 Marriage Settlement of William Cowper and Judith Booth. 1686.

D/EP T1218 Settlement of Hertford Castle on Sarah Cowper for her life. 1686.

D/EP T4445 Letter of Robert to Judith Booth. 1685.

BL Add. MSS 27351–6 Diary and Occasional Meditations of Mary Rich, Countess of Warwick. 1666–1678.

BL Add. MSS 42849 Correspondence and Diary Extracts of Sarah Savage. 1694–1732.

London Public Record Office Prob. 11:

Will of Samuel Holled, reel 305, no. 125.

Will of Anne Holled, reel 314, no. 68.

Printed Primary Sources

(Place of publication is London unless otherwise noted)

An Account of Charity Schools lately erected in England, Wales, and Ireland: with the benefactions thereto; and of the methods whereby they were set up, and are governed. 6th ed. 1707.

An Account of Charity Schools lately erected in Great Britain and Ireland: with the benefactions thereto; and of the methods whereby they were set up, and are governed. 8th ed. 1709.

An Account of the Society for Propagating the Gospel in Foreign Parts . . . With their proceedings and success. 1706.

Allestree, Richard. *The Gentleman's Calling.* 1667.

———. *The Ladies' Calling.* 1673.

———. *The Whole Duty of Man.* 1659.

Astell, Mary. *Reflections Upon Marriage.* 3d ed. 1706. In Bridget Hill, ed., *The First English Feminist: Reflections Upon Marriage and Other Writings by Mary Astell.* Aldershot, UK: Gower Publishing, 1986.

Barrow, Isaac. *The Works of the Learned Isaac Barrow.* 2nd ed. 1687.

Baxter, Richard. *Christian Directory.* 1673.

Beadle, John. *The Journal or Diary of a Thankfull Christian*. 1656.

Burnet, Gilbert. *Bishop Burnet's History of His Own Time*. Oxford: Clarendon Press, 1823.

Bury, Samuel, ed., *An Account of the Life and Death of Mrs. Elizabeth Bury . . . Chiefly Collected out of her own Diary*. Bristol, 1720.

A Chapter in English Church History: SPCK Minutes 1698–1704. 1888.

Charron, Pierre. *Of Wisdom*. Transl. George Stanhope. 1697.

Churchill, Sarah, Duchess of Marlborough. *Account of the Conduct of the Duchess of Marlborough*. Hawkin, 1742.

————. *Private Correspondence of Sarah, Duchess of Marlborough*. Colburn, 1838.

Clifford, Martin. *A Treatise of Humane Reason*. 1674.

Cocks, Richard. *The Parliamentary Diary of Sir Richard Cocks 1698–1702*. Ed. David Hayton. Oxford: Clarendon Press, 1996.

Collier, Jeremy. *Essays upon Several Moral Subjects*. 1700.

Cowper, Mary. *Diary of Mary, Countess Cowper*. Ed. Spencer Cowper. London: J. Murray, 1865.

Cowper, William. *The Private Diary of William, First Earl Cowper*. Ed. Edwin Hawtrey. Eton: Roxburghe Club, 1833.

Dodwell, Henry. *An Epistolatory Discourse, Proving, from the Scriptures and the First Fathers, that the Soul is a Principle Naturally Mortal*. 1706.

Filmer, Sir Robert. *Patriarcha*. 1680.

Fleetwood, William. *The Relative Duties of Parents and Children, Husbands and Wives, Masters and Servants*. 1705. In Randolph Trumbach, ed., *Marriage, Sex and the Family in England 1660–1800*. New York; London: Garland, 1985.

Gastrell, Francis. *Certainty of Religion and the First Grounds and Principles of Humane Duty*. Boyle Lectures, 1697.

Gouge, William. *Of Domesticall Duties*. 3d ed. 1634.

Hamilton, David. *Diary of Sir David Hamilton, 1709–1714*. Ed. Philip Roberts. Oxford: Clarendon Press, 1975.

Hammond, Henry. *Paraphrase and Annotation upon all the Books of the New Testament*. 2nd ed. 1659.

Howell, T. B. *A Complete Collection of State Trials* (or, *Cobbett's State Trials*). Hansard, 1812.

Howell, William. *An Institution of General History: or, The History of the World*. 1680.

Jones, Clyve, and Geoffrey Holmes, eds. *The London Diaries of William Nicolson, Bishop of Carlisle 1702–1718*. Oxford: Clarendon, 1985.

Latham, Robert, and William Matthews, eds. *The Diary of Samuel Pepys*. Los Angeles: University of California Press, 1970.

The Letters and Diplomatic Instructions of Queen Anne. Ed. Beatrice Curtis Brown. Cassell, 1935.

Letters of Rachel, Lady Russell. Longman, 1853.

Luttrell, Narcissus. *A Brief Historical Relation of State Affairs from September 1678 to April 1714.* Oxford: Oxford University Press, 1857.

Manley, Mary Delariviere. *Secret Memoirs and Manners of Several Persons of Quality. . . . From the New Atalantis.* Ed. Rosalind Ballaster. New York: New York University Press, 1992.

Montaigne, Michel. *Essays.* Transl. John Florio. New York, 1980.

Nicholls, William. *The Duty of Inferiours Towards their Superiours in five Practical Discourses.* 1701.

Parsons, Robert. Christian Directory. 1660.

Pascoe, C. F. *Two Hundred Years of the SPG.* 1901.

The Past and Present of the SPCK 1698–1861. 1861.

Patrick, Simon. *Advice to a Friend.* 1673.

————. *A Book for Beginners or A Help to Young Communicants that They may be Fitted for the Holy Communion.* 1679.

————. *The Christian Sacrifice.* 1671.

————. *A Commentary on the First Book of Moses.* London, 1696.

————. *A Critical Commentary Upon the Old and New Testament and the Apocrypha.* 1701.

————. *The Heart's Ease.* 1660.

————. *Mensa Mystica.* 1660.

————. *Search the Scriptures.* 1685.

————. *A Treatise on the Necessity and Frequency of Receiving the Holy Communion.* 1684.

————. *Works.* Oxford, 1858.

The Private Diary of Elizabeth, Viscountess Mordaunt. Duncairn, 1856.

Pufendorf, Samuel. *The Whole Duty of Man According to the Law of Nature.* 1691.

Ranew, Nathaniel. *Practical Discourses Concerning Death and Heaven.* 1694.

Register of Admissions to the Honorable Society of the Middle Temple from the Fifteenth Century to the Year 1944. Comp. H. A. C. Sturgess. 1949.

Savile, George, Marquess of Halifax. *The Lady's New Year's Gift, or Advice to a Daughter.* 5th ed. 1696.

The Spectator. Ed. Donald Bond. 5 vols. Oxford: Clarendon Press, 1965.

Stanhope, George. *A Paraphrase and Comment Upon the Epistles and Gospels.* 4 vols. 1705–1709.

Steele, Richard. *The Tatler.* 1710–1711.

Stillingfleet, Edward. *Irenicum.* 1661.

————. *Origines Sacrae.* 1662.

The Tatler. Ed. Donald Bond. Oxford: Clarendon, 1987.

Taylor, Jeremy. *A Discourse on the Nature, Offices, and Measures of Friendship.* 1657.

———. *Ductor Dubitantium.* 1660. 3d ed. 1696.

———. *The Marriage Ring.* In *The Whole Works of Jeremy Taylor.* London: Longman, 1861.

Tillotson, John. *The Works of the Most Reverend Dr John Tillotson.* 2d ed. London 1699.

The Tryal of Spencer Cowper, esq.; John Marson, Ellis Stevens, and William Rogers, Gent., upon an Indictment for the Murther of Mrs. Sarah Stout, A Quaker . . . Of which they were Acquitted. 1699.

Wake, William. *Sermons and discourses on several occasions.* 1690.

Whichcote, Benjamin. *Select Sermons of Dr Whichcote.* 1698.

Wilkins, John. *Of the Principles and Duties of Natural Religion.* 1675.

———. *Sermons Preached on several occasions.* 1682.

Williams, John. *The Certainty of Divine Revelation.* Boyle Lecture. 1695.

Secondary Sources

Allen, William, and Edmund MacClure. *Two Hundred Years: The History of the Society for Promoting Christian Knowledge, 1698–1898.* London: SPCK, 1898.

Allison, C. F. *The Rise of Moralism: The Proclamation of the Gospel from Hooker to Baxter.* London: SPCK, 1966.

Amussen, Susan. "Gender, Family and the Social Order 1560–1725." In Anthony Fletcher and John Stevenson, eds., *Order and Disorder in Early Modern England.* Cambridge: Cambridge University Press, 1985.

———. *An Ordered Society: Gender and Class in Early Modern England.* Oxford: Blackwell, 1988.

Anderson, Bonnie S., and Judith P. Zinnser. *A History of Their Own.* New York: Harper and Row, 1988.

Andrews, Donna. *Philanthropy and Police: London Charity in the Eighteenth Century.* Princeton, NJ: Princeton University Press, 1989.

Andrews, Herbert. *The Chronicles of Hertford Castle.* Hertford, UK: Stephen Austin and Sons, 1947.

Arditi, Jorge. *A Genealogy of Manners: Transformations of Social Relations in France and England from the Fourteenth to the Eighteenth Century.* Chicago: University of Chicago Press, 1998.

Ariès, Philippe. *Centuries of Childhood.* New York: Penguin, 1973.

Ariès, Philippe, and Georges Duby, eds. *A History of Private Life.* Cambridge, MA: Belknap Press of Harvard University Press. English ed. 1989.

Armstrong, Nancy. "The Rise of the Domestic Woman." In Nancy Armstrong and Leonard Tennenhouse, eds., *The Ideology of Conduct: Essays on Literature and the History of Sexuality*. New York: Methuen, 1987.

Ashcraft, Richard. "Latitudinarianism and Toleration." In Richard Kroll, Richard Ashcraft, and Perez Zagorin, eds. *Philosophy, Science, and Religion in Restoration England 1640–1700*. Cambridge: Cambridge University Press, 1992.

Atwood, Margaret. "Biographobia: Some Personal Reflections on the Act of Biography." In Laurence Lockridge, John Maynard, and Donald Stone, eds., *Nineteenth Century Lives: Essays Presented to Jerome Hamilton Buckley*. Cambridge: Cambridge University Press, 1989.

Aylmer, G. *The Levellers in the English Revolution*. London: Thames and Hudson, 1975.

Barash, Carol. "'The Native Liberty . . . of the Subject': Configurations of Gender and Authority in the works of Mary Chudleigh, Sarah Fyge Egerton, and Mary Astell." In Isobel Grundy and Susan Wiseman, eds., *Women, Writing, History 1640–1740*. London: Batsford, 1992.

Baugh, D. A. "Poverty, Protestantism and Political Economy: English Attitudes Toward the Poor, 1660–1800." In S. B. Baxter, ed., *England's Rise to Greatness 1660–1760*. Berkeley: University of California Press, 1983.

Beckett, J. V. *The Aristocracy in England 1660–1914*. Oxford: Blackwell, 1986.

Beier, A. L., and Roger Finlay, eds. *London 1500–1700: The Making of the Metropolis*. London: Longman, 1986.

Bell, Susan Groag, and Marilyn Yalom, eds. *Revealing Lives: Autobiography, Biography, and Gender*. Albany: State University of New York Press, 1990.

Bennett, G. V. *The Tory Crisis in Church and State: The Career of Francis Atterbury, Bishop of Rochester*. Oxford: Clarendon, 1975.

Benstock, Shari, ed. *The Private Self: Theory and Practice of Women's Autobiographical Writing*. Chapel Hill: University of North Carolina Press, 1988.

Berman, David. *A History of Atheism in Britain from Hobbes to Russell*. London: Croom Helm, 1988.

Blodgett, Harriet. *Centuries of Female Days: English Women's Private Diaries*. New Brunswick, NJ: Rutgers University Press, 1988.

Bloom, Edward, and Lillian Bloom. *Educating the Audience: Addison, Steele and Eighteenth Century Culture: Papers Presented at a Clark Library Seminar 15 November, 1980*. Los Angeles: William Andrews Clark Memorial Library, 1984.

Bonfield, Lloyd, Richard Smith, and Keith Wrightson, eds. *The World We Have Gained: Essays Presented to Peter Laslett on his Seventieth Birthday*. Oxford: Blackwell, 1986.

Borsay, Peter. *The English Urban Renaissance: Culture and Society in the Provincial Town 1660–1770*. Oxford: Clarendon, 1989; reissued 1991.

Bouce, Paul-Gabriel. *Sexuality in Eighteenth-Century Britain*. Manchester, UK: Manchester University Press, 1982.

Bourdieu, Pierre. *Outline of a Theory of Practice*. Cambridge: Cambridge University Press, 1977.

Brodzki, Bella. *Life Lines: Theorizing Women's Autobiography*. Ithaca, NY: Cornell University Press, 1988.

Bryson, Anna. *From Courtesy to Civility: Changing Codes of Conduct in Early Modern England*. Oxford: Clarendon Press, 1998.

Burns, J. H., ed. *Cambridge History of Political Thought 1450–1700*. New York: Cambridge University Press, 1991.

Cahn, Susan. *Industry of Devotion: The Transformation of Women's Work in England 1500–1660*. New York: Columbia University Press, 1987.

Campbell, John. *Lives of the Lord Chancellors and Keepers of the Great Seal of England*, vol. 4. London: Murray, 1846.

Cannon, John. *Aristocratic Century: The Peerage of Eighteenth Century England*. Cambridge: Cambridge University Press, 1984.

Champion, J. A. I. *The Pillars of Priestcraft Shaken: The Church of England and its Enemies 1660–1730*. Cambridge: Cambridge University Press, 1992.

Charles, Lindsey, and Lorna Duffin, eds. *Women and Work in Pre-Industrial England*. London: Croom Helm, 1985.

Charlton, Kenneth. *Women, Religion and Education in Early Modern England*. New York: Routledge, 1994.

Clark, Alice. *Working Life of Women in the Seventeenth Century*. London: Routledge, 1919; repr. New York: Routledge and Kegan Paul, 1982.

Clark, J. C. D. *English Society: 1688–1832*. Cambridge: Cambridge University Press, 1985.

Clay, C. G. A. "Two Families and their Estates: The Grimstones and the Cowpers, 1650–1815." PhD diss., Cambridge University, 1966.

Collinson, Patrick. *The Birthpangs of Protestant England: Religious and Cultural Change in the Sixteenth and Seventeenth Centuries*. New York: St. Martin's Press, 1988.

Copelman, Dina. "Liberal Ideology, Sexual Difference, and the Lives of Women: Recent Works in British History." *Journal of Modern History* 62 (1990): 315–45.

Cragg, G. R. "The Churchman." In James Clifford, ed., *Man vs. Society in Eighteenth Century Britain: Six Points of View*. Cambridge: Cambridge University Press, 1968.

———. *From Puritanism to the Age of Reason*. Cambridge: Cambridge University Press, 1950.

Crawford, Patricia. "The Construction and Experience of Maternity." In Valerie Fildes, ed., *Women as Mothers in Pre-Industrial England*. New York: Routledge, 1990.

———. "Katherine and Philip Henry and their Children: A Case Study in Family Ideology." *Transactions of the Historic Society, Lancashire and Cheshire* 134 (1984).

———. "Women's Published Writings 1600–1700." In Mary Prior, ed., *Women in English Society 1500–1800*. London: Methuen, 1985.

———. *Women and Religion 1500–1720*. London: Routledge, 1993.

Cressy, David. "Levels of Illiteracy in England 1530–1730." *Historical Journal* 20 (1977): 1–23.

———. *Literacy and the Social Order: Reading and Writing in Tudor and Stuart England*. Cambridge: Cambridge University Press, 1980.

Culley, Margo, ed. *A Day at a Time: The Diary Literature of American Women from 1764 to the Present*. New York: Feminist Press at City University of New York, 1985.

Davies, Kathleen. "'The Sacred Condition of Equality': How Original Were Puritan Doctrines of Marriage?" *Social History* 5 (1977): 563–80.

———. "Continuity and Change in Literary Advice on Marriage." In R. B. Outhwaite, ed., *Marriage and Society: Studies in the Social History of Marriage*. London: Europa, 1981.

Davis, Natalie. "Women's History in Transition: The European Case." *Feminist Studies* 3 (1975–76): 83–103.

de Lauretis, Teresa, ed. *Feminist Studies/Critical Studies*. Bloomington: Indiana University Press, 1986.

de Riencourt, Amaury. *Sex and Power in History*. New York: David Mac-Kay, 1974.

Dictionary of English Church History. Ed. S. L. Ollard. London: Mowbray, 1919 (3d ed. 1948).

Dictionary of National Biography. Ed. Leslie Stephen and Sidney Lee. Oxford: Oxford University Press, 1917; repr. 1950.

Douglass, Jane Dempsey. "Women and the Continental Reformation." In Rosemary Radford Ruether, ed., *Religion and Sexism: Images of Women in the Jewish and Christian Traditions*. New York: Simon and Schuster, 1974.

Duffy, E. "The Godly and the Multitude in Stuart England." *The Seventeenth Century* 1 (1986): 31–55.

Durston, Christopher. *The Family in the English Revolution*. Oxford: Basil Blackwell, 1989.

Eakin, Paul John. *Fictions in Autobiography: Studies in the Art of Self-Invention*. Princeton, NJ: Princeton University Press, 1985.

Earle, Peter. *The Making of the English Middle Class: Business, Society and Family Life in London 1660–1730*. London: Methuen, 1989.

Elias, Norbert. *The Civilizing Process*. Oxford: Blackwell, 1994 (repr. 2 vols. 1978, 1982.)

Ezell, Margaret. *The Patriarch's Wife: Literary Evidence and the History of the Family*. Chapel Hill: University of North Carolina Press, 1987.

Ferguson, A. B. *Clio Unbound: Perceptions of the Social and Cultural Past in Renaissance England*. Chapel Hill: University of North Carolina Press, 1974.

Ferguson, Moira, ed. *First Feminists: British Women Writers 1578–1799*. Bloomington: Indiana University Press, 1985.

Flandrin, J. L. *Familles: Parente, Maison, Sexualité dans l'ancienne société*. Paris: Hachette, 1976. Translated as *Families in Former Times: Kinship, Household and Sexuality*. Cambridge: Cambridge University Press, 1979.

Fletcher, Anthony. *Gender, Sex and Subordination in England 1500–1800*. New Haven: Yale University Press, 1995.

———. "The Protestant Idea of Marriage in Early Modern England." In Anthony Fletcher and Peter Roberts, eds., *Religion, Culture and Society in Early Modern Britain: Essays in Honour of Patrick Collinson*. Cambridge: Cambridge University Press, 1994.

Fletcher, Anthony, and Peter Roberts, eds. *Religion, Culture and Society in Early Modern Britain*. Cambridge: Cambridge University Press, 1994.

Fletcher, Anthony, and John Stevenson, eds. *Order and Disorder in Early Modern England*. Cambridge: Cambridge University Press, 1985.

Foss, Edward. *Biographia Juridica: A Biographical Dictionary of the Judges of England from . . . 1066 to 1870*. London: Murray, 1870.

———. *The Judges of England*. 9 vols. London: Murray, 1848–1864.

Fothergill, Robert. *Private Chronicles: A Study of English Diaries*. London: Oxford University Press, 1974.

Foucault, Michel. *Power/Knowledge: Select Interviews and Other Writings 1972–77*. Ed. Colin Gordon. New York: Pantheon Books, 1977.

Frye, R. M. "The Teachings of Classical Puritanism on Conjugal Love." *Studies in the Renaissance* 11 (1955).

Gillis, John R. *For Better for Worse: British Marriages, 1600 to the Present*. New York: Oxford University Press, 1985.

Gittings, Clare. "The Hell of Living: Reflections on Death in the Diary of Sarah, Lady Cowper." *Mortality* 2:1 (1997).

Glassey, Lionel. *Politics and the Appointments of Justices of the Peace 1675–1720*. Oxford: Oxford University Press, 1979.

Goldie, Mark. "The Theory of Religious Intolerance in Restoration England." In Ole Peter Grell, Jonathan Israel, and Nicholas Tyacke, eds., *From Persecution to Toleration*. Oxford: Oxford University Press, 1991.

Goldthorpe, J. E. *Family Life in Western Societies: A Historical Sociology of Family Relationships in Britain and North America*. Cambridge: Cambridge University Press, 1987.

Graham, Elspeth, Hilary Hinds, Elaine Hobby, and Helen Wilcox, eds. *Her Own Life: Autobiographical Writings by Seventeenth-Century Englishwomen*. London: Routledge, 1989.

Gray, Kirkman. *History of English Philanthropy*. London: P. S. King, 1905, repr. 1967.

Greaves, Richard, ed. *Triumph over Silence: Women in Protestant History*. Westport, CT: Greenwood, 1985.

Green, David. *Queen Anne*. New York: Scribner, 1970.

Greenberg, Janelle. "The Legal Status of the English Woman in Early Eighteenth-Century Common Law and Equity." *Studies in Eighteenth-Century Culture* 4 (1975).

Greenblatt, Stephen. *Renaissance Self-Fashioning: From More to Shakespeare*. Chicago: Chicago University Press, 1980.

Gregg, Edward. *Queen Anne*. London: Routledge and Kegan Paul, 1980.

Gregory, Jeremy. "Anglicanism and the Arts." In Jeremy Black and Jeremy Gregory, eds., *Culture, Politics and Society in Britain 1660–1800*. Manchester, UK: Manchester University Press, 1991.

Grell, Ole Peter, Jonathan Israel, and Nicholas Tyacke, eds. *From Persecution to Toleration*. Oxford: Clarendon Press 1990.

Griffin, Martin. *Latitudinarianism in the Seventeenth Century Church of England*. Ed. Lila Freeman. New York: Brill, 1992.

Grundy, Isobel, and Susan Wiseman, eds. *Women, Writing, History 1640–1740*. London: Batsford, 1992.

Habakkuk, H. J. "The Rise and Fall of English Landed Families 1600–1800." *Transactions of the Royal Historical Society* 29–31 (1979–1981).

Haley, K. H. D. *The First Earl of Shaftesbury*. Oxford: Clarendon Press, 1968.

Haller, William, and Malleville Haller. "The Puritan Art of Love." *Huntington Library Quarterly* 5 (1941–42).

Hanson, K. V. *A Very Social Time: Crafting Community in Ante-Bellum New England*. Berkeley: University of California Press, 1996.

Harris, Frances. *A Passion for Government: The Life of Sarah, Duchess of Marlborough*. Oxford: Clarendon Press, 1991.

Harris, Tim, Paul Seaward, and Mark Goldie, eds. *The Politics of Religion in Restoration England*. Oxford: Blackwell, 1990.

Hayton, D. "Moral Reform and Country Politics in the Late Seventeenth-Century House of Commons." *Past and Present* 128 (August 1990): 48–91.

Heal, Felicity. *Hospitality in Early Modern England*. Oxford: Clarendon, 1990.

Heal, Felicity, and Clive Holmes. *The Gentry in England and Wales 1500–1700*. London: MacMillan, 1994.

Hecht, Jean. *The Domestic Servant in Eighteenth-Century England*. London: Routledge and Kegan Paul, 1956.

Heilbrun, Carolyn. *Writing a Woman's Life*. New York: Norton, 1988.

Hemphill, C. Dallett. *Bowing to Necessities: A History of Manners in America, 1620–1860*. New York: Oxford University Press, 1999.

Henderson, Katherine, and Barbara McManus. *Half Humankind: Contexts of the Controversy About Women in England 1540–1640*. Urbana: University of Illinois Press, 1985.

Henning, B. D., ed. *The History of Parliament: The House of Commons 1660–1690*. London: Secker and Warburg for the History of Parliament Trust, 1983.

Hill, Bridget. *Servants: English Domestics in the Eighteenth Century*. Oxford: Clarendon Press, 1996.

———, ed. *The First English Feminist: Reflections Upon Marriage and Other Writings*. New York: St. Martin's, 1986.

Hirschberg, D. R. "Episcopal Incomes and Expenses, 1660–c. 1760." In Rosemary O'Day and Felicity Heal, eds., *Princes and Paupers in the English Church 1500–1800*. Leicester: Leicester University Press, 1981.

———. "The Government and Church Patronage in England, 1660–1760." *Journal of British Studies* 20 (1980–81): 109–39.

Hobby, Elaine. "'Discourse so Unsavory': Women's Published Writings of the 1650s." In Isobel Grundy and Susan Wiseman, eds., *Women, Writing, History 1640–1740*. London: Batsford, 1992.

———. *Virtue of Necessity: English Women's Writing 1649–1688*. London: Virago Press, 1988.

Hoffman, Leonore, and Margo Culley, eds. *Women's Personal Narratives: Essays in Criticism and Pedagogy*. New York: MLA, 1985.

Holderness, B. A. "Widows in Pre-Industrial Society." In R. M. Smith, ed., *Land, Kinship and the Life Cycle*. Cambridge: Cambridge University Press, 1984.

Holmes, Geoffrey. *Augustan England: Professions, State and Society, 1680–1730*. London: Allen Unwin, 1982.

————. *British Politics in the Age of Anne*. Rev. ed. London: Hambledon, 1987.

————. "Gregory King and the Social Structure of Pre-Industrial England." *Transactions of the Royal Historical Society*. 5th ser. 27 (1977).

————. *The Making of a Great Power: Later Stuart and Early Georgian Britain 1660–1722*. London: Longman, 1993.

————. *Politics, Religion and Society in England 1679–1742*. London: Hambledon, 1986.

————. *The Trial of Doctor Sacheverell*. London: Eyre Methuen, 1973.

Houlbrooke, Ralph. *The English Family 1450–1700*. London; New York: Longman, 1984.

————, ed. *English Family Life, 1576–1716: An Anthology from Diaries*. Oxford: Blackwell, 1988.

Hufton, Olwen. "Survey Article: Women in History, Early Modern Europe." *Past and Present* 101 (1983).

Hull, Suzanne. *Chaste, Silent and Obedient: English Books for Women 1475–1640*. Los Angeles: Huntington Library, 1982.

Hunt, Margaret. *The Middling Sort: Commerce, Gender and the Family 1680 –1780*. Berkeley: University of California Press, 1996.

————. *Women and the Enlightenment*. New York: Haworth, 1984.

Hunter, Michael. "Science and Heterodoxy: An Early Modern Problem Reconsidered." In D. Lindberg and R. S. Westman, eds., *Reappraisals of the Scientific Revolution*. Cambridge: Cambridge University Press, 1990.

Isaacs, Tina. "Moral Crime, Moral Reform, and the State in Early Eighteenth-Century England: A Study of Piety and Politics." Ph.D. diss., University of Rochester, 1979.

————. "The Anglican Hierarchy and the Reformation of Manners, 1688–1738." *Journal of Ecclesiastical History* 33 (1982).

Jacob, Margaret C. *The Newtonians and the English Revolution 1689–1720*. Hassocks, Sussex, UK: Harvester, 1976.

————. *The Radical Enlightenment: Pantheists, Freemasons and Republicans*. London: Allen Unwin, 1981.

Jacob, W. M. *Lay People and Religion in the Early Eighteenth Century*. Cambridge: Cambridge University Press, 1996.

Jardine, Lisa, and Anthony Grafton. "'Studied for Action': How Gabriel Harvey Read his Livy." *Past and Present* 129 (1990).

Jelinek, Estelle. *Tradition of Women's Autobiography from Antiquity to the Present*. Boston: Twayne, 1986.

————, ed. *Women's Autobiography: Essays in Criticism*. Bloomington: Indiana University Press, 1980.

Johnson, J. T. "English Puritan Thought on the Ends of Marriage." *Church History* 38 (1969).

Jones, Clyve. "Debates in the House of Commons on 'The Church in Danger,' 1705, and Dr. Sacheverell's Impeachment, 1710." *Historical Journal* 19:3 (1976).

Jones, M. G. *The Charity School Movement*. London: Cass, 1964.

Kaplan, Temma. "Female Consciousness and Collective Action: The Case of Barcelona, 1910–1918." *Signs* 7 (1982).

Kelly, Joan. "The Doubled Vision of Feminist Theory." In Judith Newton, ed., *Sex and Class in Women's History*. London: Routledge and Kegan Paul, 1983.

———. "Early Feminist Theory and The Querelle des Femmes, 1400–1789." *Signs* 8 (1982).

Kelso, Ruth. *Doctrine for the Ladies of the Renaissance*. Urbana: University of Illinois Press, 1956.

Kent, D. A. "Ubiquitous but Invisible: Female Domestic Servants." *History Workshop Journal* 28 (August 1989).

Kenyon, J. P. *Revolution Principles: The Politics of Party 1689–1720*. Cambridge: Cambridge University Press, 1977.

Klein, Lawrence. "Liberty, Manners, and Politeness in Early Eighteenth-Century England." *Historical Journal* 32 (1987): 583–605.

———. *Shaftesbury and the Culture of Politeness: Moral Discourse and Cultural Politics in Early Eighteenth-Century England*. Cambridge: Cambridge University Press, 1994.

Kroll, Richard, Richard Ashcraft, and Perez Zagorin, eds. *Philosophy, Science, and Religion in Restoration England 1640–1700*. Cambridge: Cambridge University Press, 1992.

Lake, Peter. "Feminine Piety and Personal Potency: The Emancipation of Mrs. Jane Ratcliffe." *Seventeenth Century* 2 (1987): 143–65.

Langford, Paul. *A Polite and Commercial People: England 1727–1783*. Oxford: Oxford University Press, 1989.

———. *Public Life and the Propertied Englishman 1689–1798*. Oxford: Clarendon, 1991.

Laslett, Peter. *A Fresh Map of Life: The Emergence of the Third Age*. London: Weidenfeld and Nicolson, 1989.

———. *The World We Have Lost: Further Explored*. 3d ed. London: Methuen, 1983.

Latt, David. "Praising Virtuous Ladies: The Literary Image and Historical Reality of Women in Seventeenth-Century England." In Marlene Springer, ed., *What Manner of Woman: Essays on English and American Life and Literature*. New York: New York University Press, 1977.

Lensink, Judy Nolte. "Expanding the Boundaries of Criticism: The Diary as Female Autobiography." *Women's Studies* 14 (1987).

Lewalski, Barbara Kiefer. *Writing Women in Jacobean England.* Cambridge, MA: Harvard University Press, 1993.

Lilley, Kate. "True State Within: Women's Elegy 1640–1700." In Isobel Grundy and Susan Wiseman, eds., *Women, Writing, History 1640–1740.* London: Batsford, 1992.

Lummis, Trevor, and Jan Marsh. *The Woman's Domain: Women and the English Country House.* London: Penguin, 1990.

Macfarlane, Alan. *The Family Life of Ralph Josselin, a Seventeenth-Century Clergyman: An Essay in Historical Anthropology.* Cambridge: Cambridge University Press, 1970.

———. *Marriage and Love in England: Modes of Reproduction 1300–1840.* Oxford: Blackwell, 1986.

MacLean, Ian. *The Renaissance Notion of Women: A Study in the Fortunes of Scholasticism and Medical Science in European Intellectual Life.* Cambridge: Cambridge University Press, 1980.

Mandel, Barrett John. "The Autobiographer's Art." *Journal of Aesthetics and Art Criticism* 27 (1968).

Marshall, John. "The Ecclesiology of the Latitude Men 1660–1689: Stillingfleet, Tillotson and 'Hobbism.'" *Journal of Ecclesiastical History* 36 (1985): 407–27.

———. "John Locke and Latitudinarianism." In Richard Kroll, Richard Ashcraft, and Perez Zagorin, eds., *Philosophy, Science, and Religion in Restoration England 1640–1700.* Cambridge: Cambridge University Press, 1992.

Matthews, William. "The Diary, A Neglected Genre." *Sewanee Review* 85 (1977).

McLaren, Angus. *A History of Contraception: from Antiquity to the Present Day.* Oxford: Blackwell, 1990.

Meldrum, Tim. "Domestic Service, Privacy and the Eighteenth-Century Metropolitan Household." *Urban History* 26 (1999): 27–39.

Mendelson, Sara. *The Mental World of Stuart Women: Three Studies.* Hassocks, Sussex, UK: Harvester, 1987.

———. "Stuart Women's Diaries and Occasional Memoirs." In Mary Prior, ed., *Women in English Society 1500–1800.* New York: Methuen, 1985.

Mendelson, Sara, and Patricia Crawford. *Women in Early Modern England.* Oxford: Oxford University Press, 1998.

Mingay, G. E. *English Landed Society in the Eighteenth Century.* London: Routledge and Paul, 1963.

———. *The Gentry: The Rise and Fall of a Ruling Class.* London: Longman, 1976.

Minois, Georges. *History of Old Age from Antiquity to the Renaissance.* Cambridge: Cambridge University Press, 1989.

Moffatt, Mary Jane, and Charlotte Painter, eds. *Revelations: Diaries of Women*. New York: Random House, 1974.

Newton, Judith, Mary Ryan, and Judith Walkowitz. *Sex and Class in Women's History*. London: Routledge and Kegan Paul, 1983.

Nussbaum, Felicity. *The Autobiographical Subject: Gender and Ideology in Eighteenth-Century England*. Baltimore, MD: Johns Hopkins University Press, 1989.

O'Day, Rosemary. "The Anatomy of a Profession: The Clergy of the Church of England." In W. Prest, ed., *The Professions in Early Modern England*. London: Beckenham, 1989.

———. *Education and Society 1500–1800: The Social Foundations of Education in Early Modern Britain*. London: Longman, 1982.

———. *The English Clergy: The Emergence and Consolidation of a Profession 1558–1642*. Leicester, UK: Leicester University Press, 1979.

———. *The Family and Family Relationships 1500–1900: England, France, and the United States of America*. New York: St. Martin's, 1994.

O'Day, Rosemary, and Felicity Heal, eds. *Princes and Paupers in The English Church 1500–1800*. Leicester, UK: Leicester University Press, 1981.

Olney, James. *Autobiography: Essays Theoretical and Critical*. Princeton, NJ: Princeton University Press, 1980.

Owen, D. *English Philanthropy 1660–1960*. Cambridge, MA: Harvard University Press, 1965.

Parry, Graham. *The Seventeenth Century: The Intellectual and Cultural Context of English Literature 1603–1700*. London: Longman, 1989.

Pascal, Roy. *Design and Truth in Autobiography*. Cambridge, MA: Harvard University Press, 1960.

Peck, Linda Levy. *Court Patronage and Corruption in Early Stuart England*. Boston: Unwin Hyman, 1990; London: Routledge, 1993.

Perry, Ruth. *The Celebrated Mary Astell: An Early English Feminist*. Chicago: University of Chicago Press, 1986.

———. "Mary Astell's Feminism: The Veil of Chastity." *Studies in Eighteenth-Century Culture* 9 (1979): 25–43.

Pocock, J. G. A., ed. *Three British Revolutions: 1641, 1688, 1776*. Princeton, NJ: Princeton University Press, 1980.

Pollock, Linda. *Forgotten Children: Parent-Child Relations from 1500 to 1900*. Cambridge: Cambridge University Press, 1983.

Pomerleau, Cynthia. "The Emergence of Women's Autobiography." In Estelle Jelinek, ed., *Women's Autobiography: Essays in Criticism*. Bloomington: Indiana University Press, 1980.

Ponsonby, Arthur. *English Diaries. A Review of English Diaries from the Sixteenth to the Twentieth Century with an Introduction on Diary Writing*. London: Methuen, 1923.

Porter, Roy. *English Society in the Eighteenth Century.* London: Allen Lane, 1981.

Porter, Roy, and Mikulas Teich. *The Enlightenment in National Context.* Cambridge: Cambridge University Press, 1981.

Powell, Chilton. *English Domestic Relations 1487–1653.* New York: Columbia University Press, 1917.

Prest, Wilfrid. "Lawyers." In Wilfrid Prest, ed., *The Professions in Early Modern England.* London: Croom Helm, 1987.

Pritchard, Allan. "Six Letters by Cowley." *The Review of English Studies* n.s. vol. 18 no. 71 (August 1967).

Pruett, J. *The Parish Clergy under the Later Stuarts.* Urbana: University of Illinois Press, 1978.

Reay, Barry, and John MacGregor, eds. *Radical Religion in the English Revolutions.* Oxford: Oxford University Press, 1984.

Redwood, J. *Reason, Ridicule and Religion: The Age of Enlightenment in England 1660–1750.* London: Thames and Hudson, 1976.

Reedy, Gerard. *The Bible and Reason: Anglicans and Scripture in Late Seventeenth-Century England.* Philadelphia: University of Pennsylvania Press, 1985.

Register of Admissions to the Honorable Society of the Middle Temple from the Fifteenth Century to the Year 1944. Comp. H. A. C. Sturgess. London: Butterworth, 1949.

Rhode, Deborah, ed. *Theoretical Perspectives on Sexual Difference.* New Haven, CT: Yale University Press, 1990.

Rivers, Isabel. *Reason, Grace and Sentiment: A Study of the Language of Religion and Ethics in England 1660–1780.* Vol. 1, "Whichcote to Wesley." Cambridge: Cambridge University Press, 1991.

Roberts, C. "Party and Patronage in Later Stuart England." In S. B. Baxter, ed., *England's Rise to Greatness 1660–1783.* Berkeley: University of California Press, 1983.

Rogers, Katherine. *Feminism in Eighteenth-Century England.* Urbana: University of Illinois Press, 1982.

———. *The Troublesome Helpmate: A History of Misogyny in Literature.* Seattle: University of Washington Press, 1966.

Rosaldo, Michelle. "Women, Culture and Society: A Theoretical Overview." In Michelle Rosaldo and Louise Lamphere, eds., *Women, Culture and Society.* Stanford, CA: Stanford University Press, 1974.

Rose, Craig. "The Origins and Ideals of the SPCK 1699–1716." In John Walsh, Colin Haydon, and Stephen Taylor, eds., *The Church of England c. 1689–c. 1833.* Cambridge: Cambridge University Press, 1993.

Rosenthal, Joel. *Old Age in Late Medieval England.* Philadelphia: University of Pennsylvania Press, 1996.

Rupp, Gordon. *Religion in England 1688–1791*. Oxford: Clarendon Press, 1986.

Sachse, William. *Lord Somers: A Political Portrait*. Madison: University of Wisconsin Press, 1975.

Sambrook, James. *The Eighteenth Century: The Intellectual and Cultural Context of English Literature 1700–1789*. London: Longman, 1986.

Schlatter, Richard. *The Social Ideas of Religious Leaders 1660–1688*. London: Oxford University Press, 1940.

Schnorrenberg, Barbara B., and Jean E. Hunter. "The Education of the Eighteenth-Century Englishwoman." In B. Kanner, ed., *The Women of England from Anglo-Saxon Times to the Present*. Hamden, CT: Archon Books, 1979.

Schwoerer, Lois. *Lady Rachel Russell: "One of the Best of Women."* Baltimore, MD: Johns Hopkins University Press, 1988.

Scott, Joan. "Gender: A Useful Category of Historical Analysis." *American Historical Review* 91 (1986): 1053–75.

Sharpe, J. A. *Early Modern England: A Social History 1550–1760*. London: Edward Arnold, 1987.

Shumaker, Wayne. *English Autobiography: Its Emergence, Materials and Form*. Berkeley: University of California Press, 1954.

Simon, Joan. "Was there a Charity School Movement?" In B. Simon, ed., *Education in Leicestershire 1540–1940*. Leicester, UK: Leicester University Press, 1968.

Sinfield, Alan. *Literature, Politics, and Culture in Post-War Britain*. Berkeley: University of California Press, 1989.

Slack, Paul. *From Reformation to Improvement: Public Welfare in Early Modern England*. Oxford: Clarendon Press, 1999.

Slater, Miriam. *Family Life in the Seventeenth Century: The Verneys of Claydon House*. London: Routledge and Kegan Paul, 1984.

Smith, James. "Widowhood and Ageing in Traditional English Society." *Ageing and Society* 4:4 (1984): 429–49.

Smith, Sidonie. *A Poetics of Women's Autobiography: Marginality and the Fictions of Self-Representation*. Bloomington: Indiana University Press, 1987.

Sommerville, C. John. *Popular Religion in Restoration England*. Gainesville: University of Florida Press, 1977.

———. *The Secularization of Early Modern England: From Religious Culture to Religious Faith*. New York: Oxford University Press, 1992.

Spacks, Patricia Meyer. *Imagining a Self: Autobiography and Novel in Eighteenth-Century England*. Cambridge, MA: Harvard University Press, 1976.

Speck, William. *Stability and Strife: England 1714–1760.* Cambridge, MA: Harvard University Press, 1977.

Spengemann, William. *The Forms of Autobiography: Episodes in the History of a Literary Genre.* New Haven, CT: Yale University Press, 1980.

Spring, Eileen and David Spring. "The English Landed Elite 1540–1879: A Review." *Albion* 17 (Summer 1985): 149–80.

Spufford, Margaret. *Contrasting Communities: English Villages in the Sixteenth and Seventeenth Centuries.* Cambridge: Cambridge University Press, 1974.

———. "First Steps in Literacy: The Reading and Writing Experiences of the Humblest Seventeenth-Century Spiritual Autobiographers." *Social History* 4 (1979).

Spurr, John. "'Latitudinarianism' and the Restoration Church." *Historical Journal* 31 (1988): 61–82.

———. "'Rational Religion' in Restoration England." *Journal of the History of Ideas* 49 (1988): 563–85.

———. *The Restoration Church of England.* New Haven: Yale University Press, 1991.

Stanton, Domna. "Autogynography: Is the Subject Different?" In Domna Stanton, ed., *The Female Autograph.* Chicago: University of Chicago Press, 1987.

Staves, Susan. *Married Women's Separate Property in England 1660–1833.* Cambridge, MA: Harvard University Press, 1990.

Stone, Lawrence. *Broken Lives: Separation and Divorce in England 1660–1857.* Oxford: Oxford University Press, 1993.

———. *The Family, Sex and Marriage in England 1500–1800.* New York: Harper and Row, 1977.

———. *Road to Divorce: England 1530–1987.* Oxford: Oxford University Press, 1990.

———. *Uncertain Unions: Marriage in England 1660–1753.* Oxford: Oxford University Press, 1992.

Stone, Lawrence, and Jeanne Fawtier Stone. *An Open Elite? England 1540–1880.* Oxford: Clarendon Press, 1984.

Sullivan, R. *John Toland and the Deist Controversy.* Cambridge, MA: Harvard University Press, 1982.

Sundstrom, Roy. *Sidney Godolphin: Servant of the State.* Newark: University of Delaware Press, 1992.

Sykes, Norman. *Church and State in England in the Eighteenth Century.* Cambridge: Cambridge University Press, 1935.

———. *From Sheldon to Secker: Aspects of English Church History 1660–1768.* Cambridge: Cambridge University Press, 1959.

Thickstun, Margaret Olofson. *Fictions of the Feminine: Puritan Doctrine and the Representation of Women.* Ithaca, NY: Cornell University Press, 1988.

Thomas, Keith. "Age and Authority." *Proceedings of the British Academy* 62 (1976): 205–48.

———. "The Perception of the Past in Early Modern England." London: Creighton Trust Lecture, 1983.

Thompson, E. P. *Customs in Common.* London: Merlin Press, 1991.

———. "Patrician Society, Plebeian Culture." *Journal of Social History* 7 (1974).

Todd, Barbara. "The Remarrying Widow: A Stereotype Reconsidered." In Mary Prior, ed., *Women in English Society 1500–1800.* New York: Methuen, 1985.

Trumbach, Randolph. *The Rise of the Egalitarian Family: Aristocratic Kinship and Domestic Relations in Eighteenth-Century England.* New York: Academic Press, 1978.

Underdown, D. E. "The Taming of the Scold: The Enforcement of Patriarchal Authority in Early Modern England." In Anthony Fletcher and John Stevenson, eds. *Order and Disorder in Early Modern England.* Cambridge: Cambridge University Press, 1985.

Unwin, Robert. *Charity Schools and the Defense of Anglicanism.* York, UK: Saint Anthony's Press, 1984.

Vickery, Amanda. *The Gentleman's Daughter: Women's Lives in Georgian England.* New Haven, CT: Yale University Press, 1998.

———. "Golden Age to Separate Spheres? A Review of the Categories and Chronology of English Women's History." *Historical Journal* 36 (1993): 383–414.

The Victoria History of the County of Hertfordshire supp. vol. *Hertfordshire Families,* ed. Duncan Warrand. London: Constable, 1907.

Vince, Jacob. "Man's Economic Status." In James Clifford, ed., *Man Versus Society in Eighteenth-Century Britain: Six Points of View.* Cambridge: Cambridge University Press, 1968.

Virgin, P. *The Church in an Age of Negligence: Ecclesiastical Structure and Problems of Church Reform 1700–1840.* Cambridge: Cambridge University Press, 1989.

Walsh, John, and Stephen Taylor. "The Church and Anglicanism in the 'Long' Eighteenth Century." In John Walsh, Colin Haydon, and Stephen Taylor, eds., *The Church of England c. 1689–c. 1833: From Toleration to Tractarianism.* Cambridge: Cambridge University Press, 1993.

Westhauser, Karl. "Friendship and Family in Early Modern England: The Sociability of Adam Eyre and Samuel Pepys." *Journal of Social History* 27 (1994): 517–36.

Whyman, Susan. *Sociability and Power in Late-Stuart England: The Cultural World of the Verneys 1660–1720.* Oxford: University of Oxford Press, 1999.

Williams, J. D. "The Finances of an Eighteenth-Century Essex Nobleman." *Essex Archaeology and History* 9 (for 1977; 1979).

Wright, S. J. "The Elderly and the Bereaved in Eighteenth-Century Ludlow." In Margaret Pelling and Richard M. Smith, eds., *Life, Death, and the Elderly: Historical Perspectives.* London: Routledge, 1991.

Wrightson, Keith. *English Society 1580–1680.* New Brunswick, NJ: Rutgers University Press, 1982.

Index

Asterisked entries refer directly to Sarah Cowper's experiences, practices, or perceptions.